T0335554

'The authors provide an impressive and valuable resource for educators, leaders, and administrators in law enforcement, and for a community served by volunteers in policing. Today, law enforcement around the globe faces complex challenges with limited resources and law enforcement professionals and educators, at all levels, should understand the history, roles, impact, deployment, future, and best practices of volunteers in policing, a valuable community resource. This book is a complete guide for volunteer policing.'

– Dr. Jeffrey W. Goltz, School of Public Safety Executive Dean, Valencia College, Orlando, Florida

'This book is the most complete study on volunteer policing to date! My belief is that there is no better example of the current trend of "community policing" than that of a robust reserve program. I call them "citizen cops." This book explores both the positives and the negatives of reserve or volunteer policing and is a must read for anyone interested in current law enforcement trends.'

– Deputy Chief of Police Stephan Brody, Reserve Division, City of Dallas Police Department, Texas

'This book gives a fascinating and thought-provoking insight into an area of policing that has seen too little research in the past – the reserve or auxiliary police officer. Past studies have tended to be within individual countries and have not looked internationally. As a result, the obvious opportunity to learn from the practices and experiences of others has been neglected. By comparing and contrasting the different approaches to reserve policing across the US, and between the US and the UK, the authors provide a unique opportunity to consider how policing can benefit even more from reserve officers.'

– Ian Miller MBE, Special Commander, City of London Police

'Volunteers in policing make an enormous but often little-recognized contribution to policing. This important book explores this contribution internationally, identifying the roles that volunteers play and the impact that they make to policing both in the United Kingdom and the United States, and discusses what the future holds for volunteer policing."

– Iain Britton, Director at the Institute of Public safety, Crime and Justice at the University of Northampton; Head of the Centre for Citizens in Policing; Director at CoPaCC

Volunteer Police, Choosing to Serve

Volunteer Police, Choosing to Serve provides an in-depth comparison between volunteer policing in the United States and in the United Kingdom, and examines the shared past and similar – yet sometimes divergent – evolution of special constables, auxiliaries, and reserves. It discusses the history of volunteer policing, contemporary authority, functions, and training. The book also examines part-time, auxiliary, and special constable policing roles around the globe. The text contains original research comparing British and American volunteer police, and concludes with a discussion of the future of volunteer policing in UK and US contexts.

Dr. Ross Wolf is Associate Dean in the College of Health and Public Affairs and Associate Professor in the Department of Criminal Justice at the University of Central Florida. He also serves as Reserve Chief Deputy with the Orange County (Florida) Sheriff's Office. He was appointed to and serves on the International Association of Chiefs of Police (IACP) Police Administration Committee and on the National Sheriffs' Association (NSA) Outreach Committee and Reserve Law Enforcement Subcommittee. In 2017 he was appointed to the Board of Governors for the Global Society of Homeland and National Security Professionals and was named Visiting Fellow by the University of Northampton's Institute for Public Safety, Crime, and Justice in the United Kingdom. Dr. Wolf has authored over 30 refereed articles, book chapters, and books on police interviewing, police administration and management, reserve and volunteer policing, police use of force, tourism policing, and international policing. Among other achievements, he has received the United States "Daily Point of Light" Award, the National Sheriffs' Association "Medal of Merit" Award, and the United States Presidential "Lifetime Call to Service" Award for his work with volunteer and reserve policing.

Dr. Carol Borland Jones is a Research Associate at the University of Northampton's Institute for Public Safety, Crime, and Justice. Prior to taking on this role, she worked as a Senior Lecturer at the University of Chester and the University of Gloucestershire. She has authored refereed articles, book chapters, and books on reserve and volunteer policing, tourism and crime, policing tourism, and victims. Dr. Borland Jones has worked on a number of research programs and is currently collaborating on studies into the role of volunteers in UK policing. She has worked as consultant to Victim Support, Republic of Mauritius, and collaborated with academics in Australia, Ghana, Ireland, the Netherlands, and the United States.

Volunteer Police, Choosing to Serve

Exploring, Comparing, and Assessing Volunteer Policing in the United States and the United Kingdom

Ross Wolf and Carol Borland Jones

Routledge
Taylor & Francis Group

NEW YORK AND LONDON

First published 2018
by Routledge
711 Third Avenue, New York, NY 10017

and by Routledge
2 Park Square, Milton Park, Abingdon, Oxon, OX14 4RN

Routledge is an imprint of the Taylor & Francis Group, an informa business

© 2018 Taylor & Francis

Library of Congress Cataloging-in-Publication Data
Names: Wolf, Ross, author. | Jones, Carol Borland, author.
Title: Volunteer police, choosing to serve : exploring, comparing, and
assessing volunteer policing in the United States and the United Kingdom /
Ross Wolf, Carol Borland Jones.
Description: 1 Edition. | New York : Routledge, 2018. |
Includes bibliographical references and index.
Identifiers: LCCN 2017057706 | ISBN 9781466564954 (hardback) |
ISBN 9781351030786 (master)
Subjects: LCSH: Volunteer workers in law enforcement–United States. |
Volunteer workers in law enforcement–Great Britain. |
Auxiliary police–United States. | Auxiliary police–Great Britain.
Classification: LCC HV8143 .W635 2018 | DDC 363.2/20941–dc23
LC record available at https://lccn.loc.gov/2017057706

ISBN: 978-1-466-56495-4 (hbk)
ISBN: 978-1-351-03078-6 (ebk)

Typeset in Sabon
by Out of House Publishing

This book is dedicated to the men and women around the world who freely give of their time to serve their communities as volunteer police.

It is also dedicated to Professor John Borland, an inspiration to so many.

Contents

About the Authors

Dr. Ross Wolf is Associate Dean in the College of Health and Public Affairs and Associate Professor in the Department of Criminal Justice at the University of Central Florida. He also serves as Reserve Chief Deputy with the Orange County (Florida) Sheriff's Office. He was appointed to and serves on the International Association of Chiefs of Police (IACP) Police Administration Committee, and on the National Sheriffs' Association (NSA) Outreach Committee and Reserve Law Enforcement Subcommittee. In 2017 he was appointed to the Board of Governors for the Global Society of Homeland and National Security Professionals and was named Visiting Fellow by the University of Northampton's Institute for Public Safety, Crime and Justice in the United Kingdom. He has authored over 30 refereed articles, book chapters, and books on police interviewing, police administration and management, reserve and volunteer policing, police use of force, tourism policing, and international policing. In addition to his work with police agencies throughout the United States, he has worked with the police in the Caribbean, the United Kingdom, Russia, Hong Kong, and Singapore. He has received the Orange County Sheriff's Office Administrative Excellence Award, Sheriff's Citation, and Distinguished Service Award, and has been presented with the United States "Daily Point of Light" Award, the National Sheriffs' Association "Medal of Merit" Award, and the United States Presidential "Lifetime Call to Service" Award for his work with volunteer and reserve policing. Dr. Wolf is a former gubernatorial - appointed member of the State of Florida Board of Regents.

Dr. Carol Borland Jones is a Research Associate at the University of Northampton's Institute for Public Safety, Crime and Justice. Prior to taking on this role she worked as a Senior Lecturer at the University of Chester and the University of Gloucestershire. She has authored refereed articles, book chapters, and books on reserve and volunteer policing, tourism and crime, policing tourism and victims. Carol has worked on a number of research programs and is currently collaborating on studies into the role of volunteers in UK policing. She has worked as consultant to Victim Support, Republic of Mauritius, and collaborated with academics in Australia, Ghana, Ireland, the Netherlands, and the United States.

Chapter 1

Introduction

Defining Volunteer Policing

In 1999 Mawby identified the problem of definitions in comparative research; while this book does not require interpreters, as with Bayley's Japanese study (1976; see also Mawby, 1999), it does necessitate an understanding of the terminology, a way to place the reader in one location on an "equal footing" with a reader in another. Therefore, while volunteer policing in every jurisdiction throughout the world would, on the surface, appear to be self-explanatory, this work shows that definitions vary, and volunteer policing as a concept varies greatly. Where necessary explanations of terms will be given throughout this text, but "volunteer policing" is a central term that needs addressing from the very beginning. To introduce the concepts of the terms "volunteer," "policing," and "volunteer policing," each section will begin with quotes from the literature that have attempted to define these terms in the past.

Volunteer

Volunteering (England and Wales)

> We define volunteering as any activity that involves spending time, unpaid, doing something that aims to benefit the environment or someone (individuals or groups) other than, or in addition to, close relatives. Central to this definition is the fact that volunteering must be a choice freely made by each individual.
>
> (National Council for Voluntary Organisations, n.d.)

> [A] person engaged in an activity which involves spending time, unpaid (except for travel and other approved out-of-pocket expenses), doing something which aims to benefit some third party other than or in addition to a close relative.
>
> (Legislation.gov.uk, n.d.)

Volunteering (United States)

Many definitions of volunteering exclude activities that may benefit the volunteer's family or friends, although it is unclear how this volunteer work is different from the same work performed for a stranger.

(Carson, 2000, p. 68)

[A] woman who teaches acting to children through a local theater would be considered a volunteer; by contrast, a woman who, on her own, organizes softball games for the children in her neighborhood would not be counted as a volunteer for the purpose of the survey.

(Boraas, 2003, p. 11)

To volunteer is to choose to act in recognition of a need, with an attitude of social responsibility and without concern for monetary profit, going beyond one's basic obligations.

(Ellis & Noyes, 1990, p. 4)

Volunteering (United Nations)

The terms *volunteering, volunteerism* and *voluntary activities* refer to a wide range of activities...undertaken of free will, for the general public good and where monetary reward is not the principal motivating factor.

(United Nations Volunteers, 2015, p. xxiii)

Psychologists have struggled to understand why certain people volunteer their time for certain efforts, while other people do not. In 2015, over a billion people globally volunteered to provide service to their communities (United Nations Volunteers, 2015), but what generally inspires them to do so remains largely elusive (Stukas, Snyder, & Clary, 1999; see also Krebs & Miller, 1985).[1] Because the term *volunteer* has been used to mean dissimilar things to diverse cultures, communities, and people and is also used differently in different academic studies, it is difficult to determine how one's efforts may or may not be considered *volunteerism* (Stukas et al., 1999). Can an individual who is required to participate be considered a volunteer? For example, if a school or university requires students to volunteer for community service in order to receive some sort of credit necessary for graduation, is that true volunteerism?

Another confusing piece of the definition is that most people equate volunteerism with work that is done without any remuneration. If someone volunteers for a function that is normally a requirement, then is that also volunteerism? For example, the militaries of both the United States and the United Kingdom are made up entirely of "volunteers."

This means that no one is forced to serve in the military if they do not choose to do so. However, members of the US military are paid (many would argue that they are not paid enough) to perform this function. Some other countries in the world require that their citizenry, when they reach a certain age, perform certain societal services such as work with the military, the police, or with emergency response. Once this obligation is complete, citizens may continue to volunteer part-time to work in the same service area and get paid for their time. Is this volunteerism? Police services in both the United States and the United Kingdom may provide certain privileges to volunteers in policing; this may include transportation reimbursement, equipment reimbursement, a meal allowance, or a stipend for time. If this funding is at an amount far less than would be paid a full-time employee providing the same services, is it still volunteerism, or does the fact that they receive any payment negate the volunteer effort?

Finally, as mentioned in the quotes above, volunteerism may occur when it is not part of an organized effort. For example, citizens may take it upon themselves to walk their neighborhood at dusk and report to the police any suspicious activities. Although the time the individuals spend walking their neighborhood and reporting issues to the police by phone or internet they may consider to be time they spend volunteering, it is not an official activity. This would not be an example of a volunteer in policing. However, an individual who joins a neighborhood watch organization, and does the same activity, might be considered a volunteer in policing.

The United Nations reports that the terminology, categories, and definitions of volunteerism throughout the world have led to difficulty in evaluating programs and the impact of volunteerism on governments and civil organizations (United Nations Volunteers, 2015). By utilizing the definition of volunteerism found in Ellis and Noyes (1990), a volunteer acts with an "attitude of social responsibility" and goes beyond "one's basic obligations" (p. 4). For the purposes of this book, the following definition is therefore adopted for the term "volunteer." We will discuss other types of volunteerism in policing throughout the world, but we will clearly indicate where we deviate from this definition.

Volunteer: An individual who provides time for a recognized organization or governmental service without significant remuneration for his or her services or imposed requirement.

However, the term "volunteer" should not be confused with the term "amateur." An amateur is an individual who may not be trained or accomplished or as professional as a non-amateur. While some volunteers in policing may not have the same training as their full-time counterparts, many are as well-trained, recognized, and highly regarded as those who serve full-time in these positions (Carson, 2000).

Policing

Policing (England and Wales)

> Across England and Wales the police are not primarily seen as providers of a narrow sense of personal security, held responsible for crime and safety. Instead the police stand as symbolic "guardians" of social stability and order, held responsible for community values and informal social controls.
>
> (Jackson & Bradford, 2009, p. 2)

> The simple answer to the question "What is policing?" is that policing is what police officers do.
>
> (Waddington, 1999, p. 1)

Policing (United States)

> [T]hrough reform, our policing systems must identify not just the roles and responsibilities of the police but the roles and responsibilities of the community as well… The level of community involvement in the policing system and the level of personal responsibility each community member assumes by cooperating or collaborating with the police greatly impact the outcome of the system.
>
> (Davis, 2016)

> [T]he decisions which police must make are political, social, and psychological and very much affected by the democratic nature of American society.
>
> (Remington, 1965, p. 361)

The above descriptions of policing, each provided by well-established academics and experts in their field, suggest very different interpretations but are all legitimate. Policing has been difficult to define since academics began to research the concept. To some, policing is a positive application of the law to society, giving order to civilization, a social function that stresses the development of norms and standards of behaviors that are acceptable (Rowe, 2014). To others, it is an extension of government that tries to infiltrate their lives and take away freedoms.

> The broader notion of [good and fair] policing still survives in the American constitutional doctrine of police powers, in which the Supreme Court explicitly treats policing as encompassing the tasks of governance.
>
> (Walker, 2011, p. 578)

However one may view policing, the term was not associated with a particular government institution until very recently in history. While the Greek word *polis* and the Latin word *politia* both referred to the state, it was not until the early eighteenth century that *la police* and *die Polizei* were used to explain the internal administration, surveillance, and protection of a territory (Rowe, 2014). Before we venture further in to this study we should perhaps indicate that the modern meaning of the word "policing" varies not only across borders but also within borders.

Crawford's definition of policing (2003; see also Reiner, 2000) clearly indicates that the act of "policing" is carried out both formally and informally; passersby, for example, routinely provide informal policing through natural surveillance in much the same way as members of the police service on routine patrol. In the case of "the police," however, such surveillance is formal, but both are examples of "policing." Security guards and store detectives in both the United Kingdom and the United States undertake "policing" without powers of arrest beyond those of an ordinary citizen but the presence of those in uniform acts as a deterrent while store detectives provide policing through surveillance. Davis (2016) said that the police cannot be separated from the communities they serve, that this would be "akin to separating patients from the health care system or students from the educational system." The level of community involvement in the policing system, which is the foundation of this current book, greatly influences the effectiveness of the police (Davis, 2016).

Policing, often presumed to be a government function, can also be undertaken by private entities. Although the function of a private security guard may be easily differentiated from that of a public police officer, in some American jurisdictions the differences are not so easily demarcated. Some states in the United States allow certain private entities to employ individuals as private police officers; they are privately funded but publicly certified, with sworn/warranted law enforcement powers (MacDonald, Klick, & Grunwald, 2015). Private police forces have been a part of American history since the early nineteenth century, when residents would pay for individuals or organizations to patrol their neighborhoods and protect individual businesses (Stringham, 2015). Current Virginia law, for example, allows private citizens to petition the courts for the authority to carry a gun, carry a badge, and make arrests with only limited amounts of training. These Virginia Special Conservators of the Peace (SCOP) patrol businesses and neighborhoods, are loosely regulated, and may legally identify themselves as "police" (Jouvenal, 2015).

A different type of commercialization of policing can be found in the "provision of legal activities for which the police receive money in exchange for service...through a formal contractual agreement and from a voluntary customer" (Mulone, 2011, p. 166). Private organizations in the United States can contract with policing agencies to provide private security services under the umbrella of the legal protections and authority provided to government police officers. However, this type of policing is seen as a practice that is legal and legitimate in the United States, and therefore can be considered as part of the general definition of policing. This privatization of policing raises questions that are beyond the scope of this book, but do have implications to volunteer policing. As will be discussed later in this text, volunteer police in certain jurisdictions participate in this type of "off-duty" or "moonlighting" work. Mulone (2011) raises significant questions about this type of policing. What rules and policies should the policing organization adopt to ensure the ethical delivery of services? In what way do the activities of the police in this type of private policing differ from usual police work? Does this type of private policing give rise to a private police, "intended solely for the wealthy" (Mulone, 2011, p. 178)?

For clarification, the following definition is therefore adopted for the term "police" in this book. We will discuss other types of policing throughout the world, but we will clearly indicate where we deviate from this definition.

Police: An individual who works directly for a government entity and who is authorized with lawful powers for the prevention, investigation, and prosecution of criminal activity and the preservation of public order.

Because of the differences between "police" and "sheriff" law enforcement officers in the United States, the term "police" may still lead to some confusion. In this book the term "police" will also include the duties of sheriff's offices, though not all sheriff's offices in the United States have primary responsibility for law enforcement functions. British police services can also be included in this definition by the role that they take in their governmental police organizations. Although the term "law enforcement officer" may seem to be more generalized and therefore a more appropriate terminology, police in England and Wales generally do not consider their primary function to be law enforcement.

While many of the issues that surround the organizational and cultural questions of full-time police also exist for volunteer police, they can be significantly different. One condition that has been studied within policing over the past several decades, beginning with the seminal study of Tyler (1990), is the legitimacy of police. People who feel that the police treat them unfairly were more likely to question the fairness of the process, and the legitimacy of the criminal justice process and professionals, and therefore were less likely to comply with regulations, laws, and regulations (Tyler, 1990; see also Tankebe, Reisig, & Wang, 2016). Police officers should enforce the law, but remain within the boundaries of their authority to do so, and the allocation of police resources should be fair and equitably distributed. Tyler (1990) found that citizens were concerned with respect, courtesy, and dignity during their encounters with the police, and that even short, common police-citizen encounters can build or challenge community and individual perceptions of the police, and therefore their legitimacy (see also Tankebe et al., 2016; Reisig, Bratton, & Gertz, 2007). The level of legitimacy that one police officer or one police agency has within the community can affect the level of cooperation with the police, even when controlling for known predictors of criminal activity, including individual low self-control (Tankebe et al., 2016).

Legitimacy is essential for the role of policing (Mulone, 2016), and, so far as most citizens do not discern between full-time and volunteer police, it is important for volunteer police to ensure their legitimacy in the communities that use them. The United States and the United Kingdom have both experienced a new era in policing legitimacy over the past decade, and police are extremely aware of the new transparency in today's technological world. Issues of questionable police conduct have not been limited to full-time police, and the dubious actions of any who act under the guise of government authority brings often harsh criticism to everyone else in the profession. Perceptions of policing can influence citizen attitudes toward the police and impact the effectiveness of police organizations. "I expect that fair leadership shapes fair policing by stimulating trust in citizens" (Van Craen, 2016, p. 8). If volunteer police are a nexus between the police organization and the citizenry, one potential outcome is a greater sense of police legitimacy for the volunteer policing organization, the policing service, and the government.

Volunteer Police

Providing a definition of "volunteer" and "police" creates a strong foundation for this book, but it is important to realize that the combination of the two terms creates a phrase that is even more difficult to demarcate clearly across cultures, languages, countries, unions, states, and local jurisdictions. Although some volunteers may clearly be labeled as "volunteer police," such as the example of special constables (SCs) in England and Wales, or reserve police officers in California, Texas, or Florida, there are volunteers in those jurisdictions and elsewhere who do not have full police powers. The auxiliary police of the New York City Police Department (NYPD) will be discussed later in this book. However, the severely limited authority of the NYPD auxiliary police officers makes them less police, more volunteer citizens. The same could be said for police support volunteers (PSVs) in the United Kingdom, a type of volunteerism that has shown recent expansion across the country. These volunteers assist the police, but do not have police powers. Conversely, there are individuals who might be granted full police powers or authority, but do not meet the definition of a volunteer provided above: individuals who may provide less than full-time service as police officers, but who are provided a significant remuneration for their services.

As the use of volunteers in policing has expanded throughout the United States and the United Kingdom, the ability to clearly define key terms related to their functions has become increasingly problematic. Defining a "special constable" in the United Kingdom is fairly straightforward, even though their role has expanded within the last decade. A special constable, or "special," is a voluntary member of a UK police service who has the authority to make arrests and investigate criminal activity. Specials are not paid for their service, other than reimbursement for travel or meals. Specials historically had police powers only within the jurisdiction of their constabulary, as granted by the Chief Constable. However, with the 2012 Queen's Diamond Jubilee, the 2012 London Olympics, and the 2010 and 2011 London riots, the powers of the special constabulary were expanded to include all of England and Wales.

As we will discuss further in this book, the terms "auxiliary" and "reserve" are often used interchangeably, and either definition may include officers who have full or partial police powers and may or may not perform the functions of police. Greenberg (2005) chose to merge the definitions of "auxiliary" or "reserve" police in the United States by considering the concept of "volunteer police." Greenberg (p. 14) defined volunteer police as

> members of a permanent organization (or one established during wartime mobilization) authorized by either governmental or societal action for the purpose of performing one or more functions of policing in an overt manner (i.e., functions that go beyond surveillance or communications work) for minimal or no salary.

This definition allows for the many varied ways that different jurisdictions may utilize police volunteers, and also takes into account that some of these "volunteers" may actually receive some sort of nominal financial support in exchange for their participation in the program. The definition does not include organized groups that may tend to be police-related; groups such as the Guardian Angels or Mothers Against Drunk Driving (MADD) would therefore not be considered volunteer police, even though they may claim or appear to have a policing, or police-related, function. However, volunteer police should not be confused with the term "Volunteers in Police Service," or VIPS, which is a category of volunteers that is tracked by the International Association of Chiefs of Police (IACP) and which is funded through the Bureau of Justice Assistance and the Department of Justice. VIPS programs utilize volunteers in a variety of roles to assist police agencies. While Volunteers in Police Service include reserve and auxiliary officers, they also include volunteers who serve as receptionists and document managers, and on neighborhood watch, citizen patrol, and child safety ID programs, among others (Godshall, 2009). These are volunteers who work in police agencies, all doing a variety of necessary and often thankless jobs, but they are not necessarily "volunteer police" according to Greenberg's definition above.

However, even the term "volunteer police" may fail to discern many similar types of personnel within police organizations who perform analogous duties. Police Explorers, a Boy Scouts subgroup, may perform subsidiary law enforcement functions such as parking details, honor guard details, minor traffic direction, or site security, and therefore seem to fit into the definition listed above for volunteer police. Police Explorers are often provided with uniforms similar to police (though usually with some distinct differences) and may seem to be very young police officers (the maximum age for membership in the Police Explorer program is 21) to a casual observer. Police interns, usually college students who "volunteer" with a policing agency, may also seem to fit in the definition listed above for volunteer police. Most police interns are not provided with any pay for their time, yet they often participate in investigations, report writing, and other tasks that may seem to fit them into Greenberg's definition. For the purposes of this book, the following definition is therefore adopted for the term "volunteer police." We will discuss other types of volunteer police throughout the world, but we will clearly indicate where we deviate from this definition.

Volunteer police: An individual who works directly for a government entity and is authorized with lawful powers for the prevention, investigation, and prosecution of criminal activity and the preservation of public order, and who provides this service without an imposed requirement and without significant remuneration for his or her services.

Police agencies throughout the United States have varied in their way of addressing the power, authority, job responsibilities, and functions of members of a volunteer policing unit. An example of one way to utilize volunteer police can be found in New York Police Department's auxiliary unit, consisting of approximately 4,500 volunteers; this unit has been mentioned already, and is discussed at greater length in Chapter 8 in this book. Auxiliary police officers with the NYPD have no arrest powers and are used as a visual deterrent to crime, for minor traffic control, and as a public relations resource, rather than as a supplement to police power. At the opposite end in terms of the utilization of volunteers from the way the NYPD uses auxiliary police, however, is the City of Los Angeles, California. Los Angeles utilizes approximately 650 volunteer reserve officers, who have demarcated training requirements and have the same responsibilities and roles as full-time officers, including the power of arrest. Throughout the United States (see Photo 1), agencies utilize their

Photo 1 Volunteer police in the United States and in the United Kingdom provide a variety of services, including crowd and traffic control

reserve or auxiliary officers from one end of this spectrum to the other (Dobrin & Wolf, 2016; Wolf, Albrecht, & Dobrin, 2015).

In England and Wales, while volunteering within the police service is undertaken by a range of non-waged individuals, special constables have the same powers as their regular counterparts and can, dependent upon the individual force area, assume a wide range of duties (currently excluding positions that carry firearms). UK police agencies use volunteer special constables to serve as unarmed warranted police officers in all police forces across England, Wales, and Scotland. While they are entrusted with the same powers to uphold the law as their full-time counterparts, they have significantly less initial training. Specials often work in teams, either with other specials or full-time officers, but they can also be approved to patrol alone (Wolf, Pepper, & Dobrin, 2016; Seth, 2006).

How Many Volunteer Police Are There?

Although many American police agencies and organizations utilize volunteer, reserve, and auxiliary officers, the precise number of volunteer police units and the number of volunteer officers in the United States is not known (Berg & Doerner, 1988; Kakalik & Wildhorn, 1971). However, recently Dobrin and Wolf (2016) used data provided by the United States Department of Justice to determine that there are approximately 58,500 reserve or auxiliary volunteer police and deputy sheriffs with sworn police powers, and approximately 19,000 volunteer reserve and auxiliary police and deputy sheriffs who have limited police powers. Combined,

Photo 2 Volunteer special constables make up approximately 14 percent of the number of full-time police in the United Kingdom

this totals over 77,500 citizen volunteers who serve in these roles in the United States, or approximately 20 percent of the 404,000 who serve as full-time law enforcement officers (Dobrin & Wolf, 2016).[2] Some of these volunteer police in the United States have law enforcement authority, as will be discussed later in this text, and others do not. Some are authorized to carry firearms, while others are not. Wolf, Holmes, and Jones (2016) reported that, in a study of sheriff's office reserves in the United States, respondents indicated that they are given most, if not all, of the same job functions that are given to full-time law enforcement officers.

There are approximately 17,000 special constables in England and Wales, or approximately 14 percent of the 125,000 full-time police (see Photo 2). As police are not generally armed in the United Kingdom, only certain specially trained regular police officers are able to carry guns, while special constables are not currently permitted or authorized to become armed officers.

This book will examine the history and role of volunteer police in both the United Kingdom and the United States, but will also utilize case studies from other countries to show differences and similarities throughout the world, including former British colonies such as Singapore and Hong Kong, and not all of these programs cleanly fit the definition we have provided above. The utilization of volunteer police in these countries and their similarities to and differences from the volunteer police utilized in the United States and the United Kingdom will be discussed. In addition, the text will examine the role of volunteers in functions that are primarily considered government services. The role of volunteer police in community-oriented policing, tourism-oriented policing, intelligence-led policing, and problem-oriented policing will also be examined.

Notes

1 Clary et al. (1998) developed a measurement tool to collect data as to why people are motivated to volunteer called the Volunteer Function Inventory (VFI). The VFI is a 30-item survey that collects functional motives individuals have for choosing to volunteer. The scale is divided into six factors: protective motives, values, career, social, understanding, and enhancement. The tool has been used to analyze motivations for people who are required to provide "volunteer service" against those who are not required, and their findings suggest that many people who perform volunteer functions do so to fulfill multiple motivations (Stukas et al., 1999).

2 Interestingly, the number of sworn volunteer police officers in the United States reported here by Dobrin and Wolf (2016) is vastly different from the number estimated by Hedlund and Burke (2006). Hedlund and Burke reported that there may be as many as 400,000 police reserves in the United States, but their data relied on a now defunct reserve policing association, and there is no way to determine how this number was derived. Dempsey and Forst (2007) used the estimate provided by Hedlund and Burke in their textbook, which may be a significant overestimation.

References

Bayley, D. H. (1976). *Forces of order: Policing modern Japan*. Berkeley, CA: University of California Press.

Berg, B. L., & Doerner, W. G. (1988). Volunteer police officers: An unexamined personnel dimension in law enforcement. *American Journal of Police*, 7(1), 81–89.

Boraas, S. (2003). Volunteerism in the United States. *Monthly Labor Review*, 126(8), 3–11.

Carson, E. (2000). On defining and measuring volunteering in the United States and abroad. *Law and Contemporary Problems*, 62(4), 67–71.

Clary, E. G., Snyder, M., Ridge, R. D., Copeland, J., Stukas, A. A., Haugen, J., & Meine, P. (1998). Understanding and assessing the motivations of volunteers: A functional approach. *Journal of Personality and Social Psychology*, 74(6), 1516–1530.

Crawford, A. (2003). The pattern of policing in the UK: Policing beyond the police, in T. Newburn (Ed.), *Handbook of Policing*, pp. 136–168. Cullompton, UK: Willan Publishing.

Davis, R. L. (2016). Police reform vs. policing reform. *Community Policing Dispatch*, 9(8). Retrieved August 12, 2017, from https://cops.usdoj.gov/html/dispatch/08-2016/police_reform.asp.

Dempsey, J. S., & Forst, L. S. (2007). *Police*, 2nd Edition. Boston: Cengage.

Dobrin, A., & Wolf, R. (2016). What we know and what we don't know about volunteer policing in the United States. *International Journal of Police Science and Management*, 18(3), 220–227.

Ellis, S. J., & Noyes, K. H. (1990). *By the people: A history of Americans as volunteers.* San Francisco: Jossey-Bass.

Godshall, S. L. (2009). Engaging volunteers in your law enforcement agency: The Volunteers in Police Service (VIPS) program. *Sheriff* (September/October), 48–52.

Greenberg, M. A. (2005). *Citizens defending America: From colonial times to the age of terrorism.* Pittsburgh: University of Pittsburgh Press.

Hedlund, K., & Burke, T. W. (2006). Reserve officers: A valuable resource. *FBI Law Enforcement Bulletin, 75*(12), 11–15.

Jackson, J., & Bradford, B. (2009). Crime, policing and social order: On the expressive nature of public confidence in policing. *British Journal of Sociology, 60*(3), 493–521.

Jouvenal, J. (2015, February 28). Private police carry guns and make arrests, and their ranks are swelling. *The Washington Post.* Retrieved August 12, 2017, from www.washingtonpost.com/local/crime/private-police-carry-guns-and-make-arrests-and-their-ranks-are-swelling/2015/02/28/29f6e02e-8f79-11e4-a900-9960214d4cd7_story.html?utm_term=.8d9853f5e911.

Kakalik, J. S., & Wildhorn, S. (1971). *Special-purpose public police.* Santa Monica, CA: Rand Corporation.

Krebs, D. L., & Miller, D. T. (1985). Altruism and aggression. In G. Lindzey & E. Aronson (Eds.), *Handbook of social psychology,* Volume 2, 3rd Edition, pp. 1–71. New York: Random House.

Legislation.gov.uk (n.d.). The Police Act 1997 (Criminal Records) Regulations 2002. Retrieved August 12, 2017, from www.legislation.gov.uk/uksi/2002/233/regulation/2/made.

MacDonald, J. M., Klick, J., & Grunwald, B. (2015). The effect of private police on crime: Evidence from a geographic regression discontinuity design. *Journal of the Royal Statistical Society, 179*(3), 831–846.

Mawby, R. I. (1999). *Policing across the world: Issues for the twenty-first century.* Abingdon, UK: Routledge.

Mulone, M. (2011). When private and public policing merge: Thoughts on commercial policing. *Social Justice, 38*(1/2), 165–183.

Mulone, M. (2016). The politics of private policing: No force and no legitimacy. In M. Deflem (Ed.), *The politics of policing: Between force and legitimacy,* pp. 277–294. Bingley, UK: Emerald Group Publishing.

National Council of Voluntary Organisations (n.d.). Volunteering. NCVO. Retrieved August 12, 2017, from www.ncvo.org.uk/policy-and-research/volunteering-policy.

Reiner, R. (2000). *The Politics of the Police,* 3rd Edition. Oxford: Oxford University Press.

Reisig, M. D., Bratton, J., & Gertz, M. (2007). The construct validity and refinement of process-based policing measures. *Criminal Justice and Behavior, 34*(8), 1005–1028.

Remington, F. J. (1965). The role of police in a democratic society. *Journal of Criminal Law and Criminology, 56*(3), 361–365.

Rowe, M. (2014). *Introduction to policing,* 2nd Edition. London: Sage.

Seth, R. (2006). *The specials.* Trowbridge, UK: Cromwell Press.

Stringham, E. (2015). San Francisco's private police force. *Reason, 47*(4), 48–54.

Stukas, A. A., Snyder, M., & Clary, E. G. (1999). The effects of "mandatory volunteerism" on intentions to volunteer. *Psychological Science*, *10*(1), 59–64.

Tankebe, J., Reisig, M. D., & Wang X. (2016). A multidimensional model of police legitimacy: A cross-cultural assessment. *Law and Human Behavior*, *40*(1), 11–22.

Tyler, T. R. (1990). *Why people obey the law*. New Haven, CT: Yale University Press.

United Nations Volunteers (2015). *2015 state of the world's volunteerism report: Transforming governance*. Washington, DC: United Nations Volunteers. Retrieved August 12, 2017, from www.unv.org/sites/default/files/2015%20State%20of%20the%20World%27s%20Volunteerism%20Report%20-%20Transforming%20Governance.pdf.

Van Craen, M. (2016). Fair policing from the inside out. In M. Deflem (Ed.), *The politics of policing: Between force and legitimacy*, pp. 3–20. Bingley, UK: Emerald Group Publishing.

Waddington, P. A. J. (1999). *Policing citizens*. Abingdon, UK: Routledge.

Walker, A. (2011). Racial profiling – separate and unequal keeping the minorities in line: The role of law enforcement in America. *St. Thomas Law Review*, *23*(4), 576–619.

Wolf, R., Albrecht, J., & Dobrin, A. (2015). Reserve policing in the United States: Citizens volunteering for public service. *The Police Chief*, *82*(10), 38–47.

Wolf, R., Holmes, S. T., & Jones, C. (2016). Utilization and satisfaction of volunteer law enforcement officers in the office of the American sheriff: An exploratory nationwide study. *Police Practice and Research: An International Journal*, *17*(5), 448–462.

Wolf, R., Pepper, I. K., & Dobrin, A. (2017). An exploratory international comparison of professional confidence in volunteer policing. *The Police Journal: Theory, Practice and Principles*, *90*(2), 91–106.

Chapter 2

The Impact of Volunteer Policing

On March 20, 2011, Florida Agricultural and Mechanical University (FAMU) drum major Robert Champion was found unconscious on the band's charter bus outside a busy hotel in the Orlando tourist area. The case would soon turn into national news in America, reporting on the tragedy of a young life brought to an end by a hazing ritual[1] and the deeply embedded hazing culture of the marching band. However, what would never make the news was the fact that the first responding uniformed law enforcement officers to the incident – officers who would perform mouth-to-mouth resuscitation and CPR in an attempt to save Mr. Champion's life, and who would then begin the preliminary investigation of the incident and who were dispatched to the emergency call – were not full-time, nor paid, employees of the sheriff's office. Although they drove marked sheriff's office cars, wore uniforms that were identical to full-time deputies with the sheriff's office, wore badges and side arms, and were sworn law enforcement officers, they were in fact volunteer reserve deputies. Both of these volunteers had retired from full-time employment with the Orange County Sheriff's Office (OCSO) and were serving in a capacity as reserves. Upon separating from his full-time position with the sheriff's office, Reserve Captain Tim Wood had moved into the private sector as head of security for a private university in Orlando and then as head of security for what is arguably the largest convention center in the United States. Reserve Deputy Stew Blackton had retired from a long career in the sheriff's office and was enjoying retirement and working as a consultant. Both were in uniform that night working as volunteers in the tourist area after the football game at which the FAMU band had played.[2]

In early January of 2012 hundreds of California law enforcement officers were on the lookout for a suspect in a string of arson fires in the West Hollywood area of Los Angeles. Reserve Deputy Shervin Lalezary, a full-time Beverly Hills real estate attorney, had volunteered to work overtime after an eight-hour volunteer shift, and spotted the driver of a van who matched the description of the arsonist seen on surveillance video. Lalezary had only recently completed his field training program which allowed him to patrol in a solo capacity, and on this date he was working just his fourth solo patrol shift. He stopped the vehicle and, after an investigation at the traffic stop, the driver was arrested and charged with at least one count of arson to an occupied dwelling. The driver, Harry Burkhart, was eventually charged with setting more than 53 fires in less than a week, causing more than US$3 million in damage (Johnson, Bonner, & Hanser, 2017). Los Angeles County Sheriff Lee Baca commented to news reporters that Reserve Deputy Lalezary had made an arrest of the suspect in one of the worst arson sprees in California history. In contrast with the first case described in this chapter, however, this incident publicized the crucial role that volunteer officers play in making our communities safer. Lalezary was awarded several local, state, and national awards, including a guest spot on the American television talk show *Ellen*, where he was very publicly congratulated for his investigation skills.

In September 2014 off-duty Reserve Deputy Sheriff Mark Vaughan in Oklahoma County, Oklahoma, shot a suspect during a workplace violence incident resulting from the suspect's earlier termination from his employment. Reserve Vaughan had served as a reserve with the Oklahoma County Sheriff's Office in the patrol division since 2010, and also served on the agency's tactical unit as a sniper and on the firearms training team. His full-time position was as chief operating officer of Vaughan Foods, a company he had founded in 1988. The suspect in this incident had been suspended from work at the Vaughan plant after getting into an argument with fellow employees, when he had allegedly stated that he did not like white people. The suspect drove to the plant, crashed his car into a parked vehicle, and entered the administrative offices, where he beheaded one female employee and attacked another, apparently trying to behead her as well. Reserve Vaughan responded to the emergency by exiting his office at the plant, and gathering his firearm and vest that identified him as a "County Sheriff" from his vehicle. He then confronted the suspect, who was still armed with a knife and attacking the second female. The suspect suddenly ran toward Vaughan, who fired three rounds, striking the suspect. The suspect was arrested by responding police and pled guilty to the homicide late in 2016. However, the judge in the case would not accept his plea, questioning the mental competence of the accused. During the investigation of the incident the suspect's apparent infatuation with Islamic extremism was discovered. Reserve Deputy Vaughan was recognized by the Oklahoma County Sheriff's Office for his heroic actions with the Award of Valor (Liu, 2014). In a statement to the public about the incident, Oklahoma County Sheriff John Whetsel stated: "Reserve deputies serve a very important role in the ability of the Oklahoma County Sheriff's Office to provide law enforcement services and protection to the citizens of Oklahoma County. Reserve deputies are citizens who attended rigorous law enforcement training and volunteer their time to serve. Mark Vaughan is an example of just how significant these men and women are to our citizens."

On June 12, 2016, a lone gunman entered the Pulse nightclub in Orlando, Florida, and carried out the deadliest terror attack on US soil since September 11, 2001, killing 49 people and wounding 53 others. While entering the club, the gunman fired shots at a police officer working a detail nearby, who returned fire at the gunman and then made a "Shots fired/officer needs help" radio call. Immediately, over a hundred law enforcement officers working throughout the area, from agencies including the Orlando Police Department, the Florida Highway Patrol, the University of Central Florida Police Department, Orange and Seminole County Sheriff's Offices, and others, responded and encountered the horrific event, with an active shooter still inside. Among the law enforcement officers who responded were three Orange County Sheriff's Office reserve deputies who had been preparing to end their volunteer shift, on which they had been working a reserve unit patrol detail on the east side of Orange County. These volunteers were among the first police officers to arrive on the scene, and included computer software professional Reserve Lieutenant James Montgomery, business owner Reserve Sergeant Jesus "Jay" Rosario, and retired law enforcement officer Reserve Sergeant Robert Knight. These unpaid, volunteer, citizen police officers mobilized with other full-time officers on scene and entered the still unsafe nightclub, with the suspect armed with a powerful assault-type rifle and semi-automatic pistol and still inside, to extract the wounded. Law enforcement efforts to assist the wounded and trapped continued even when the suspect claimed to have explosives.[3] Reserve Sergeant Knight's report of the incident was released by the sheriff's office and has been widely publicized, and depicts the heroic actions of these volunteers, who entered the club numerous times to assist the wounded in evacuating and then searched through "piles" of bodies with horrific wounds for survivors. The volunteer officers were awarded the highest honor for their bravery by the agency, the Orange County Sheriff's Office Medal of Valor. Reserve Sergeant Robert Knight and two full-time OCSO deputies were awarded the National Sheriffs' Association National Medal of Valor for their heroism.

As these examples show, being a reserve officer can be dangerous. But other incidents have occurred when the situation turned deadly for the volunteer police. A reserve deputy from Johnson County, Arkansas, was killed on May 15, 2015, after he confronted a suspect of a burglary. Reserve Deputy Sonny Smith and other deputies were searching for and confronted a suspect, who then shot Smith. Smith was able to return fire but the bullet that had struck him had punctured his lung, and he was later pronounced dead at the hospital. The reserve deputy was a father of five, and was an 11-year veteran of the Johnson County Sheriff's Office. The suspect, who was 72 years old, was found guilty of first- and second-degree murder, and was sentenced to 28 years in prison (Rains, 2016).

On March 14, 2007, two NYPD auxiliary police officers, wearing uniforms that look very similar to regular NYPD officers,[4] were killed when they began to follow the suspect of a robbery homicide in Greenwich Village in New York City. The incident began when the suspect, a former US marine, fired shots "inexplicably" at an employee inside a restaurant, killing him. Two regular police officers heard the shots and began chasing the suspect, who then ran into the path of the auxiliary police officers. NYPD auxiliary officers are not armed, and when the suspect turned back on them they tried to hide behind parked vehicles as he shot at them. The two auxiliary officers, Nicholas Pekearo, who was 28, and Yevgeniy Marshalik, who was 19, both died at the scene. The suspect was shot and killed by responding NYPD police officers (Hope, 2007).[5] Marshalik had joined the NYPD auxiliary unit about 18 months prior to the incident, and was an immigrant to New York from Chechnya, where he and his family had fled the violence of war. He was also a student at New York University, and intended to go to law school to be a prosecutor. Pekearo had been an auxiliary officer for about four years, and worked as a salesman at a bookstore while he attended Empire State College in Manhattan (Wilson, 2007).

Being a volunteer officer may also involve a deadly situation, even when doing something that may be considered "routine," such as directing traffic. One example of this occurred on May 14, 2005. Washington DC Metropolitan Police Reserve Officer Joseph Pozell was directing traffic at an intersection in Georgetown when he was struck by a vehicle. He died from his injuries. Another similar example is found in the circumstance of Ramsey County (Minnesota) Sheriff's Department Reserve Deputy Mike Wilken. Reserve Deputy Wilken was directing traffic at an annual Halloween haunted house on October 25, 2009, when he was struck and killed by a vehicle (Officer Down Memorial Page, n.d.).

In England and Wales incidents similar to those above are not only very rare but also generally localized in areas where gang and drug activity is most common. Handguns are not permitted and licenses for other firearms are issued only after extensive background searches of the applicant and an examination of the property where the firearm is to be kept. While armed police officers are more commonplace since the increased tensions around terrorism, they are by no means a routine part of the day-to-day policing in the United Kingdom. Volunteer police (special constables) are not currently permitted to carry Tasers® or firearms but these weapons are used in a wide range of operations by regular, full-time officers.

On Sunday June 7, 1992, Police Constable Sandy Kelly and Special Constable Glenn Goodman were on routine patrol in their police vehicle in Tadcaster, North Yorkshire, when they noted a car parked close to a brewery in the town. The car sped off and was pursued by Kelly and Goodman, who were then fired on by Paul Magee, a known IRA terrorist. Goodman was shot twice in the chest by Magee and died. Kelly was then shot four times by the same gunman and was injured, but survived his wounds. Mr. Goodman was 37 years old and his regular job was as a truck driver. He was married and father to an 11-month-old son. He was the first special constable to be murdered while on duty since 1942. Mr. Goodman had joined the specials only a few months earlier as a step to applying for the regular police service (Kirby, 1993).

In 2016 Special Constable George Brown received an award from the Metropolitan Police Commissioner after he successfully caught and apprehended a man, armed with a samurai sword, who was also wanted for attempted murder. In January 2017 a quick-thinking special constable was suspicious when he noted a vehicle parked across a gate. The driver took off on foot and was caught by the volunteer police officer. Following the driver's arrest, an array of stolen gardening equipment was found in the van. This event took place in a village in rural Somerset in the southwest of England. Such areas are perceived to have few crime problems, so policing is sparse; it is often only the service of SCs which enables such areas to be policed to any degree.

The importance of appropriate training to address a wide range of potential incidents is fundamental, and in particular the ability of both regular officers and volunteer police officers to work together. An example of unit deployment, in December of 2013, saw bad weather and tidal surges that led to flooding on the east coast of Essex in the United Kingdom, which called for the mobilization of the volunteer Essex Police Special Constabulary. During a single 24-hour period the volunteer constables responded to over 150 calls for service, with some officers working shifts in excess of 18 hours. The chief officer of the Essex Special Constabulary commented on the hard work of the volunteer officers and the unit's ability to respond to this type of disaster with "resilience at times of peak demand" (Deller, 2013).

The 2012 Olympic Games in London provided an operational scenario that demanded a high police presence requiring the import of extra personnel. Originally it was thought that these special constables, who have police authority and wear police uniforms, would be sent to help with the policing of the games in London and other sites where heats were taking place, an opportunity that some specials looked forward to. In the end, though, plans changed and full-time officers were deployed, resulting in specials filling the roles of the relocated officers. Nonetheless, the London Metropolitan Police reported an all-time high number of 5,677 special constables during the Olympics in 2012, a figure which dropped by 43 percent in the four years that followed, down to 3,253 in mid-2016

(Davenport, 2016). In March 2015 there were 16,101 special constables across all of England and Wales (Home Office, 2015).

These events exemplify what it means to go "above and beyond" for reserves, auxiliaries, and special constables. Often the public do not differentiate the act performed by the volunteer, because they do not recognize, due to the similar uniforms and the professionalism displayed, that the individual is a volunteer or "part-time" police officer. Many people may not even realize that volunteers exist in policing in the United Kingdom or the United States. Unfortunately, this also means that, as regular police can become the subject of violence just because they are police, so can volunteer police. In February of 2016 four gang members were convicted of the murder of 45-year-old Waynesboro, Virginia, Reserve Police Captain Kevin Quick. Reserve Captain Quick had been killed in February of 2014 when he was attacked and forced to give his personal banking information so that the gang members could steal US$400 from his account. When they discovered Quick's police identification, they shot him once in the head and hid his body, which was not found for four days. The leader of the attack has been sentenced to life plus 132 years for the abduction and murder, two of his accomplices were sentenced to life plus 82 years, and the fourth to life plus 10 years (Bryan & Burns, 2016).

Unfortunately, there have also been instances when volunteer policing has been "under the microscope" for reasons that are not admirable. Similar to any profession, there are people in volunteer policing who have made poor decisions, have made mistakes, or have committed outright criminal acts. Such a situation was brought to the attention of the worldwide media when a Tulsa, Oklahoma, reserve deputy shot and killed a suspected armed drug dealer in April of 2015 when he apparently fired his revolver when he thought he had his Taser in his hand. Media outlets focused on the fact that the reserve, Robert Bates, was a police volunteer, and questioned whether he should have been in a position to be involved in such a dangerous situation with a gun. Because the reserve deputy was also wealthy and had contributed money to the sheriff's office where he volunteered, the media (and the Civil Liberties Union) questioned whether the reserve had "bought" his position as a reserve. The charge of manslaughter led the media and the public to use this instance as a condemnation of volunteer policing in the United States (Campoy & Elinson, 2015). A jury found the former volunteer reserve deputy guilty of second-degree manslaughter and recommended a sentence of four years in prison (Ellis, Lett, & Sidner, 2016). The judge in the case agreed with the jury and sentenced him to four years in prison, even though Bates' attorney provided sentencing data indicating that probation was the standard sentence for a second-degree manslaughter conviction (Pickard & Jones, 2016).

Early in 2016, in the United Kingdom, Special Constable Andrew Blades was forced to resign and was given a criminal record after he had used the patrol vehicle he was driving as a barrier to stop a biker who was driving toward a fellow police officer. "Police top brass claimed he had not been trained to carry out such a manoeuvre and he was yesterday convicted of dangerous driving" (Mansfield, 2016).

These examples are important illustrations of how volunteer police can make either a positive or a negative impact on policing in communities in both the United Kingdom and the United States.

Unfortunately, academic literature and public knowledge about the role of volunteer police has been lacking. With the United States' fragmented police system, even the number of active police reserves is difficult to estimate; there is no one single entity responsible for maintaining records on volunteer police, and no two states keep similar data (Dobrin & Wolf, 2016; Berg & Doerner, 1988). Policing agencies in the United States that utilize reserves, auxiliaries, and other types of volunteer police have no singular best practice on how to organize their workforce, and there is little research on the organizational structure of reserves (Dobrin & Wolf, 2016). The lack of uniformity in the United States regarding the definition of a reserve or auxiliary officer, as well as the inconsistency in training for these officers, will be discussed at greater length in this book.

Contrary to the situation in the United States, in England and Wales all police forces are required to follow central policies, although individual forces' strategies do vary. While in the United States all full-time or regular law enforcement officers are armed with firearms, and in many jurisdictions reserve and auxiliary police are too, police officers in England and Wales do not routinely carry firearms. Across UK police forces, selected full-time personnel carry firearms as part of special response units according to the strategic decision making of each force. Therefore, full-time police are issued stab vests, sprays, batons, and increasingly Tasers, or may be assigned to specialized units and carry firearms. Special constables carry similar equipment, but are issued with neither Tasers nor firearms.

The Role of Police

With the creation of the first modern police force in London in 1829, Sir Robert Peel focused on crime prevention and an organization that was a civilian rather than a military force. The Act for Improving the Police in and near the Metropolis, also known as the Metropolitan Police Act, emphasized the preventative aspects of law enforcement. This reflected the notion that it is better to prevent crime than it is to respond to calls for help. These officers, or "bobbies," as they later became known in recognition of their founder, were structured along military lines – that is, with a rank structure and located in proximity so that they were accessible to citizens, and distributed according to time and area. This organization became the model for many other police organizations that are or formerly were a part of the British Empire, including the United States. Although policing in the United Kingdom and in other countries that followed the British example may have deviated in some ways, the central focus of these organizations is that police cannot be successful without the willing participation and involvement of the communities that are policed. The police have therefore endeavored to encourage the resources of the community to participate in keeping a watchful eye out for criminal activity, and share in various policing functions. This has been more successful in some areas and at different times than in others.

Modern policing in both the United States and the United Kingdom developed systems based on the "Peelian principles," but strikingly different models have evolved. When English colonists first arrived in America in the early seventeenth century and created their own "policing" agencies, they borrowed from the English model of the time. The sheriff, the constable, and the watch were adapted to fit distinctly American needs. However, these were inefficient and often corrupt organizations that acceded to political interference. Even after Sir Robert Peel implemented the English model of policing in London, American police agencies struggled with corruption and inefficiency in light of urbanization, industrialization, immigration, and riots between ethnic groups. The American cities that developed police agencies based on the London model were met with uncertainty by citizens, largely due to a fear that the police would be controlled by political parties – a fear that was largely realized (Archbold, 2013).

Police officers in the United States in the "political era" of policing (1830s–1920s) were selected based on their political connections or their contributions to the political party in power. In this early era of policing in America, police departments were immersed in local politics and there was a political stronghold over the functions and actions of the police, including promotion. In Britain, however, this same political influence into the daily routine of policing did not occur, and the commissioners of the London police were essentially free from outside political influence, largely insulating them from the corruption that was occurring in America.

This difference continues today, with many local policing agencies in the United States having elected or politically appointed chief officers, while the British model has only recently begun to utilize newly created and elected police and crime commissioners (PCCs). The role of the PCCs came into being in 2012, and was considered to be preferable to the previous police authorities in an era of local accountability and community policing. The Policy Exchange think tank set the mood for American-style police commissioners, who would be locally elected and take on responsibility for the budget in their force area, as well as holding senior officers to account (Bullock, 2014). According to the Association of Police and Crime Commissioners (APCC), "The role of the PCCs is to be the voice of the people and hold the police to account. They are responsible for the totality of policing" (Association of Police and Crime Commissioners, n.d.). The introduction of PCCs was poorly supported, generally because of a lack of knowledge on the part of the electorate, resulting in only 15.1 percent overall submitting valid voting forms, with many spoiling their voting papers. When the vote took place, on November 15, 2012, turnout by the electorate varied between 11.6 percent and 19.8 percent in the 41 eligible police areas (Electoral Commission, 2013). Many of the candidates canvassed as members of political parties: in 2012 27.5 percent of successful contenders declared themselves as "independent," but in the most recent election, in 2016, this figure had reduced to 7.5 percent. In spite of this apparent affiliation, PCCs are required to fulfill the role with impartiality.

The election of the PCCs came about while the United Kingdom remained in recession, and a pledge given by many of the candidates called for a significant increase in special constables to fill the gap left by the reduction in the number of full-time police officers, an issue that was fueled by much of the media (see, for example, Sussex, Cheshire, and Humberside).

Walker and Katz (2013) illustrate that from their inception the police in London became increasingly professionalized, while American police were entrenched in racial and religious tensions, instability of assignments, and unprofessional conduct. "The difference was that the Commissioners of the London Metropolitan Police were free from political interference and able to maintain high personnel standards. As a result, London bobbies eventually won public respect" (p. 32). Certainly, this respect has been questioned at various times, but English police have striven to maintain the essence of Sir Robert Peel's first concept: that of policing citizens by citizens. The police, and the criminal justice system itself, rely heavily on the public on many different levels, and "it is no exaggeration to state that the system is dependent upon both public involvement and co-operation" (Gill & Mawby, 1990, p. 5).

A further separation between the British and American models of policing can be found in the use of force options available. American police began to carry firearms early in their history as a result of increasing violence and the nature of firearms in American society. Firearms are an arguably accepted part of society in the United States, based largely upon the American Constitution's Bill of Rights, which included requirements to maintain a well-armed militia in light of prior military action by the

Photo 3 An American volunteer sheriff's deputy trains in the use of firearms

British monarchy. This has permeated modern American society, and today allows for very liberal gun laws in many states. Police in the United Kingdom have not had to react to a similar culture, and therefore have been able to resist this change. Modern armed response teams can also be found today in English policing, but this underlying cultural difference has created a significantly dissimilar way of responding to violent activity when comparing American and English police officers. This difference is also noted in the training and equipment utilized by volunteer police in the two countries. Reserve or auxiliary police in the United States may or may not be trained on firearms and the use of deadly force, while special constables in the United Kingdom are not. American volunteer police may tend to see themselves as equal to their paid, full-time counterparts only if they have received firearm training and are authorized to carry a firearm while on duty (see Photo 3). Those volunteer police in the United States who have not received this training may feel as if they are "second class," or as being functionally different from their full-time counterparts.

Volunteering to Police

Both American and British policing have significant histories with regard to volunteerism relating to policing duties. Volunteers have supported policing efforts in the United States both in formal and informal ways, through volunteer posse, search and rescue, communications, and government-supported auxiliary or reserve police functions. In the American British colonies, local volunteers were the first peace officers, serving the night watch. Many major cities then moved to a paid night-watch system, or variations of town marshals, constables, and police justices (Greenberg, 1984). However, volunteerism in policing has continued, and today can be seen in neighborhood watch programs, victim advocates, language interpreters, youth explorer or cadet programs, citizens on patrol, and reserve and auxiliary programs.

While the use of uncompensated policing dates back at least 1,000 years, Greenberg (2005) divided the history of volunteer policing in the United States into five periods. He defined these as 1) the Lay Justice Era, including slave patrols and the constable and watch systems; 2) the Vigilant Era, including the use of posses and detective societies; 3) the Spy Era, including individuals from the Anti-Saloon League and the American Protective League; 4) the Transformation Era, including the evolution of special-purpose police reserves; and 5) the Assimilation Era, when civil defense workers and other volunteer police became part of the community policing of many police agencies. The history of volunteer policing and the history of regular policing will be examined more closely in Chapter 4 of this text.

In modern policing in the United States there is no standard definition for what the title of "auxiliary" or "reserve" officer means. In 1971 the Rand Corporation produced a report on special-purpose police in the United States, and, as part of that report, addressed the issue of police reserves. "Reserve police forces, typically composed of volunteers who operate under the guidance and control of the regular public police organization, serve as an emergency reserve manpower pool for use in the event of civil or natural disaster" (Kakalik & Wildhorn, 1971, p. 4). American reserve and auxiliary officers are still used to serve as reserve personnel for specific large-scale police needs. Often reserves serve as supplementary to "regular" police officers, and they may be utilized as back-up officers in two-person patrols, or in posts during times of heavy demand for law enforcement personnel. However, the understanding of what reserves might actually do as law enforcement officers can be confusing because of the many varied ways that states have adopted their use.

In many states in America, an auxiliary officer has limited or no authority and serves in a public support, rather than a law enforcement, role. In other states, an auxiliary officer may be armed and have arrest powers and may perform the same duties and functions of a full-time officer but as a volunteer. Some agencies may also utilize volunteer officers to perform functions that are not needed on a day-to-day basis, such as mounted patrol or in riot control teams or underwater search and rescue teams (Kakalik & Wildhorn, 1971). Although some agencies may limit the duties and assignments of police volunteers to specific, and often more mundane, tasks, others may provide police training to volunteers plus additional specialized training (Greenberg, 1984).

Americans are encouraged to volunteer in general, and American policy makers have developed initiatives to promote volunteerism.

Recent US Presidents George H. W. Bush and Barack Obama have both started programs to recognize the importance of volunteering (Nesbit & Brudney, 2010). The horrific events of September 11, 2001, also had a positive influence on volunteer utilization in the United States; county governments and highly populated cities saw an increase in people who had an interest in volunteering, especially those communities that already had some public volunteers (Gazley & Brudney, 2005). In 2011 64.3 million Americans volunteered in all types of civic engagement, volunteering approximately 7.9 billion hours, estimated to be worth over US$171 billion (Corporation for National and Community Service, 2012). The benefits of citizens volunteering in police work relates to both local governments and the citizens of the community (Ren, Zhao, Lovrich, & Gaffney, 2006). Hanser, Bonner, and Johnson (2017) suggest that "the use of volunteers in police agencies is a concept that has been fully embraced in the United States" (p. 25), but actually only a limited number of the over 18,000 law enforcement agencies in the country have formal programs. Recent literature suggests that only 30 percent of all public safety organizations in the United States have volunteer units or organizations (Brudney & Kellough, 2000).

Britain has mirrored the expansion of the use of volunteers in policing, engaging volunteers in programs such as Police and Communities Together (PACT), Neighborhood Watch, and the special constabulary, resulting in Her Majesty's Inspectorate for Constabulary noting "that the role of the volunteer was essential" in British policing (Gravelle & Rogers, 2009). However, the role of the special constabulary, first formally recognized in 1662 in Britain, was initially to enforce the law (Pepper, 2012). In 1831 the role of the special constabulary became more consistent with that of the British police, including protecting the peace (Pepper, 2012). The term "special" may also create confusion, as many different police agencies tend to utilize the word in describing other police functions or units, such as Special Branch, special response, and Special Patrol Groups (Gill & Mawby, 1990). More recently the relatively new National Crime Agency also recruits special constables, whose role is far more specialist and their powers somewhat different from "normal" volunteer police officers (National Crime Agency, n.d.). The term may also create confusion with those who work as "special police" or with private police forces. Modern special constables are volunteers who work under the direction of a chief constable and function as duly authorized members of a police force (Gill & Mawby, 1990). More than 30 percent of volunteer police special constables in the United Kingdom are female, and 10 percent from a minority ethnic group. These rates are higher than those found among regular British police officers (Strickland & Lalic, 2010).

Most special constables spend a few hours each week as volunteers in their local police force. They receive training, are provided a police uniform (sometimes with special markings which indicate their volunteer status), have full police powers, and are responsible for carrying out many of the same functions as full-time regular officers, including foot patrol, mobile community patrol, and traffic duty (Strickland & Lalic, 2010).

Why Volunteer in Policing?

Throughout the United States and the United Kingdom individuals decide to volunteer to serve in policing programs for a variety of reasons. In both countries some volunteer because they see the training and experience necessary to apply for full-time positions in policing (Pepper, 2014; Wolf, Holmes, & Jones, 2016). In fact, some policing agencies in the United States have proposed requiring new applicants to their organization to have volunteer law enforcement service as a prerequisite before an individual is considered for a full-time position (Scoville, 2014). Others are allowing police reserve time to count toward time needed for promotion once a volunteer becomes a full-time police officer (Police Department Disciplinary Bulletin, 2006). Most policing agencies require volunteer police to participate in "on-the-job" training programs, a field training (or mentored accompanied patrol) program, or similar in addition to having any additional required training. This "in-house" preparation by the agencies allows the potential police agency employer to get a better understanding of the capabilities and any potential pitfalls a particular candidate for hire might have before offering him or her a position. Agencies can screen new volunteer officers for their ability to solve problems and show initiative, take direction, learn new skills, use good judgment and demonstrate integrity, show compassion and respect, and communicate effectively.

Another subgroup of American volunteer law enforcement officers is those who have retired from full-time policing positions and who want to stay in touch with the profession, community, and those who they worked with for years (Ferranto, 2011; Hunter, 2012). This seems to be an anomaly of American policing, and is rarely found in other countries that use volunteer police. Members of this group may decide to stay in volunteer policing for fear of giving up their police powers; or they may stay for personal gain, or to use their training and expertise to acquire part-time or private security positions. Some of these officers become volunteers after a short full-time stint in law enforcement, and have moved on to other careers or opportunities for a variety of reasons. Others may have been in long-term careers as police, possibly even holding high-ranking positions within the same or another agency before retiring and becoming a volunteer. This allows agencies to keep some of the institutional knowledge that might normally vanish upon senior leadership retirement, but it also allows the agency to use the expertise, contacts, training, and abilities of those moving to retirement or other positions for current projects, special details, and investigations.

The last subgroup of volunteer law enforcement officers is those who have never held full-time law enforcement positions and have no plans to do so. Instead, they view volunteer policing to be an avenue of community service that fits their interests, and they donate their time as an exciting and rewarding way to contribute to society's welfare. Volunteer law enforcement officers report that they enjoy the excitement of helping citizens, learning new things, and interacting with others as part of the experience (Berg & Doerner, 1988). This category has many commonalities in American and British policing.

While this classifies the types of people who work in volunteer policing functions into subsets, this does not answer the question "Why?" Although it may be easiest, when reviewing these reasons for participation, to understand why those who wish to apply for full-time position may volunteer, the other categories are not self-explanatory. Why would someone who has invested 20 or 30 years in a career, who is able to draw a retirement allowance, continue to work in the same capacity as a volunteer? Why would someone with no interest in being employed full-time as a police officer choose to succumb to the rigorous training, time commitments, evaluation, and retraining required of a volunteer police officer rather than to some other, potentially less dangerous, community involvement? Undoubtedly, volunteer police are not the only individuals who serve in this capacity; volunteer firefighters also place their lives and well-being at risk for society.

Pepper and Wolf (2015) studied two agencies that utilized volunteer police, one from the United States and one from the United Kingdom. American respondents in this study indicated that they were motivated to serve as volunteer police for a variety of reasons, but 25 percent because they "used to be a regular officer and want to keep in touch with colleagues" or "used to be a regular officer and want to make use of knowledge and/or expertise" (Pepper & Wolf, 2015, p. 217). None of the UK respondents indicated that they held any prior regular full-time police positions. Pepper (2014) followed 20 new special constables as they began their careers with a UK police service. One-half of the respondents in this study indicated that they had previously applied to be regular police officers, or had applied for full-time positions in other paid policing roles. Pepper also reported that volunteer motivations include a desire to give back to the community or to make a difference in the community.

Crime-related variables, such as fear of crime, social disorder, and citizen perceptions of the level and legitimacy of police services, may influence the decisions of citizens to participate in community-based policing. Additionally, studies have shown that citizens that participate in crime prevention tend to have more positive attitudes toward the police and are more supportive of the community policing philosophy (Randol & Gaffney, 2014).

Who Volunteers in Policing?

American law enforcement volunteers in policing are generally white males with a college education, and almost half are older than 40 years of age. They are more likely than other types of volunteers to hold full-time positions other than in law enforcement (Hilal & Olsen, 2010), which means that they generally have other time commitments and work requirements apart from their volunteer role. American police reserves are more likely than other types of volunteers to hold full-time jobs and may also be more likely to donate to more than one organization (Hilal & Olsen, 2010; see also Wolf et al., 2016). Volunteer law enforcement officers indicate that they are motivated to serve as volunteer police because they want to contribute to their community, they want to "develop as a person," they have an interest in law and policing in general, or they have previous skills and knowledge that they want to use to enhance policing in their community (Wolf et al., 2016; Dobrin & Wolf, 2016).

With regard to those who volunteer to join the special constabulary in England and Wales, their reasons, too, are manifold (see Photo 4). Historically the police in England and Wales have recruited and trained their own, with every one of the 43 force areas recruiting to suit their

Photo 4 Volunteers join the special constabulary for a variety of reasons in the United Kingdom, including a desire to learn more about policing and to give back to their community

individual needs for full-time or volunteer officers. In the past decade or so, however, many forces have undertaken their training through universities, which has the benefit of offsetting costs of training on to the students themselves.

Recent research (Britton, 2016) has indicated that there are a number of reasons why special constables join as volunteer police. Respondents were asked to put in order, from a list, their top three options. Number one was "I was interested in a career in policing and wanted to learn more about it and/or to gain skills and experience to strengthen a future application for a paid policing role" (41.0 percent) and the second most common reply was "I wanted to give something back to my local community and to play an important part in making my local community safer" (31.2 percent) (Britton, 2016, p. 17).

According to government statistics, in March 2016 special constables were the most ethnically diverse section of all policing groups, with 11.6 percent declaring themselves to be non-white compared to only 5.9 percent of regular officers. At the time, 14 percent of the population was similarly categorized (Hargreaves, Linehan, Husband, & McKee, 2017).

Why Would a Police Agency Use a Volunteer Program?

As will be identified throughout this book, volunteers continue to provide a breadth of benefits to both the provider and the recipient/s, be they individuals or communities. Volunteer programs can also be used to develop cooperation between public organizations and communities. Beyond these immediate benefits, involvement in volunteer programs can also provide citizens with a sense of connection to their own government. Voluntary activities often help to enhance the services that government and non-profit entities provide (Fredericksen & Levin, 2004), and bridge the gap in coverage from governmental organizations (Nesbit & Brudney, 2010). Fear of crime is regularly identified as a contributor to public perceptions of crime and disorder (Lee, 2007), and volunteer programs within criminal justice agencies can go some way to reduce such feelings through their very presence and increase positive perceptions of local police and other public institutions. American volunteer officers may enhance citizen understanding of the problems, demands, and activities of government because of the variety of backgrounds and experiences brought into the agency and utilized within the community (Ren et al., 2006). In England and Wales, however, the specialist skills that volunteers may hold have only recently begun to be utilized by the forces in which they serve.

There are other advantages, however, to a volunteer policing unit. In addition to improved engagement with the local community and an increased confidence in the police, volunteer police also provide greater transparency to policing functions (Gravelle & Rogers, 2009). For example, by allowing volunteers into the organization with free access to police tactics, intelligence, and the decision-making process, departments are opening themselves up for greater transparency and community involvement. This is something that is in contrast to the "veil" of secrecy that police departments have historically held, or have been perceived to hold, over their operations. Volunteer policing programs also provide the potential for inexpensive (not necessarily "free") and potentially highly skilled labor. The use of police volunteers may reduce or eliminate the human resources financial impact (there are some places that "pay" their volunteers, either in the form of allowances, or as stipends to offset costs), there are still costs involved with hosting personnel in such a unit, including recruitment, training, and operational costs. Examples of operational costs include uniforms and equipment, medical or worker's compensation insurance, liability insurance, and the need for full-time staff to supervise or organize the volunteers (Wolf et al., 2016; Brudney, 2000).

Although many volunteer police participate in foot patrol or vehicle patrol, American police agencies may also use them for other tasks, including public record investigations, creating public visibility for large events, traffic control, background investigations, report writing, case investigations, automobile accident investigations, parking regulations enforcement, or participation in a specialized unit within the agency (Arwood, Hilal, Karsky, & Norman, 2005). In England and Wales the job functions are similarly diverse, though they may vary slightly from those in the United States.

American police agencies also benefit from the experience that their volunteers bring from other public-sector and private-sector professions. Many agencies in the United States have begun utilizing fully trained or certified emergency medical technicians (EMTs) or medical doctors in law enforcement medical roles for special response teams. Criminal investigation units within policing agencies have begun utilizing volunteer police who are certified accountants in the investigation of white-collar crime. Training units have utilized experienced educators as agency trainers, and this knowledge is now expanding to online education, as many agencies begin to put short training courses in online formats assisted by volunteer police with educational experience. Retired or former full-time officers can also be utilized for their knowledge and experience. This may include using former criminal investigators, field training officers, background investigators, recruiters, or crime scene investigators in the same role they once worked in, or to train new people who have moved into these roles. Finally, agencies may decide to build a ready reserve for specialized functions, including providing advanced training in such areas as motorcycle or mounted patrols, search and rescue or dive teams, bomb squads, aviation, or other similar, highly specialized positions (Wolf et al., 2016).

In England and Wales, forces have generally been much slower in recognizing the benefits of special constables (and, indeed, police support volunteers) who have specialist skills. Police services throughout the United Kingdom focus on the benefits that service as a special constable can offer to the individual, not the other way around. This is gradually changing, however, with experts in a range of specialisms being recruited as both special constables and PSVs, the latter having fewer powers. Indeed, there are many examples of special constables and volunteers being sought and utilized in areas where expertise is needed and the cost of training police officers is expensive. In addition, since 2010 policing numbers have decreased in most of the 43 force areas, therefore resulting in less spare capacity (Allen & Uberoi, 2016). As in the United States, opportunities are wide-reaching and can provide a significant financial saving to individual forces and to tight budgets.

In the past several decades policing agencies have had an increased realization that crime control cannot be effective without community support. Communities and the citizens who make them up must be involved and play an assertive role in crime prevention efforts (Randol & Gaffney, 2014). Gravelle and Rogers (2010) examined the advantages within England and Wales for a police service to utilize civilian police volunteers, especially in light of the economic downturn. They reported three distinct benefits: the economic advantages of using volunteers, an increase in community cohesion, and increased public confidence in the police. In addition to improved engagement with the local community and an increased confidence in the police, volunteer police also provide greater transparency in terms of policing functions (Gravelle & Rogers, 2009; see also Dobrin, 2016).

As mentioned earlier, there also is a wide range of events that require increased personnel resources, to assist with planned high-need occasions, including parades, sporting events, and political events, and also to respond to weather emergencies and natural or man-made disasters (Greenberg, 1984; Dobrin, 2016). The ability to have a ready reserve of personnel for a police agency can be priceless (see Photo 5). To have a readily available pool of fully trained, full-time personnel is impractical and economically not viable, so the availability of trained and warranted volunteer officers provides a ready reserve pool of personnel. Volunteer officers also serve as potential applicants for full-time positions. "Volunteer programs can serve as an *ad hoc* apprentice program from which departments might recruit potential full-time officers" (Dobrin, 2016, p. 720).

Volunteer police can help ease the burden on full-time personnel when there is a need to move personnel resources from one area to another.

Photo 5 Volunteer police can be a ready reserve of personnel for emergencies or planned large-scale events

Volunteers with full police powers can "backfill" patrol zones and answer calls if regular full-time personnel are needed to respond to a high-risk or more serious event. Additionally, specially trained volunteers can serve as an agency on-call unit when it does not make sense to have a full-time unit or use full-time resources (Dobrin, 2016). Examples may include special operations units, such as technical diving teams, boat operators, medics, or bicycle patrol units. As needed, investigative units might be useful, including those with expertise in cybercrime, technological expertise, or financial crimes units. Smaller police agencies (such as many of those found in the United States) may find it cost-effective to use volunteers as honor guard units or mounted patrol units, rather than pay the expenses to try to maintain these full-time.

Phillips and Terrell-Orr (2013) reported that police supervisors, even those who hold attitudes that may be considered reflective of aggressive law enforcement, do not appear to resist volunteers in policing. This study reported that many police supervisors may value citizen involvement in policing, especially when dealing with order maintenance. Police supervisors, contrary to what may be expected, did not view volunteers as outsiders in the policing world, nor did they view volunteers as more trouble for the agency than they are worth.

In fieldwork over a number of years in England and Wales conversations suggest that, while many senior officers value the availability of SCs, there are those who are more dismissive of the role, and even some of those who are supportive fail to recognize the extent to which they can benefit the service.

Why Might an Agency Not Want to Use a Volunteer Program?

Agencies may hesitate to create volunteer units because of concerns about the authority, job responsibilities, and functions of members of a volunteer policing unit. While these are clearly outlined in some jurisdictions (such as those in the United Kingdom), this is not true in all cases in the United States. As discussed in Chapter 1 of this book, New York City's 4,500 auxiliary officers have no arrest powers and are considered a visual deterrent for crime rather than law enforcement officers, while the City of Los Angeles utilizes approximately 650 volunteer reserve officers who do have the power of arrest. Specific job functions for volunteer officers throughout the United States and the United Kingdom vary greatly, but may include office tasks, public record investigations, public events, traffic control, background investigations, patrol functions, report writing, case investigations, crash investigations, or participation in a specialized unit within the agency. Many agencies today also attempt to utilize the full-time job or experience of volunteer officers in their role with the police. This may include having EMTs or medical doctors serving in medic roles for special response teams, or utilizing accountants in the investigations of white-collar crime or having educators as agency trainers.

There are also arguments that can be made against having a reserve or auxiliary unit entirely. These arguments include the fact that it may be difficult to get volunteers for such a dangerous and potentially litigious position. Arguments also include the potentially high cost of initial and continual training, the potential threat of liability to the agency (Kakalik & Wildhorn, 1971), objections from full-time (or "regular") police officers, and potential public distrust and disrespect for "weekend warrior" officers (Phillips & Terrell-Orr, 2013; National Advisory Commission on Criminal Justice Standards and Goals, 1973).

Zhao, Gibson, Lovrich, and Gaffney (2002) reported that those citizens who participated in crime prevention efforts demonstrated higher levels of social cohesion than those that did not, but Randol and Gaffney (2014) reported that "practitioners should consider that it will be most difficult to encourage citizens that have lower incomes, less favorable attitudes toward the police, and citizens that do not normally engage in volunteerism to participate" (p. 244) in volunteer policing activities.

Notes

1 "Hazing" is defined by Florida statute 1006.63 as "any action or situation that recklessly or intentionally endangers the mental or physical health or safety of a student for purposes including, but not limited to, initiation or admission into or affiliation with any organization operating under the sanction of a postsecondary institution."

2 In contrast with the US experience, regular police officers who leave the police service are far less likely to continue as volunteers in the United Kingdom's Special Constabulary, an issue that will be explored later in this book.

3 9-1-1 emergency operators were warned by patrons being held as hostages, still inside, that the suspect claimed to have explosives. Officers utilized bomb detection canine teams, including a team from the University of Central Florida Police Department, to sweep the area and the suspect's car, which was found in a nearby parking lot. Special tactical team members killed the gunman when they breached the wall of the bathroom where the gunman was holding hostages.

4 Members of the NYPD auxiliary wear uniforms that are largely identical to full-time police officers in New York. The auxiliary police uniform shirt sleeve has a "rocker" on top of the NYPD patch that states "Auxiliary" and the auxiliary badge is shaped like a star, instead of like a police shield. NYPD Auxiliary Police are not authorized to carry a firearm on duty, but are required to complete an "Auxiliary Police Basic Training Course," which provides "Peace Officer without Firearm Training" status, and they must complete an auxiliary field training program.

5 Initially the US Justice Department refused to provide line-of-duty death benefits to the families of the fallen NYPD auxiliary officers killed in 2007, but in 2008 they reversed that decision. NYPD Auxiliary Officer Milton Clarke was slain in December 1993 when he ran in the direction of gunfire when he was off duty. His family was finally provided line-of-duty death benefits in 2010, following the US Justice Department's reversal in the Pekearo and Marshalik homicide.

References

Allen, G., & Uberoi, E. (2016). *Police service strength*, Briefing Paper 00634. London: House of Commons Library. Retrieved January 13, 2017, from http://researchbriefings.files.parliament.uk/documents/SN00634/SN00634.pdf.

Archbold, C. (2013). *Policing: A text/reader*. Thousand Oaks, CA: Sage.

Arwood, D. E., Hilal, S. M., Karsky, J., & Norman, J. M. (2005). Police reserve officers: Structural embeddedness of self-role merger and volunteering. *Great Plains Sociologists*, 17(2), 36–60.

Association of Police and Crime Commissioners (n.d.). Role of the PCC. APCC. Retrieved December 4, 2015, from www.apccs.police.uk/role-of-the-pcc.

Berg, B. L., & Doerner, W. G. (1988). Volunteer police officers: An unexamined personnel dimension in law enforcement. *American Journal of Police*, 7(1), 81–89.

Britton, I. (2016). *National survey of special constables and police support volunteers: Initial findings report*. Northampton, UK: University of Northampton, Institute for Public Safety, Crime and Justice.

Brudney, J. L. (2000). The effective use of volunteers: Best practices for the public sector. *Law Enforcement and Contemporary Problems*, 4(11), 219–255.

Brudney, J. L., & Kellough, J. E. (2000). Volunteers in state government: Involvement, management, and benefits. *Nonprofit and Voluntary Sector Quarterly*, 29(1), 111–130.

Bryan, A., & Burns, J. (2016, September 19). Gang members sentenced to life in prison for Cpt. Kevin Quick's murder. WTVR News. Retrieved September 22, 2016, from wtvr.com/2016/09/19/gang-members-sentenced-to-life-in-prison-for-cpt-kevin-quicks-murder.

Bullock, K. (2014). *Citizens, community and crime control*. Basingstoke, UK: Palgrave Macmillan.

Campoy, A., & Elinson, Z. (2015, April 15). Volunteer deputy in Tulsa shooting turns himself in. *The Wall Street Journal*, A3.

Corporation for National and Community Service (2012). Volunteering and civic life in America 2012. CNCS. Retrieved May 16, 2013, from www.volunteeringinamerica.gov.

Davenport, J. (2016, March 3). Huge fall in number of special constables puts "immense strain" on Met. *Evening Standard*. Retrieved August 1, 2016, from www.standard.co.uk/news/crime/huge-fall-in-number-of-special-constables-puts-immense-strain-on-met-a3194641.html.

Deller, J. (2013, December 10). Special constables mobilised in force to assist with the policing response to the recent tidal surges on the East Coast. Association of Special Constabulary Chief Officers. Retrieved June 10, 2014, from www.ascco.org.uk/index.php/news/63-essex-specials-answer-call-to-action.

Dobrin, A. (2016). Volunteer police: History, benefits, costs and current descriptions. *Security Journal, 30*(3), 717–733.

Dobrin, A., & Wolf, R. (2016). What is known and not known about volunteer policing in the United States. *International Journal of Police Science and Management, 18*(3), 220–227.

Electoral Commission (2013). *Police and crime commissioner elections in England and Wales: Report on the administration of the elections held on 15 November 2012*. London: Electoral Commission.

Ellis, R., Lett, C., & Sidner, S. (2016, April 28). Ex-Oklahoma deputy Robert Bates guilty of killing unarmed suspect. CNN News. Retrieved August 1, 2016, from www.cnn.com/2016/04/27/us/tulsa-deputy-manslaughter-trial.

Ferranto, D. (2011). Not "just a reserve." *Sheriff, 63*(3), 36.

Fredericksen, P. J., & Levin, D. (2004). Accountability and the use of volunteer officers in public safety organizations. *Public Performance and Management, 27*(4), 118–143.

Gazley, B., & Brudney, J. L. (2005). Volunteer involvement in local government after September 11: The continuing question of capacity. *Public Administration Review, 65*(2), 131–142.

Gill, M. L., & Mawby, R. I. (1990). *A special constable: A study of the police reserve*. Aldershot, UK: Avebury Publishing.

Gravelle, J., & Rogers, C. (2009). Your country needs you! The economic viability of volunteers in the police. *Safer Communities, 8*(3), 34–38.

Gravelle, J., & Rogers, C. (2010). The economy of policing: The impact of the volunteer. *Policing: A Journal of Policy and Practice, 41*(1), 56–63.

Greenberg, M. A. (1984). *Auxiliary police: The citizen's approach to public safety*. Westport, CT: Greenwood Press.

Greenberg, M. A. (2005). *Citizens defending America: From colonial times to the age of terrorism*. Pittsburgh: University of Pittsburgh Press.

Hanser, R. D., Bonner, M., & Johnson, M. S. (2017). Volunteers in policing in the United States. In J. Albrecht (Ed.), *Police reserves and volunteers: Enhancing organizational effectiveness and public trust*, pp. 7–28. Boca Raton, FL: CRC Press.

Hargreaves, J., Linehan, C., Husband, H., & McKee, C. (2017). *Police workforce, England and Wales, 30 September 2016*, Statistical Bulletin 02/17. London: Office for National Statistics. Retrieved May 22, 2017, from www.gov.uk/government/uploads/system/uploads/attachment_data/file/586508/police-workforce-sep16-hosb0217.pdf.

Hilal, S. M., & Olsen, D. P. (2010). Police reserve officers: Essential in today's economy and an opportunity to increase diversity in the law enforcement profession. *The Police Chief*, 77(10), 92–94.

Home Office (2015). National statistics: Police workforce, England and Wales, 31 March 2015. Retrieved September 18, 2016, on www.gov.uk/government/publications/police-workforce-england-and-wales-31-march-2015/police-workforce-england-and-wales-31-march-2015.

Hope, B. (2007, March 15). Two auxiliary police officers killed in Greenwich Village. *The New York Sun*. Retrieved September 22, 2016, from www.nysun.com/new-york/two-auxiliary-police-officers-killed-in-greenwich/50486.

Hunter, G. (2012, June 23). Detroit police chief signs order to beef up reserves. *The Detroit News*, A1.

Johnson, M. S., Bonner, M., & Hanser, R. D. (2017). "Doing more with less": The professional model of the Los Angeles Police Department. In J. Albrecht (Ed.), *Police reserves and volunteers: Enhancing organizational effectiveness and public trust*, pp. 101–112. Boca Raton, FL: CRC Press.

Kakalik, J. S., & Wildhorn, S. (1971). *Special-purpose public police*. Santa Monica, CA: Rand Corporation.

Kirby, T. (1993, March 29). Veteran IRA gunman convicted of murder: Two Irishmen guilty of Yorkshire police shootings. *The Independent*. Retrieved March 22, 2017, from www.independent.co.uk/news/uk/veteran-ira-gunman-convicted-of-murder-two-irishmen-guilty-of-yorkshire-police-shootings-1500766.html.

Lee, M. (2007). *Inventing fear of crime: Criminology and the politics of anxiety*. Cullompton, UK: Willan Publishing.

Liu, X. X. (2014, December 9). Reserve Deputy Mark Vaughan honored with award of valor. News9.com. Retrieved February 10, 2016, from www.news9.com/story/27584381/reserve-deputy-mark-vaughan-honored-with-award-of-valor.

Mansfield, K. (2016, February 11). Special constable CONVICTED after helping save colleague from motorbike thugs. *Daily Express*. Retrieved January 10, 2018, from www.express.co.uk/news/uk/643159/special-constable-convicted-dangerous-driving-save-colleagues-motorbike-thugs.

National Advisory Commission on Criminal Justice Standards and Goals (1973). *Police: A report*. Washington, DC: US Government Printing Office.

National Crime Agency (n.d.). NCA specials. Retrieved December 30, 2016, from www.nationalcrimeagency.gov.uk/careers/specials.

Nesbit, R., & Brudney, J. L. (2010). At your service? Volunteering and national service in 2020. *Public Administration Review*, 70(Supplement S1), S107–S113.

Officer Down Memorial Page (n.d.). Officer Down Memorial Page. Retrieved April 16, 2013, from www.odmp.org.

Pepper, I. K. (2012). Research study: "Special" or not. Unpublished research. Teesside University, School of Social Sciences and Law, Middlesbrough, UK.

Pepper, I. K. (2014). Do part-time volunteer police officers aspire to be regular police officers? *Police Journal: Theory, Practice and Principles*, 87(2), 105–113.

Pepper, I. K., & Wolf, R. (2015). Volunteering to serve: An international comparison of volunteer police officers in a UK north east police force and a US Florida sheriff's office. *The Police Journal: Theory, Practice and Principles*, 88(3), 209–219.

Phillips, S. W., & Terrell-Orr, A. (2013). Attitudes of police supervisors: Do volunteers fit into policing? *Policing: An International Journal of Police Strategies and Management*, 36(4), 683–701.

Pickard, A., & Jones, C. (2016, June 1). Former reserve deputy Robert Bates sentenced to four years in prison for death of Eric Harris. *The Tulsa World*. Retrieved December 27, 2016, from www.tulsaworld.com/homepagelatest/former-reserve-deputy-robert-bates-sentenced-to-four-years-in/article_ec042b6d-11d2-5ee1-95d9-cf9e5ee78aba.html.

Police Department Disciplinary Bulletin (2006). City allows police reserve time to count toward promotion. *Police Department Disciplinary Bulletin*, 17(7), 8.

Rains, B. (2016, May 27). Kauffeld sentenced for murder of Johnson County deputy: Jury recommends sentence of 28 years, judge agrees. 40/29 News on Demand. Retrieved December 28, 2016, from www.4029tv.com/article/kauffeld-sentenced-for-murder-of-johnson-county-deputy/4959435.

Randol, B. M., & Gaffney, M. J. (2014). Are block watch volunteers different than volunteers in community-oriented policing programs? Findings from a mature COPS setting. *Police Practice and Research: An International Journal*, 15(3), 234–248.

Ren, L., Zhao, J., Lovrich, N. P., & Gaffney, M. J. (2006). Participation community crime prevention: Who volunteers for police work? *Policing: An International Journal of Police Strategies and Management*, 29(3), 464–481.

Scoville, D. (2014). Reserve officers: For love of the job. *Police*, 38(March), 34–41.

Strickland, P., & Lalic, M. (2010, June 9). Special constables, Standard Note SN/HA/1154. London: House of Commons Library.

Walker, S., & Katz, C. M. (2013). *The police in America: An introduction*. New York: McGraw-Hill.

Wilson, M. (2007, March 16). Lives intersect violently on busy city street. *The New York Times*. Retrieved December 28, 2016, from www.nytimes.com/2007/03/16/myregion/16cops.html.

Wolf, R., Holmes, S. T., & Jones, C. (2016). Utilization and satisfaction of volunteer law enforcement officers in the office of the American sheriff: An exploratory nationwide study. *Police Practice and Research: An International Journal*, 17(5), 448–462.

Zhao, J., Gibson, C., Lovrich, N. P., & Gaffney, M. J. (2002). Participation in community crime prevention: Are volunteers more or less fearful of crime than other citizens? *Journal of Crime and Justice*, 25(1), 41–61.

Chapter 3

The Utilization and Deployment of Volunteer Police in the United Kingdom and the United States

The United Nations takes a strong interest in volunteering as a way for people in marginalized or lower socio-economic areas to have access to the services, resources, and opportunities they need to improve their lives. In its *2015 State of the World's Volunteerism Report* the United Nations recommends that volunteers should work hand in hand with local governments to improve the quality of life of resident citizenry; but, while stressing the importance of cooperating with local governments, hospitals, police, and court services to ensure accountability and responsiveness of service, it fails to include any mention of volunteers who serve as police throughout the world (United Nations Volunteers, 2015). Volunteer police serve most often in uniformed patrol functions completing regular policing tasks, but many police services utilize them in differing ways.

In England and Wales, volunteer police serve in non-patrol functions, including in the Ministry of Defence Police, community policing, problem-oriented policing, intelligence-led policing, tourism policing, and rural policing. In addition, many UK police organizations have begun to utilize skills that special constables may bring to their policing roles, and expanded training for both specials and regular officers.

In the United States the utilization of volunteers varies greatly according to local jurisdiction and state law, but examples may include volunteer police at the local, county, and state levels, including state highway patrol, fish and wildlife offices, and marine patrol agencies. Additionally, many American policing agencies utilize volunteers in positions without police authority, but assist the police in their work, including volunteer office assistants, investigators, and human resources volunteers. Volunteers may also work in specialized roles, such as tourism policing, search and rescue, and other areas requiring specialized knowledge and/or training, and may have varying levels of training; some receive "less than regular" police training, and others have full police training and certification.

The Expanded Role of Volunteers in UK Policing

At best, the voluntary sector is connected to people at a local and a personal level. It can empower people to fulfil their potential, as well as creating active communities, adding to the quality of life. This is reflected in the values that define, support and sustain voluntary organisations. The sector is not part of our formal democracy but it enriches democratic life through engagement with communities and participation of trustees and volunteers.

(Panel on the Independence of the Voluntary Sector, 2011, p. 5)

The timing of this book is apposite not only in the United Kingdom and the United States but also in a vast number of countries globally, where economic downturns have enhanced and, in some cases, underpinned the role of volunteers across societies and their communities.[1] Volunteering is not new but its importance has been growing; 2001 was declared the International Year of Volunteers (Rochester, 2006) in the United Kingdom, and five years later a Commission on the Future of Volunteering was established by the England Volunteering Development Council. The commission's initial publication (Rochester, 2006), with a foreword written by Baroness Neuberger,[2] indicated that they intended to look at both formal and informal volunteering and in all sectors – in other words, not just those who work in the community and voluntary sectors. In January 2008 the commission identified and made a number of recommendations for a future volunteering model (Commission on the Future of Volunteering, 2008). Research for this book and other projects would suggest that the management and organization of police volunteers does not always follow the suggestions put forward in the commission's *Manifesto for Change*.

However, the promotion of the use of volunteers has grown in numbers and breadth over recent years, and their importance in policing in the United Kingdom was made even more apparent in 2012 when police and crime commissioners were campaigning for election throughout England and Wales. In Cheshire, for example, the elected PCC canvassed for an increase to 1,000 specials in that force, while PCCs in many other forces also called for an increase in their numbers. The Chief Constable in Thames Valley called for a real transformation in policing during the same time period, reporting that the 719 special constables in her police force were a significant part of her ability to police, and questioned whether community policing should be left solely to professional officers (Whitehead, 2012). The Police Federation, an organization that had previously represented only full-time officers, voted in 2014 to allow volunteer special constables to join as members for the first time. The federation maintained that special constables should continue to support full-time police in back-up rather than core police functions, and not replace officers (Warrell, 2014).

Rochester, Paine, and Howlett (2012) suggested that in the twenty-first century the context in which volunteering takes place has changed in a number of important ways. They first suggested that the population in England and Wales is an aging one; additionally, the economic constraints which have impacted upon health and welfare services have led to higher demands for support for the elderly and the vulnerable, who are often represented to be lonely and isolated. To compound this situation, work patterns have changed so that, increasingly, women as well as men are in paid employment, with a significant proportion working both paid and unpaid overtime (see Smith, 2016; Conway & Sturges, 2014). Rochester et al. (2012) provided a succinct outline regarding modern society and the changes that have taken place over the last 20 years. Furthermore, they indicated that perceived dangers have resulted in a society that is risk-averse and populated by individuals ready to blame governments in failing to reduce risks (Rochester, 2001, cited in Rochester et al., 2012). This seems somewhat contrary to the announcement in 1997 by the Labour government of the introduction of anti-social behaviour orders (ASBOs), which are civil contracts issued by the police or local authorities in response to complaints against people who were harassing members of the public.[3] ASBOs were considered to be a way in which members of a community could be regarded as "policing" their locality and putting some level of autonomy in the hands of a neighborhood. More cynically, one might contend that they provided an opportunity for authorities to hand a level of responsibility to members of the public. It can be argued, therefore, that this was a form of volunteering, in that those who took on board the task of recording and reporting anti-social behavior were, in fact, forerunners of police support volunteers. However, results were initially disappointing and subsequently somewhat mixed, and, in 2011, a change of direction was announced.

The growth in the use of volunteers in law enforcement has resulted in cries of "policing on the cheap," however, though this is not a new suggestion; according to Gill and Mawby (1990) an article by a Police Federation deputy secretary in *The Police Review* raised concerns about the negative impact of special constables on the amount of overtime that regular police may have available and therefore be able to work for additional money. The same article went on to report that specials were "public spirited but completely misguided people" (p. 51). Gill and Mawby (1990) similarly referred to a line of questioning regarding how much the government had saved by the policing of an event using special constables rather than regulars.

The perception of the underlying role of special constables has also taken to the internet. In 2013, in an online discussion among both special constables and regular officers, one of the contributors said,

> Many years ago I had a conversation with my tutor. He was not a fan of specials. My view was better to have anyone with you rather than no one. He told me it was the thin end of the wedge and that one day we would rue their role. I once observed him having a conversation with a special who worked in a car factory where redundancies were taking place. My tutor asked the bloke, "How would you feel if I dropped into your job for 16 hours or more a month, doing it for free when your jobs are on the line?" The special hit back saying our jobs weren't at risk. My tutor hit back that our overtime was cut back because specials came on and did lates at the weekend when otherwise we'd get O/T and that it was the thin end of the wedge.
>
> (Police UK, 2013)

The attitude of the tutor depicted in this online post is not exclusive. Specials have been faced with criticism from full-time officers for a variety of reasons, although this may not be true to an individual. Millie (2016) reported on the experiences of volunteers with the Lancashire Constabulary in a project funded through the Citizens in Policing program. This qualitative study was designed to determine the factors that inhibit or facilitate volunteering, recruitment, supervision, and the operation of special constables and police support volunteers.[4] The report found that the respondents felt largely positive about the experience of volunteering, but some felt underutilized, had little contact with other volunteers, and did not feel to be a part of the policing team. Some of the volunteers in this study felt that they did not feel valued, and one of the conclusions of the report was that "[m]ost volunteers enjoy their time with the police and get a lot out of it; yet some feel underused or under-informed, a concern for volunteer retention" (p. 21). While Millie reported that special constables felt positive about the training they received, there was a concern over using the special constabulary as a training ground for prospective applicants for the regular police. "Instead of being cheap labour until they join as regulars, they could look at what the police call career specials, which are people like me really that have no intention of joining, and using us better" (p. 14).

Volunteers in Service of the Public Good

Altruistic individuals who rush to the aid of their neighbors in need and those who routinely assist strangers without a second thought are demonstrating volunteer behavior. Often their actions go overlooked and unrecognized other than by the immediate recipients of their support. More formally, charities and other organizations have depended on the time and effort given by individuals since the latter part of the nineteenth century (Brewis, 2013). The Guild of Help Movement acknowledged that "personal service and not almsgiving is the highest form of charity" (cited in Brewis, 2013, p. 6). Brewis (2013) also recognized that there was a growth in the development of training opportunities for those who were keen to embrace the "social service" movement within Edwardian society.

The role of volunteers during and after the Second World War was significant, but the introduction of the welfare state with the 1945 Family Allowance Act saw social want put in the hands of the newly established National Health Service and other services, funded through taxation and offering universal support. British politician William Beveridge identified five obstacles to reconstruction in the United Kingdom: poverty, disease, ignorance, squalor, and idleness. In order to overcome these obstacles, Beveridge proposed setting up a social security program, a nationalized health service, free education, council housing, and employment opportunities. As a consequence, volunteering by some was deemed less necessary. However, volunteering continued, to greater and lesser extents, depending upon the mores of administrations. The National Council of Social Service (NCSS), which had been founded in 1919, was an important institution in the development and significance of social service. In 1952 a report commissioned by the NCSS on voluntary service and the state suggested that the extensive use of "social service" during the First World War was a "turning point," and in the years between the two world wars "voluntary service had ceased to be charity or patronage and had become personal service by people from all walks of society" (cited in Brewis, 2013, p. 8).

However, it was not until the 1960s that governments once again began to actively promote volunteering. In the latter part of the 1970s and throughout the 1980s economic constraints provided the platform for Conservative governments to pick up from Labour prime minister Jim Callaghan's national "Be a Good Neighbour" campaign, launched in 1976. This was an informal scheme which was supposed to encourage people to voluntarily look out for vulnerable residents in their neighborhood. By this time it had been recognized that public services could not provide for all and volunteers could be a beneficial and useful asset, and the idea was to reduce the pressures on health and social services. As demands grew and resources became ever more stretched, successive governments, both Conservative and Labour, began to see volunteers as an essential asset. There was no single motivation for this; the reasons were manifold, including the agendas of specific political parties. This was made clear in the adoption of the Conservative Party's "Make a Difference" campaign, during John Major's government in 1994–97, that a more holistic approach was needed. An important feature of this campaign was that, for the first time consultation and agreement across the four nations of the United Kingdom attempted to produce a policy on volunteering that satisfied all participants. Significantly, the campaign saw volunteering as a "vehicle for participation in and contributing to society" (cited in Rochester et al., 2012, p. 90) as opposed to delivery of service. In the end, however, and as is often the case, funding was very limited from government, so that, while the recommendations were promising, results fell short.

Crime-related organizations have evolved through the use of volunteers, and a good example of this is Victim Support, which began in the United Kingdom in the southwest of England in the 1970s. Initially a wholly volunteer organization, within twenty years it had begun to receive a proportion of its income from government. It may be argued that by taking such funding the organization could risk losing some of its autonomy; it would appear that the issue of independence is concerning, particularly at a time when economic constraints have been identified.

The top-down and bureaucratic nature of the state that has existed in the United Kingdom for a number of decades has, according to Brannan, John, and Stoker (2006), given way to a "[s]tate [that] appears to need to forge a new relationship with the realm of the civic if it is to retain its capacity to act" (p. 994). Neighbourhood Watch (NW) was introduced in England in 1982 and demonstrates an example of citizen engagement in crime prevention. Neighbourhood Watch is sanctioned by the police service and aims to "bring neighbours together to create strong, friendly, active communities" (Neighbourhood Watch, n.d.) through community collaboration to deter and reduce crime and anti-social activity. Within the ethos of community engagement and crime prevention, Kirkholt (a housing estate on the outskirts of Rochdale, in the north of England) developed a burglary reduction project in the late 1980s. The program developed "Cocoon" Neighbourhood Watch, wherein surrounding homes were alerted after a burglary to remove opportunities and motivations for burglars, and was an important element of the success of the project without evidence of crime displacement (Wakefield & Fleming, 2009; see also Office of Justice Programs, 2011). Cocoon Neighbourhood Watch works on a micro level: when one property has been victimized (in the case of Kirkholt, the problem was residential burglary) the residents of the properties surrounding the victim property volunteer to maintain natural surveillance to reduce the risk of repeat victimization.

Aside from such endorsed volunteering programs, the police service in England and Wales uses a wide array of volunteers in a number of differing scenarios. As mentioned earlier, the use of police support volunteers (including cadets) has gone through varying fortunes; according to data from the national PSV and specials survey undertaken in 2016, numbers of PSVs in each force area often reflect the "will" of senior officers in supporting and encouraging their recruitment and application. Conversations and interviews with a range of personnel have also suggested that the loss of volunteer coordinators and similar at a time of fiscal constraints has resulted in a lack of focus and enthusiasm. As a result, comments by PSVs suggest that these volunteers may feel that they are "being ignored, with nothing to do," or that there is a "lack of understanding of our role and place within the general police family, especially amongst the bosses and the benefits of utilising us as another resource. I think this is caused by a lack of knowledge around what experiences we can bring to the team" (Britton, 2016). While such comments cannot be taken as applicable to all volunteers in all forces, it is clear from year-on-year statistics that volunteer numbers are tending to go down in a significant number. Furthermore, the data does not indicate levels of activity, so that recorded numbers of PSVs may not be reflected in the actual level of engagement. It may be significant to note that there is no senior police representation for PSVs, as there is for special constables.

The *Report of the Working Group on the Special Constabulary in England and Wales 1995–96* (Home Office, 1996) gave rise to 91 advisory recommendations, many of which related to provision of allowances. Significantly, the second recommendation suggests that "[s]pecials should continue not to be reckoned formally as part of a force's establishment or strength, nor taken into permanent account for operational planning purposes in calculating the optimum number of constables for a particular division or area" (p. 47). The subsequent New Labour government elected in 1997 took a far more robust approach to volunteering. Examples that support its somewhat forceful approach to volunteering included incorporating performance measures. A distinct feature of New Labour policies was the centrality of targets across all spheres of public policy delivery

The *Manifesto for Change* report of the Commission on the Future of Volunteering (2008) identified the increasing importance of citizenship in a progressively multicultural society in which the bridging of different faiths, cultures, and ethnicities is needed to give a sense of inclusivity. To that end, this manifesto identified six recommendations at a time that coincided with austerity and the restructuring of many organizations. Another government report suggested that "[w]orld class services are characterised not only by collaboration between citizens and public service professionals, but also by empowering people to make a greater contribution to meeting their own needs" (Cabinet Office, 2008, p. 22) and that this stance would result in a shared responsibility.

The Baring Foundation, in partnership with the Civil Exchange, produced a report entitled *Voluntary Sector Independence* in 2011 (Panel on the Independence of the Voluntary Sector, 2011). The report by this consultation panel, which was chaired by a former Chief Inspector of Prisons, was the precursor to a series of publications on the state of the voluntary sector and its independence. More recently citizen empowerment has become increasingly central to government policies and in relation to the criminal justice system in England and Wales, and in 2016 the Citizens in Policing strategy was unveiled. The strategy hopes to develop new and creative approaches to maximize the use of police volunteers in three areas: special constables, police support volunteers, and Volunteer Police Cadets (VPCs). The strategy provides an initial proposal to address the vision of "connecting communities to policing and policing to communities" and "will enhance capabilities and achieve value for money by scaling up specialist capabilities and standardising functions where appropriate" (Jones, 2016, p. 7).

Volunteering in the criminal justice system has a long history, including magistrates, prison visitors, police support volunteers, and parish constables, as well as special constables. Within the court system there are currently some 23,000 magistrates in England and Wales (Courts and Tribunal Judiciary, n.d.), 450 in Scotland (Judiciary of Scotland, n.d.), and 21 in Northern Ireland (Northern Ireland Courts and Tribunals Service, n.d.), though this "voluntary" management of summary offences continues to undergo reform, including the increased use of paid district judges in magistrates' courts in England and Wales. As another example, the growth of the number of police cadets through the Volunteer Police Cadet scheme across the country has encouraged young people aged between 13 and 18, particularly those from vulnerable backgrounds, to participate in force-based structures.

One possible reason that citizens may join the Special Constabulary was uncovered in an assessment of volunteer policing in London. Not only is the Metropolitan Police the largest force in England and Wales, it also has the largest number of special constables. In 2016 a strategic review of the Metropolitan Special Constabulary (MSC) was undertaken, and the findings were disappointing (D'Orsi, 2016). Commander D'Orsi, who headed the review panel, was quoted in an interview as saying: "One in ten Met special constables exists in the force without completing any duty hours at all, and two in ten exit less than a year after joining" (Loeb, 2016). The report went on to indicate that some 20 percent of serving Metropolitan special constables did not live in London, and, since traveling expenses can be claimed by such officers up to 70 miles from central London, the MSCs who lived the furthest away cost more than those who lived close by. In the relevant financial year there were 646 non-London-based MSCs who claimed £69,640, while the 2,580 officers resident in London claimed £41,340 (D'Orsi, 2016). While free travel may be a way to encourage those who are interested in volunteering to make the time-consuming commitment to serve, volunteering for a policing role should not be, argued Loeb (2016), an excuse to get free travel. Because MSCs and regular police in London are authorized to travel on public transportation for nothing, suggestions are that there should be both financial and accountability implications.[5]

The United Kingdom's 43 Jurisdictions, One Force

It is commonly accepted that the formalization of policing came about in 1829 when Robert Peel, the then British home secretary, oversaw the passing of the Metropolitan Police Act. However, Emsley (2009) suggested that the Cheshire Constabulary Act, which pre-dated the 1829 Metropolitan Police Act by a few weeks, saw the appointment of the first constabulary, because magistrates had wanted to recruit a Mr. George Burgess as a paid special constable, but due to legislation found that they couldn't pay him a salary. The Cheshire Constabulary was a largely rural force but its officers were concentrated in the newly developed industrial areas; concentrated levels of policing were not regarded as necessary in the rural areas.

Following the passing of the Metropolitan Police Act some 1,000 officers, uniformed and regulated, started patrolling the streets of London under the direction of two commissioners of police (Emsley, 2009). Within a very short time numbers had increased significantly, so that in May of 1830, less than a year after their introduction, there were 3,300; however, turnover was rapid, with a range of issues being identified, drunkenness being regularly cited (Emsley, 2009).

In spite of the size and rapid expansion of the Metropolitan force, the Cheshire force was used as the model for many other county forces. During the nineteenth century policing across England and Wales was not the homogeneous organization that exists in the twenty-first century, with regulation being at the behest of watch committees. In spite of the 1856 County and Borough Act, which made policing compulsory across England and Wales, it was not until the police strikes in 1918–1919 and the subsequent Desborough Committee that uniformity, through the introduction of standardized salaries, established the notion of a national body rather than independent policing agencies. In 1900 there were 243 separate police forces, a number which, following the Police Act of 1946, was reduced to 117 when small town forces were merged into the county constabularies. In order to improve efficiency this number was again reduced to 47 under the 1964 Police Act. The same act saw the establishment of 20 forces across Scotland.

A Royal Commission in 1962 led to the merging of city and borough police forces, so that, by 1974, England and Wales was policed by 43 forces. At around the same time the number of forces across Scotland was set at eight. The size of each of the forces varies, as do the population and geography, so that, while Gloucestershire, North Wales, and Cheshire have large rural areas, Greater Manchester Police (GMP), Merseyside, and the Metropolitan Police are more urban, albeit with parks and agricultural land.

The largest force in England is the London Metropolitan Police service, which protects 7.2 million individuals in an area covering 620 square miles (London Metropolitan Police, n.d.). It does not, however, include "the Square Mile" which accounts for the City of London itself, which has 11,000 residents but, by day, accommodates 300,000 plus workers, shoppers, and tourists (City of London, n.d.). The multiplicity of additional people within that area suggests a diversity of ethnicities, calculated at somewhere between 40 and 55 percent (Lammy, 2014), but the percentage of officers from such backgrounds falls far below the population that it serves, as only 6 percent of those who declared their ethnic background in the City of London Special Constabulary were of black, Asian, or minority ethnic (BAME) origin.

Volunteers in Policing in the United States

As discussed earlier in this book, volunteers have always been a part of American policing, and police volunteers currently represent about 20 percent of the total number of paid police officers in the United States (Dobrin & Wolf, 2016), though some states and forces do not use volunteer police (defined here as volunteers with "sworn" or "warranted" police powers) at all. As far back as the middle of the seventeenth century the local sheriff would organize a "posse" of volunteers from the community that would assist with maintaining order, tracking down fugitives, and providing community resources against violent criminals. In the urban cities of the east, the nightwatch system used volunteers to patrol city streets until the more formal introduction of paid police based on the UK Metropolitan Police Act. The New York Police Department, for example, was created in 1845 and based largely on the model created in London.

A major difference between police in the United States and in the United Kingdom, however, is that all police officers in the United States carry firearms. This is largely due to the proliferation of firearms in American society, where many states have "right to carry" laws which allow citizens to possess firearms (though not necessarily on their person or concealed) without any type of permit or license.[6] Another significant difference between US and UK policing is that it is rare to find a police agency with a mandatory retirement age in the United States, where over 80 percent of the 100 largest policing agencies have no such requirement (Pepper & Wolf, 2015).

Probably the largest difference between policing in the two countries, however, is the nationalization of the police force in the United

Kingdom and the purposeful decentralization that has evolved in the United States. With over 18,000 law enforcement agencies in the United States, it is rare to find any two that do things exactly the same. This stems from "federalism," the principle that stresses the rights and powers of the states, and not the federal government. The formation of the Constitution of the United States granted vague and virtually unlimited powers to the states: "The powers not delegated to the United States by the Constitution, nor prohibited by it to the States, are reserved for the States respectively, or to the people" (Gerstle, 2010). Although state and local governments used this power granted within the Constitution to regulate commerce, manufacturing, and labor, they also criminalized activities, such as gambling, prostitution, and other immoral behaviors. This is also where the states began to diverge in their interpretations of some acts, such as slavery. "The extraordinary power vested by common law and the Constitution in the hands of governments became 'states' rights': a doctrine that white southerners were willing to – and did – defend with their lives" (Gerstle, 2010, p. 31). It is also important to note that for most of American history the police have been used to maintain a political order that has promoted segregation, discrimination, and slavery (Greenberg, 2005).

Although it was one of the most disgraceful institutions in American history, slavery did give rise to official armed groups of community members called "slave patrols," which were a type of volunteer police. These patrols, which were incentivized differently throughout history (coercion, pay, rewards), were responsible for searching slave quarters, for dispersing unauthorized slave gatherings, and for hunting down wayward slaves. The patrols came into conflict not just with slaves but also with their owners, who complained that these groups whipped slaves brutally and arbitrarily. In larger cities this loosely knit system of citizen patrols evolved into the beginnings of a well-regulated and paid police force (Hadden, 2001), which certainly contributes to the poor relationship between African Americans and other minority groups and police agencies in the United States, even today.

While slave patrols continued in the south through the end of the Civil War, volunteer police roles were also forming in other parts of the United States. Anti-horse-thief and detective societies were created, as were other organizations provided with some sort of law enforcement authority, such as vice suppression leagues. Such societies first came into existence in the 1790s and became even more prevalent over the next century, largely due to the lack of competent policing throughout the country. These official and legalized protective associations were created to identify and arrest criminals. For example, Anthony Comstock, a New Yorker who served from 1872 to 1915 as secretary of the New York Society for the Suppression of Vice (NYSSV), nearly single-handedly policed the US mails as a volunteer postal "special federal agent." Comstock had helped to write legislation banning the mailing of obscene, lewd, and filthy material, and then was eventually appointed to enforce this new law. He asked that he be paid no salary, to avoid any inference of political gain. In a brief span of time, during the mid-1870s, Comstock confiscated more than 3 million pictures and postcards from the mail, and boasted that he sent nearly 3,000 criminals to jail (Greenberg, 2005; Werbel, 2014). Organizations designed to detect and prosecute crime grew in popularity, and several midwestern and eastern states passed laws to allow the establishment of volunteer organizations. These organizations were commonly known as anti-horse-thief associations or public aid societies, and the laws often granted the power of arrest to organization members (Greenberg, 2005).

In the midwest's more rural regions, however, volunteer law enforcement began to grow through the use of the sheriff's posse. In the American frontier, sheriffs could summon a posse to assist in keeping the peace, and allowed for the sheriff to call upon armed citizenry to aid in law enforcement. Americans were reliant upon the citizenry to assist in self-governance, and it was argued that the security of citizens against undue government powers led to the *posse comitatus*,[7] habeas corpus,[8] and the jury system. A posse was and is distinctly different from a militia, in that a posse has no compulsory training requirements, and is created when summoned. A militia has a regular command structure, and serves as a standing body of trained members (Kopel, 2015).

The federal courts were eventually able to force states to recognize the primacy of individual rights as set forth in the Constitution, the Bill of Rights, and other amendments to the Constitution. The civil rights movement of the 1960s helped to move more power back to the federal government, including federals laws that forbid states to racially discriminate in the distribution of federal grants. The states and local authorities, however, numbering more than 89,000 distinct jurisdictional units, continue today to push back against the federal government (Gerstle, 2010), and were part of the political rise of the Republican Party in the 2016 election cycle.

Because there is such separation amongst the states, policing has evolved differently throughout the country, and so too has volunteer policing. Reserve and auxiliary units began to appear throughout the country in the 1920s in large American cities, but they rarely were called upon to perform law enforcement functions, and citizens were often appointed to these positions as political favors (Greenberg, 2005). One example today of auxiliary police with extremely limited powers can be found in the northeast United States, where many cities use volunteers called "auxiliary" police; although they are uniformed to look very similar to regular police officers, they have no law enforcement authority. The south and west are more likely to use "reserve" police, who have full police authority but varying amounts of training.

Even the terminology of "reserve" and "auxiliary" police are used throughout the United States to mean different things. While auxiliary police with the NYPD have no police powers, an alternative example can be found in the auxiliary police in Florida. Florida's certified auxiliary officers are authorized to carry firearms and make arrests, and have full police authority when working with a fully certified law enforcement officer. In the midwest and central parts of the United States, volunteer police are provided with varying amounts of training and authority. Some states have reserve police who must attend training, wear a uniform, and provide patrol functions, but are not authorized to carry firearms or make arrests. Other states provide significant amounts of training, and authorize volunteer police to make arrests and carry a firearm, and in some jurisdictions they are authorized to use their own personal vehicles as emergency police vehicles. Examples of the variation in volunteer policing units can be found in Chapter 8.

Because it is so difficult to define the term "volunteer police" in the United States, many scholars have limited their research to those public organizations that have assumed or been empowered to work in varying policing functions (including the functions of criminal investigation, arrest, and prosecution), or that have been given the authority to provide peacekeeping functions (including traffic and crowd control, and efforts to increase police visibility). These organizations are also authorized by legitimate governmental police forces or government entities (Greenberg, 2005). Volunteer police share some common characteristics, and for the purposes of this book are individuals who work directly for a government entity and are authorized with legal authority for the prevention, investigation, and prosecution of criminal activity and the preservation of public order. This service is provided without being an imposed requirement, and without significant remuneration. The level of the legal authority and the amount of possible remuneration are malleable concepts, however.

Much like their special constable counterparts in the United Kingdom, however, American volunteer police are sometimes seen as "scabs"[9] or "misguided do-gooders" (Greenberg, 2005, p. 11). Police unions are rarely accepting of volunteer police programs or officers, and it has been reported that regular officers have mixed views on the worth of volunteer police. As reported by Crary (2015), the head of the Oklahoma chapter of the American Civil Liberties Union does not feel that volunteers should serve in sworn policing roles. "If somebody wants to volunteer with a police department and help hold someone's hand to cross the street… that's fine. But to allow someone to play police officer with real bullets and a gun is reckless. That should never happen." Wyllie (2017) reported the mixed feelings of regular police officers when asked about volunteer policing, and most supporters pointed at the cost-effectiveness of having a ready reserve to assist with the day-to-day functions of policing, particularly in times of shrinking budgets. But Wyllie (2017) also reported on some of the negative perceptions by regular police officers of volunteer police: "I believe the 'part time' system of policing is absolutely ridiculous... We contend with more anti-police groups, 24/7 videotaping, and more charging and law suits [than] ever before. As such, to do this job without a full salary and full benefits is insane." DeLord, Burpo, Shannon, and Spearing (2008) looked at police unions and how reserve and volunteer police fit into modern policing agencies, and asked if police unions work to eliminate reserve programs, or "[f]ully integrate reserves into the association" (p. 283).

Recognition and Specialization of Volunteer Policing

Volunteering has become increasingly desirable in an era of fiscal shrinkage and political ideology, and both American and British residents are encouraged to donate their time, talent, and treasure in a plethora of public service and non-profit agencies. The use of police volunteers in both the United Kingdom and the United States means that law enforcement agencies are able to provide an additional level of service in order to meet citizen expectations.

Because police volunteers receive little or no financial remuneration, recognition of the importance of volunteers in the United States by national programs such as the President's Volunteer Service Award,[10] George H. W. Bush's "Points of Light," and Barack Obama's Edward M. Kennedy Serve America Act validate the important work that these individuals do (Nesbit and Brudney, 2010; Wolf, 2013; Wolf, Holmes, and Jones, 2016). However, none of these programs are specific to the role of volunteer policing; instead, they recognize volunteering in general, and volunteer police are eligible to earn these awards. However, the National Sheriffs' Association (NSA) has created an award to recognize one or more individuals for significant contributions to reserve and volunteer policing in sheriffs' offices through the Reserve Deputy of the Year Award,[11] and the International Association of Chiefs of Police awards the Leadership in Law Enforcement Volunteer Programs Award to volunteer policing organizations.[12] In the United Kingdom the Lord Ferrers Awards[13] have, for 23 years, recognized outstanding contributions by groups as well as individual special constables (Lord Ferrers Awards, 2017). In both the United Sates and the United Kingdom, these national-level awards are in addition to force-wide ceremonies acknowledging the contributions made by their own volunteers.

While recognition programs may provide a means to identify and distinguish volunteers, horrific events, such as the terrorist attacks of

September 11, 2001, in New York, may also have a resultant positive effect on volunteerism. As discussed earlier, the United States saw an increase in volunteerism after the September 11 attacks as county governments and highly populated cities saw an upsurge in the number of people who had an interest in volunteering (Gazley & Brudney, 2005). National pride may similarly influence volunteerism, as the London Olympics in 2012 saw a successful call for up to 70,000 volunteers from 240,000 applications (International Olympic Committee, 2012). However, this momentum in the United Kingdom has not been maintained.

With diminishing resources and the demands for personnel qualified in particular specialisms continuing to rise, many police agencies rely on volunteers to help offset their costs (Hilal & Olsen, 2010; Wolf et al., 2016). However, while police agencies utilize these volunteers in numerous ways, many members of the public are unaware of the extent of use of volunteers in both the United States and the United Kingdom to increase the police presence in the communities they serve. In the United Kingdom, special constables were traditionally warranted to a specific police force, and their duties tended to reflect those of "jack of all trades," though predominantly for patrols and special events. Recently, however, there has been recognition of the value of expertise that special constables can bring to the role, and increasingly this is being used in areas such as cybercrime and medical services. For example, both the Greater Manchester and West Yorkshire Police Services have recruited junior doctors into their SC ranks while, as discussed in Chapter 5, Hampshire and Gloucestershire have enlisted cybercrime experts.

In the United States, volunteer units within police agencies are often specialized entities that may be integrated into community functions in order to create a positive tie between members of the community and local government (Ren, Zhao, Lovrich, and Gaffney, 2006). Law enforcement agencies in the United States use volunteers in a variety of ways, as sworn reserve, auxiliary, or special deputies, as victim advocates, as interpreters, and other specialized functions (Hilal & Olsen, 2010). However, as detailed in Chapter 2, only 30 percent of all public safety organizations in the United States utilize volunteers (Brudney & Kellough, 2000), and even fewer allow police volunteers the full powers of arrest and/or ability to carry a service weapon. Specialized training for volunteer police is discussed in Chapter 6.

Notes

1 In times of economic downturn there is most often an increase in the needs for human services and less funding to meet those needs. Social issues such as homelessness, mental health, and crime may rise, and the people who normally volunteer to provide those services or donate to fund organizations that

provide the services may no longer have the time or money to do so, as they also struggle to meet their own personal needs (Ellis, 2008).

2 Baroness Julia Neuberger became Britain's second woman rabbi in 1977. She took a rabbinic post in London and a professorship at Leo Baeck College, where she taught for 20 years, before being named a Dame of the British Empire (DBE). She was elevated to baroness the following year.

3 Anti-social behaviour orders were introduced by section 1 of the Crime and Disorder Act of 1998, which took effect on April 1, 1999. The act has since been amended numerous times, including in 2002, 2003, and 2005. In October 2014 the criminal behaviour order (CBO) was enacted to replace the ASBO on conviction. ASBOs are civil orders that are intended to protect the public from anti-social behaviors such as harassment and trespassing. The behaviors must cause or be likely to cause harassment, alarm, or distress to any person or people not in the same household as the offender. The orders are not criminal in nature, and are intended to be preventative rather than punitive (Crown Prosecution Service, n.d.).

4 PSVs began in England and Wales in the early 1990s (Bullock, 2017). The original concept was to allow volunteer roles to undertake specific duties that would free up warranted officers to work in the field. This has included acting as support staff to provide information on cases to victims and witnesses, act as liaisons between the police and the public, or serve as police chaplains or headquarters volunteers (Millie, 2016). PSVs volunteer to serve as non-warranted "civilian" police staff, and in January 2014 there were approximately 9,000 PSVs in England and Wales (Bullock, 2017).

5 Between February 2013 and January 2015 58 complaints of officers (both special constables and regular London Metropolitan police) were exposed in a Freedom of Information Act request by the *Daily Mail*. According to the report, the London Met has investigated staff for misusing their warrant cards for access to pubs and nightclubs, football (soccer) matches, and to get free travel on trains. In one case, a special constable was dismissed for showing his Metropolitan Police Service (MPS) warrant card when he did not have a correct ticket for a train. In order to use the MPS free travel benefit, police officers and SCs must have in their possession both their warrant card and an appropriately issued Police Oyster card for travel (Boyle, 2015). Unfortunately, this type of news report makes it difficult for those who are not taking advantage of the system to continue to receive the benefits they deserve without attracting negative public opinion.

6 For example, Florida laws allow any citizen who has not been convicted of a felony (or otherwise had their right to carry removed by the courts) to possess a firearm. There is no requirement to have a license in Florida to own or possess that weapon, and in fact the government is forbidden from tracking those who own firearms. In order to carry a firearm concealed on their person, however, the citizen must apply for and obtain a "Concealed Weapon License." In order to obtain a Concealed Weapon License the applicant must be a citizen of the United States (not necessarily a citizen of Florida), be 21 years of age or older, and pass a limited criminal background check. In addition, the applicant must be able to demonstrate the physical

ability to handle a firearm (which can be accomplished in a very short hands-on training class for a small fee), and pay a fee of less than $100. Other states are on the other end of the spectrum of allowing firearm carrying, however, and some states forbid carrying a firearm at all without special, very difficult to obtain, permits. Fourteen other US states have reciprocal license agreements with Florida, so that a concealed weapon permit in Florida is accepted as a concealed weapon permit in those states.

7 *Posse comitatus* originated in Anglo-Saxon England. A core power of the sheriff has been the authority to summon citizens to serve in protection of the territory, and posse service was a common feature of life in colonial times in America. "Like jury service, it was embraced as the right and duty of a responsible citizen of a republic" (Kopel, 2014). This power still exists today, and is used by county sheriffs throughout the United States to assemble volunteers for various needs of the sheriff's office.

8 *Habeas corpus*: a writ requiring that a person who has been arrested be brought before a judge or into court to secure that person's release unless lawful grounds are shown for his or her detention.

9 A "scab" is a worker who stays on the job or begins working at a job when others are on strike. In the 1500s the term expanded from its original definition of the crust that forms on skin after a wound and took on the meaning of a rascal or a scoundrel, and it may have been based on bad habits and lack of cleanliness. By the late 1700s it took on the meaning used here: the workman who would not join a strike or take part in organized labor.

10 The President's Volunteer Service Award is administered by the Corporation for National and Community Service, a federal agency that recognizes service in community and faith-based organizations. Anyone who has participated in a certified organization as a volunteer can be recognized for levels of volunteerism, bracketed according to the volunteer's age. In addition, volunteers can be awarded the President's Lifetime Achievement Award for contributing more than 4,000 hours as a volunteer in their lifetime (the President's Volunteer Service Award, n.d.).

11 The NSA Reserve Deputy of the Year Award program was created in 2013 by the NSA Reserve Law Enforcement Officer Committee to recognize individuals who have made "significant contributions or accomplishments directly related to volunteer law enforcement." While meritorious or heroic acts can be considered, the award was established to recognize unusual initiative. Only volunteer deputy sheriffs are eligible (National Sheriffs' Association, 2017), and not volunteers who work in police departments.

12 The IACP awards the Leadership in Law Enforcement Volunteer Programs Award to programs that demonstrate "innovative, effective practices for augmenting sworn or civilian staff and/or improving service delivery to their communities" to those volunteer programs that are decidedly multipurpose, and include as many facets of volunteering as possible, including non-sworn support (International Association of Chiefs of Police, n.d.); volunteer reserve and auxiliary programs that are solely used for policing duties are not considered for the award. Both local police agency and sheriff's office volunteer programs are eligible to apply, as are state-level policing units.

13 The Lord Ferrers Awards were previously known as the Special Constable and Police Support Volunteer Awards, and recognize the vital role that police volunteers play in UK policing. In 2013 they were renamed the Lord Ferrers Awards after the former Home Office minister who created the awards in 1993. The awards recognize both individual and team-level performance for special constables, police support volunteers, police cadets, and employer-supported policing organizations, and contributions to technology in the support of policing (Lord Ferrers Awards, 2017).

References

Boyle, D. (2015, April 29). Let me through, I'm a cop! Dozens of police officers disciplined for abusing their warrant cards to get into bars and football matches and blag free train travel. *Daily Mail*. Retrieved August 13, 2017, from www.dailymail.co.uk/news/article-3060513/Let-m-cop-Dozens-police-officers-discplined-abusing-warrant-cards-bars-blag-free-train-travel.html.

Brannan, T., John, P., & Stoker, G. (2006). Active citizenship and effective public services and programmes: How can we know what really works? *Urban Studies, 43*(5/6), 993–1008.

Brewis, G. (2013). *Towards a new understanding of volunteering in England before 1960?*, Working Paper 2. London: Institute for Volunteering Research. Retrieved April 14, 2017, from http://eprints.ioe.ac.uk/18258/1/IVR_working_paper_two_history_of_volunteering.pdf.

Britton, I. (2016). *National survey of special constables and police support volunteers: Initial findings report*. Northampton, UK: University of Northampton, Institute for Public Safety, Crime and Justice.

Brudney, J. L., & Kellough, J. E. (2000). Volunteers in state government: Involvement, management and benefits. *Nonprofit and voluntary sector quarterly, 29*(1), 111–130.

Bullock, K. (2017). Shoring up the "home guard"? Reflections on the development and deployment of police support volunteer programmes in England and Wales. *Policing and Society, 27*(4), 341–358.

Cabinet Office (2008). *Excellence and fairness: Achieving world class public services*. London: HMSO.

City of London (n.d.). Police authority. Retrieved April 14, 2017, from www.cityoflondon.gov.uk/about-the-city/how-we-make-decisions/Pages/police-authority.aspx.

Commission on the Future of Volunteering (2008). *Report of the Commission on the Future of Volunteering and manifesto for change*. London: Commission on the Future of Volunteering. Retrieved April 14, 2017, from www.fairplayforchildren.org/pdf/1216564640.pdf.

Conway, N., & Sturges, J. (2014). Investigating unpaid overtime working among the part-time workforce. *British Journal of Management, 25*(4), 755–771.

Courts and Tribunal Judiciary (n.d.). Magistrates' court. Retrieved April 14, 2017, from www.judiciary.gov.uk/you-and-the-judiciary/going-to-court/magistrates-court.

Crary, D. (2015, April 13). Amid tight budgets, use of police reserve officers is common. *The San Diego Union-Tribune*. Retrieved August 13, 2017, from www.sandiegouniontribune.com/sdut-amid-tight-budgets-use-of-police-reserve-officers-2015apr13-story.html.

Crown Prosecution Service (n.d.). Anti-social behaviour orders on conviction (ASBOs). Retrieved August 13, 2017, from www.cps.gov.uk/legal-guidance/anti_social_behaviour-orders-conviction-asbos.

DeLord, R., Burpo, J., Shannon, M., & Spearing, J. (2008). *Police union power, politics, and confrontation in the 21st century: New challenges, new issues*, 2nd Edition. Springfield, IL: Charles C. Thomas Publishing.

Dobrin, A., & Wolf, R. (2016). What is known and not known about volunteer policing in the United States. *International Journal of Police Science and Management, 18*(3), 220–227.

D'Orsi, L. (2016). *Metropolitan Special Constabulary: Strategic review*. London: Metropolitan Police. Retrieved February 9, 2017, from www.met.police.uk/foi/pdfs/priorities_and_how_we_are_doing/corporate/msc_strategic_review.pdf.

Ellis, S. J. (2008, November). How will the economic crisis affect volunteering? Energize. Retrieved August 13, 2017, from www.energizeinc.com/hot-topics/2008/november.

Emsley, C. (2009). *The Great British bobby: A history of British policing from the 18th century to the present*. London: Quercus.

Gazley, B., & Brudney, J. L. (2005). Volunteer involvement in local government after September 11: The continuing question of capacity. *Public Administration Review, 65*(2), 131–142.

Gerstle, G. (2010). Federalism in America: Beyond the Tea Partiers. *Dissent, 57*(4), 29–36.

Gill, M. L., & Mawby, R. I. (1990). *A special constable: A study of the police reserve*. Aldershot, UK: Avebury Publishing.

Greenberg, M. A. (2005). *Citizens defending America: From colonial times to the age of terrorism*. Pittsburgh: University of Pittsburgh Press.

Hadden, S. E. (2001). *Slave patrols: Law and violence in Virginia and the Carolinas*. Cambridge, MA: Harvard University Press.

Hilal, S. M., & Olsen, D. P. (2010). Police reserve officers: Essential in today's economy and an opportunity to increase diversity in the law enforcement profession. *The Police Chief, 77*(10), 92–94.

Home Office (1996). *Report of the Working Group on the Special Constabulary in England and Wales 1995–96*. London: Home Office Communications Directorate.

International Association of Chiefs of Police (n.d.). IACP/BodyWorn Leadership in Law Enforcement Volunteer Programs Award. Retrieved August 27, 2017, from www.theiacp.org/IACP-Award-for-Outstanding-Achievement-in-Law-Enforcement-Volunteer-Programs.

International Olympic Committee (2012, July 21). Volunteers: Helping to make the games happen. Retrieved March 13, 2017, from www.olympic.org/news/volunteers-helping-to-make-the-games-happen.

Jewish Women's Archive (n.d.). Women rabbis: Julia Neuberger. Retrieved September 9, 2017, from https://jwa.org/rabbis/narrators/neuberger-julia.

Jones, D. (2016). Citizens in policing strategy 2016–2019. London: National Police Chiefs' Council.

Judiciary of Scotland (n.d.). Justices of the Peace. Retrieved December 15, 2016, from www.scotland-judiciary.org.uk/38/0/Justices-of-the-Peace.

Kopel, D. B. (2015). The *posse comitatus* and the office of the sheriff: Armed citizens summoned to the aid of law enforcement. *The Journal of Criminal Law and Criminology, 104*(4), 761–850.

Lammy, D. (2014, January 13). Does the Metropolitan Police reflect London's ethnic diversity? *Daily Mirror.* Retrieved April 14, 2017, from https://fullfact.org/crime/does-metropolitan-police-reflect-londons-ethnic-diversity.

Loeb, J. (2016, April 8). Specials not complying with 16 hours per month volunteering role. Police Oracle. Retrieved April 11, 2016, from www.policeoracle.com/news/special_constabulary/2016/Apr/08/-specials-not-complying-with-16-hours-per-month-volunteering-rule-_91506.html.

London Metropolitan Police (n.d.). Who we are. Retrieved April 14, 2017, from http://content.met.police.uk/Site/About.

Lord Ferrers Awards (2017, August 18). Lord Ferrers Awards 2017. Retrieved March 13, 2017, from www.gov.uk/government/publications/lord-ferrers-awards-2017.

Millie, A. (2016). *Volunteering within the police: Experiences of special constables and police support volunteers.* Ormskirk, UK: Edge Hill University, Department of Law and Criminology. Retrieved May 25, 2016, from https://repository.edgehill.ac.uk/8206/1/MILLIE%20-%20police%20volunteers%20report%20-%20FINAL.pdf.

National Sheriffs' Association (2017). 2017 awards. Retrieved August 27, 2017, from www.sheriffs.org/sites/default/files/NSA%20Awards%202017.pdf.

Neighbourhood Watch (n.d.). About us. Retrieved February 20, 2017, from www.ourwatch.org.uk/about-us.

Nesbit, R., & Brudney, J. L. (2010). At your service? Volunteering and national service in 2020. *Public Administration Review, 70*(S1), S107–S113.

Northern Ireland Courts and Tribunals Service (n.d.). Judiciary of Northern Ireland. Retrieved December 15, 2016, from www.courtsni.gov.uk/en-GB/AboutUs/OrganisationalStructure/Pages/Judiciary-of-Northern-Ireland.aspx.

Office of Justice Programs (2011, June 10). Program profile: Kirkholt (England) burglary prevention project. Retrieved May 24, 2017, from www.crimesolutions.gov/ProgramDetails.aspx?ID=71.

Panel on the Independence of the Voluntary Sector (2011). *Voluntary sector independence.* London: Baring Foundation. Retrieved April 14, 2017, from http://baringfoundation.org.uk/wp-content/uploads/2011/03/POIreport2011.pdf.

Pepper, I. K., & Wolf, R. (2015). Volunteering to serve: An international comparison of volunteer police officers in a UK north east police force and a US Florida sheriff's office. *The Police Journal: Theory, Practice and Principles, 88*(3), 209–219.

Police UK (2013, July 6). General police discussion. Retrieved June 7, 2017, from www.policeuk.com/forum/index.php?/topic/18198-specials.

President's Volunteer Service Award (n.d.). The award. Retrieved August 27, 2017, from www.presidentialserviceawards.gov/the-award.

Ren, L., Zhao, J., Lovrich, N. P., & Gaffney, M. J. (2006). Participation community crime prevention: Who volunteers for police work? *Policing: An International Journal of Police Strategies and Management, 29*(3), 464–481.

Rochester, C. (2006). *Making sense of volunteering: A literature review.* London: Commission on the Future of Volunteering.

Rochester, C., Paine, A. E., & Howlett, S. (2012). *Volunteering and society in the 21st century.* Basingstoke, UK: Palgrave Macmillan.

Smith, A. (2016). "The Magnificent 7[am]?" Work–life articulation beyond the 9[am] to 5[pm] "norm." *New Technology, Work and Employment, 31*(3), 209–222.

United Nations Volunteers (2015). *2015 state of the world's volunteerism report: Transforming governance.* Washington, DC: United Nations Volunteers. Retrieved August 12, 2017, from www.unv.org/sites/default/files/2015%20 State%20of%20the%20World%27s%20Volunteerism%20Report%20-%20Transforming%20Governance.pdf.

Wakefield, A., & Fleming, J. (Eds.) (2009). *The Sage dictionary of policing.* London: Sage.

Warrell, H. (2014, November 7). Special constables take bigger role as budget cuts hit police. *Financial Times.* Retrieved August 20, 2017, from www.ft.com/content/edcb8282-3409-11e4-8832-00144feabdc0.

Werbel, A. (2014). The crime of the nude Anthony Comstock, the Art Students League of New York, and the origins of modern American obscenity. *Winterthur Portfolio: A Journal of American Material Culture, 48*(4), 249–282.

Whitehead, T. (2012, October 9). Police cuts mean more specials and volunteers, chief signals. *The Daily Telegraph.* Retrieved August 13, 2017, from www. telegraph.co.uk/news/uknews/law-and-order/9643289/Police-cuts-mean-more-specials-and-volunteers-chief-signals.html.

Wolf, R. (2013). An exploratory study of the utilization of volunteer law enforcement officers by American sheriffs. In *Proceedings of the International Conference of Forensic Sciences and Criminalistics Research*, Volume I, pp. 37–41. Singapore: Global Science and Technology Forum.

Wolf, R., Holmes, S. T., & Jones, C. (2016). Utilization and satisfaction of volunteer law enforcement officers in the office of the American sheriff: An exploratory nationwide study. *Police Practice and Research: An International Journal, 17*(5), 448–462.

Wyllie, D. (2017, August 8). The reserve officer's role in law enforcement. PoliceOne. Retrieved August 13, 2017, from www.policeone.com/patrol-issues/articles/4239138-The-reserve-officers-role-in-law-enforcement.

Chapter 4

The History of Volunteer Policing

The use of specials in the United Kingdom has a long and integral role in the policing of crime and disorder, preceding full-time, "formal" police officers by several hundred years. The history of policing itself started with volunteers, and is provided elsewhere (see Mawby, 1999; Seth, 2006; Greenberg, 2015), but it is worth revisiting in this book, albeit briefly. The historical practice of policing in communities could be said to coincide with the establishment of "tithings"[1] over a thousand years ago. Tithings were groups of about ten households, and each was under the responsibility of a tithingman, a sort of foreman, who acted as a leader or spokesman for the group. A tithing was a territorial identification and was later known as a "township" (Seth, 2006). The term "hundred" was used to describe approximately ten tithings, or 100 households. The tithingman was, in turn, answerable to a hundredman.

Within tithings and hundreds law and order (or the "king's peace") was kept through the use of adult citizens, who, without remuneration, were responsible for the "suppression of thieves, the recovery of stolen property, and mutual insurance against losses by theft" (Seth, 2006, p. 31), and may be considered to be the first formalized voluntary police force in England. "Shires" were made up of several hundreds (later known as a county or parish) and were led by a "shire reeve" (later known as a sheriff). The reeve was responsible for keeping the peace on behalf of the king, and acted as the chief magistrate. During the later feudal system the reeve was also responsible for ensuring that crops were gathered and sold, enforcing debt repayment, and collecting money and payments on accounts.

The term "constable" during this period (and for many centuries on) was unrelated to policing, and referred to a military man (Giblin, 2007) responsible for keeping and maintaining the king's armaments. Non-military constables were introduced in the middle of the thirteenth century, when the title was given to men appointed as principle representatives of the manor. Their role evolved such that, by the end of that century, they were given powers to ensure that the king's peace was kept. As

Mawby (1999) stated, though, the role that we would more readily recognize as "policing" was introduced only with the Statute of Winchester
of 1285, with the "watch and ward" system, whereby "all able-bodied
townsmen were required to take turns to guard the town during the
hours of darkness" (Mawby, 1999, p. 29). An Act passed by King Charles
II in 1673 ruled that, when there was a threat of great disturbances, any
citizen was liable to be empowered as a temporary police officer (City of
London Special Constabulary, 2011). This system of policing by unpaid,
volunteer parish constables would continue in England[2] until the creation of the Metropolitan Police Act of 1829, and the later County Police
Constabularies Act of 1839, led to the creation of full-time, paid, police
professionals. The Metropolitan Police Act authorized the formation of
a new policing organization: "His Majesty may establish a new police
office for the metropolis and the surrounding district, and may appoint
two persons as justices, to conduct the business of the office, under the
directions of a secretary of state" (Legislation.gov.uk, n.d.). This Act saw
the introduction of Sir Robert Peel's "bobbies," whose role was to combat
"tumult, riot and felony" in "any Parish, Township or Place is situate [sic]
within the Division or Limits for which the said respective Justices usually act, and such Justices shall be of opinion that the ordinary officers
appointed for preserving the peace are not sufficient" (Kettilby Rickards,
1831, p. 254).

The role of the modern volunteer special constable was created by
An Act for amending the Laws relative to the Appointment of Special
Constables, and for the better preservation of the Peace, more commonly
referred to as the Special Constables Act of 1831, which gave rise to the
appointment of volunteer police officers. This Act permitted the selection
of volunteer police officers at times of unrest, and authorized them with
full powers of arrest. The Act further gave these unpaid constables the
authority, in extraordinary circumstances, to act in adjoining counties.
Special constables were also provided with the necessary articles and
weapons required for their position (Seth, 2006). The Act provided
Justices of the Peace with the ability to provide specials with a reasonable
allowance for their service, a provision that is still in use today to provide meal allowances and other stipends in exchange for volunteer duty.
Finally, an interesting provision of the Act required that those nominated
for service as a special constable were *required* to serve, or they would be
fined £5 (quite a hefty sum at the time) for refusal (Seth, 2006).

Although special constables are used today primarily to supplement the
full-time police forces, they have also been used extensively in England
during times of upheaval and war. In 1848, during a political uprising
in France, at least 85,000 men volunteered and were sworn in as special
constables with the London Metropolitan Police Force. In 1914, when
war between Britain and Germany broke out, 20,000 special constables

were recruited to serve. This World War I effort forced a revision of the Special Constables Act of 1831, which was amended to include a grant of allowances for payment of lost time, payments for injuries, and payments to dependents for constables killed, and provided that an appointed special constable could resign if he wished (Seth, 2006).

The next time that specials were called upon nationally was during the General Strike of 1926,[3] and by 1930 the number of SCs had risen to 136,000, but, as at all other times, the numbers who turned out were a different matter. Because of the nature of "volunteerism," whereby individuals where asked to donate their time and energy for the benefit of others without financial reward, individuals could not be required to go on duty.

As full-time police officers were conscripted or volunteered for the military during World War II (1939–1945) their places were taken by around 130,000 special constables, many of them retired regular officers. In common with other post-emergency demands, at the end of the wartime period the number of SCs declined significantly. In 1949 women were finally admitted into the Special Constabulary, over a hundred years after its modern structure had been introduced.

In spite of the relatively small size and large population of England and Wales, more than half the area is rural, and the policing of the countryside has been a thorny issue for many years. Rural areas are perceived to be idyllic and tranquil, with less crime and fewer threats. In reality, however, estimates suggest that the cost of crime in such areas is actually significantly higher than previously thought. The National Rural Crime Network (NRCN) has estimated that rural crime cost £800 million in 2015, rather than the previous calculation by NFU Mutual in 2014 of £38.4 million (BBC, 2016). Policing these sparsely populated areas provides a challenge to many of the 43 police forces in England and Wales. Levels of rurality do vary from force to force, but some, such as Devon and Cornwall and North Wales, are predominantly rural.

Historically, policing in urban and rural areas was very different, with urban police officers working together while those covering rural areas were very much a part of their community and generally worked in isolation (Cain, 1973). As Mawby and Yarwood (2016) clearly demonstrated, however, advances in technology and increased mobility reduce differences in methods and patterns of working. Forces around the United Kingdom have addressed some of these differences in novel and cost-effective ways. Since 2009 Hertfordshire Constabulary has recruited and utilized SCs who have their own horses to patrol rural areas, thus covering locations that are inaccessible by car (Hertfordshire Constabulary, n.d.).

In 1993 the home secretary proposed the Parish Constables Scheme, whereby the recruitment of additional SCs in rural areas was intended to improve the relationship between the police service and residents in rural areas that felt neglected (Southgate, Bucke, & Byron, 1995).

The Specials in Northern Ireland

The evolution of specials in Northern Ireland is somewhat different from the development of special constables on the mainland of Great Britain. Ireland was a place of torment and upheaval through much of the twentieth century, and this has been underlined by its militaristic form of policing – a distinct contrast with its unarmed English counterparts.

Prior to 1920 there were two police forces in Ireland (which was, at that time, one country under rule from Westminster on the mainland): the Royal Irish Constabulary (RIC), which was some ten thousand strong and armed with pistols and rifles; and the Dublin Metropolitan Police (DMP), which was unarmed and consisted of around 1,100 men. As the political upheaval grew as the south of the country sought home rule, the unarmed Dublin Metropolitan Police found themselves increasingly under attack, resulting in the closure of many rural police stations so that those officers could be redirected to the urban areas (Hezlet, 1972).

The closure of so many stations in the north of the country led to demands for an armed special constabulary to support the RIC, and in 1920 the Ulster Special Constabulary (USC) was introduced in Northern Ireland and aligned to a political/militaristic structure (Farrell, 1983).

The Special Constabulary in Northern Ireland was actually made up of three separate sections: "A," "B," and "C" Specials. "A" Specials were full-time, made up of able-bodied men aged between 21 and 45 (the authorities hoped that they would be experienced ex-servicemen). They were to be employed for six months at a time and be paid the same rate as RIC officers plus an additional bounty, payable on discharge. This was considerably higher pay than even skilled workers. They were to bear arms, wear similar uniforms to the RIC officers, and have the same legal rights. They came under the command of their own senior officers and were warranted to serve only in the six counties of Northern Ireland (Farrell, 1983). So, while they were called "specials," their terms of engagement contrasted with those of voluntary officers on the mainland.

"B" Specials were a force made up of part-time officers who were generally deployed in such exercises as the manning of road blocks (a common feature), mounting patrols, and guarding buildings during the nighttime hours. They were required to go on duty one night per week and were unpaid, though they were eligible for an allowance of £5 every six months plus a small meal allowance each time they went on duty. They had to attend periodical training sessions and a condition of their service was that they could be mobilized for full-time duty in times of emergency. They were warranted only to serve in their own locality and, at their introduction, were allocated only caps and armbands to distinguish them. In 1922 they were issued with full uniforms. When they were on duty they were fully armed but were required to leave the arms at the police station when they were not on duty. Opposition resulted in this being partially overturned, with rural "B" Specials being allowed to keep their arms at home while those in urban areas continued to have to leave them at the police barracks (Farrell, 1983).

A good illustration of the activity of the "B" Specials is provided by the following extract from Gamble's (2009, p. 2) recollections of Bill Balmer:

> In October 1953 I joined the Ballymoney Platoon of the B Specials Major John Munnis was in charge.
>
> Karl Carton was the man who formed the B Specials in Ballymoney. When he died Major John Munnis succeeded him. Major John Munnis was the last County Commandant in the Ballymoney area. He joined the Ulster Defence Regiment in 1970 when the Bs were disbanded. In his civilian capacity he was the manager of Dixon's shoe shop in Coleraine.
>
> When Major Munnis was promoted to County Commandant, Tommy McMullan took over as Platoon Sergeant of the Ballymoney Platoon with the support of William Hill and Alfie Hanna. When Tommy McMullin went to England to live I was promoted to Platoon Sergeant of the Ballymoney Platoon…
>
> …I worked in the Post Office at that time and I was expected to start work at 4am every morning and start my postal deliveries at 6am. After some incidents I would still be out on the road patrolling and was late for work in the Post Office. One day I was very late and the supervisor took me to the side and complained. When I told him that I was out on patrol and came straight into work after the patrol he told me to go home, as he did not want me in the job. He threatened to sack me on the spot but unfortunately for him most of the staff were ex-service. One of these men pinned the supervisor to the wall and informed him that he would not be walking the streets of Ballymoney a free man if it were not for men like myself out guarding him. He was left in no doubt that if he sacked me he would have a "serious problem" on his hands.

The third group, the "C" Specials, was a wholly reserve force that had no regular duties other than occasional drill and training exercises. Their role was to step in during emergencies to undertake localized duties similar to those covered by the "B" Specials or to provide some short-term full-time duty. They did not have uniforms, merely the caps and armbands similar to those issued that had been issued to "B" Specials in their early days. They were unpaid other than an allowance when they were called out and were issued with arms only when they were on duty. However, they were encouraged to provide their own weapons and would be issued with appropriate licenses at a time when such paperwork was almost impossible to acquire (Farrell, 1983).

Ireland was formally partitioned and its border between north and south finally fixed in December 1925. As a consequence, the "A" Specials were the first to be disbanded, and soon afterwards recruitment to the "C" Specials was ended in order to diminish the size of the force. In April 1926 the allowances for "B" Specials were reduced to £3 per year, and they were required only to undertake drilling and ceased to be an active police force (Hezlet, 1972).

Political upheaval and violence continued in Northern Ireland, and in the 1930s the "B" Specials, who had been largely ignored since the mid-1920s, were suddenly brought into dispute as they were used as replacements for police in regular duties as well as for guarding military buildings. This was much more in line with routine policing, in contrast to being deployed only to suppress riots (Hezlet, 1972). The "B" Specials continued through an atmosphere of turmoil and aggression when, in 1969, the Hunt Report made a number of recommendations relating to the policing of Northern Ireland, including the disbandment of the "B" Specials (Advisory Committee on Police in Northern Ireland, 1969). The "B" Specials were disbanded the following year, to be replaced by the Royal Ulster Constabulary (RUC) Reserve under the terms of the 1970 Police Act (NI). The RUC was superseded by the Police Service of Northern Ireland (PSNI) in 2001, but there has not been a special constabulary in Northern Ireland since 1970; instead, the PSNI employs a small force of approximately 450 "part-time" officers, who are required to work a minimum of 144 hours/year (*Belfast Telegraph*, 2015).

The Use of Specials in Scotland

Just as there are clear differences identified between the policing of Northern Ireland and England and Wales, Donnelly and Scott (2002) have similarly indicated the Scottish application in relation to policing. Scotland is a part of the United Kingdom, but its legal and criminal justice systems remain entrenched in its own history.

In Scotland, a systematic policing organization was established before Peel's, with a local Act of parliament being introduced in Glasgow in 1800. Under this Act, householders elected police commissioners to oversee a police force, and this structure quickly spread across the remainder of the country, resulting, in 1890, with the Burgh Police (Scotland) Act, which ensured police burghs[4] throughout Scotland. Special constables in Scotland are utilized in a similar manner to those in England and Wales, particularly in the rural areas which make up a significant geographical area of the country (Donnelly & Scott, 2010).

As in England and Wales, the numbers of special constables declined significantly so that, in 2004, a pilot scheme was introduced whereby special constables in Grampian and Tayside could be provided with a remuneration of £1,000 per year. It was essential that the sum not be regarded as a payment, thus deflecting from the notion of "the volunteer." Nor was it to be used to compensate for out-of-pocket expenses, which were already provided. In 2005 the system was extended to cover all eight forces in Scotland, this system of "bounty" payments following their introduction in England and Wales a couple of years earlier. On April 1, 2013, the eight forces in Scotland were combined under the Police and Fire Reform (Scotland) Act 2012 to establish a single body. The rationale for such a move was, in part, to reduce duplication during a period of economic expediency. Among Scottish SCs, females make up a significantly higher proportion than full-time officers (37 percent against 28 percent, respectively), somewhat higher than in England and Wales. With regard to the ages of Scottish special constables, 5 percent are over the age of 55, and 50 percent are between the ages of 25 and 45.

The Evolution of Volunteer Policing in the United States

The evolution of American volunteer policing traces its roots back to the British model. American colonies and territories began using volunteers as far back as the middle of the seventeenth century, when a volunteer "posse," a group of people, could be called together by the local sheriff to assist with law enforcement, order maintenance, and fugitive apprehension. The authority to utilize armed citizens to aid in law enforcement is "deeply rooted in the Anglo-American legal system, originating no later than the ninth century" (Kopel, 2015, p. 763). During the great expansion of America from east to west, new territories and states were formed, occupied, and governed. These jurisdictional areas were comprised of counties, and most often the American people modeled the county peacekeeper on the Anglo-Saxon office of the sheriff. The common law powers of posse comitatus allowed the American sheriff, in upholding his duties to keep the peace, to summon able-bodied citizens (though women were traditionally exempt) to assist in the enforcement of the law, and allowed the sheriff complete discretion in how those citizens would be armed (Kopel, 2015). Colonial Americans took the Anglo-Saxon model of the office of the sheriff from its roots in England, with one exception. The new colonial sheriffs were elected, and became more active than their English counterparts in the apprehension of fugitives, delivering them to court, and in keeping the peace through law enforcement (Kopel, 2015).

The expanded role of the sheriff in America, particularly in the south and west, can be seen in modern policing and the more increased utilization of volunteer police even today. While many states in the northeast United States today utilize sheriffs' offices only for the security of courts, corrections, and the service of warrants,[5] states in the south and west utilize sheriffs as elected leaders of agencies with full police powers and responsibility.

The development of the US Army National Guard can be traced to the creation of militias in the early seventeenth century. On December 13, 1636, the first militia regiments in North America were organized by an order of the Massachusetts Bay Colony's General Court. This created an organized militia in the United States that required all able-bodied men (except for judges and ministers) between the ages of 16 and 60 to serve. The order declared that citizen-soldiers would be used to defend the Massachusetts colony when needed. Soon after this militia was established other colonies, such as Connecticut and Rhode Island, formed similar units, and they were quickly followed by other militias in Florida, Virginia, and New Mexico (Boehm, 2011).

The militia registry was also used in the north to organize night watch duty (Greenberg, 2015). In the northeast United States, and in many large urban population areas, the night watch system was utilized to aid in fighting criminal activity. This system, which later became famous for its inefficiency and inability to curb crime, utilized citizen volunteers, primarily at night, to patrol for criminal activity. These watches first appeared in Boston in the early seventeenth century and in New York City late that century. Night watch patrols were expected to report fires, announce the time and weather, care for street lamps, assist with nuisance animals, and keep a watchful eye for any type of criminal activity.

In the early eighteenth century southern lawmen also utilized similar groups to enforce slavery laws in the form of slave patrols. These patrols, which usually provided payment in the form of tobacco or cash to white citizens, were responsible for returning runaway slaves to their owners. Later these patrols would be made up of individuals selected from state militias. Although not an actual volunteer policing unit, which is the focus of this book, these patrols cannot be ignored in the history of American policing. The often brutal treatment of slaves by these patrols, and the utilization of these patrol to suppress insurrection and break up meetings of slaves, may be at least partially responsible for the lack of trust in the police on the part of American communities of color, and, in particular, wariness about the option of participation in volunteer policing.

Nineteenth-century policing in America was controlled by politicians, and was often brutal, corrupt, and inept. The police were accused of doing little to prevent crime, and of serving as the enforcement arm of the political party in power. Politicians determined who could be appointed to police officer occupations, which paid well. The politicians also decided who within policing would be promoted to higher ranks. Because corruption was so rampant, the police often became a part of the crime problem. Citizens generally did not like the police and outwardly disrespected them, which in turn fueled police brutality, as officers used their clubs to gain control in situations. Theodore Roosevelt,[6] as a New York City Board of Police commissioner from 1895 to 1897, focused on increasing the professionalism of police. Roosevelt fought to raise the standards for police recruits and to discipline dishonest police officers. Roosevelt worked hard to reform the police in New York City, but many of his efforts failed due to the powerful politics within policing at the time (Dempsey & Forst, 2008).

During the progressive era of government in the early 1900s, more attempts at reforming the police were attempted, but originated from outside of policing agencies by reformers. The progressive movement aimed at eliminating the corruption of government. Again, however, most of these reforms failed and corrupt, inept, and brutal policing continued (Dempsey & Forst, 2008).

As the United States moved into World Wars I and II, the increased use of volunteers to assist in routine public safety was formalized in 1941 with the United States Citizen Service Corps, and later in 1950 with the Federal Civil Defense Act. Wartime drafts had created a shortage of able men to serve as police, and many veteran police officers were called to active duty in the military. The Citizen Service Corps was created so that civilian volunteers could be charged with leading the fight against insecurity and poor health in communities during World War II. Any "able-bodied" person was encouraged to join, and were organized into committees of the local Defense Council. Later, during the years of the perceived threat in America of the Cold War, volunteer police programs flourished, partially due to the availability of federal grant programs to assist in their funding. This included service in the Air Raid Protective Service and the Auxiliary Police Service, which were responsible for guarding and patrolling targets of interest for saboteurs, including power stations, public works facilities, and gas tanks (Greenberg, 2015).

The political turmoil of the 1960s in America was reflected in the assassinations of President John F. Kennedy (1963), Senator Robert Kennedy (1968), and Dr. Martin Luther King (1968). The era was turbulent, with anti-war demonstrations, civil disobedience, and violent clashes between police and the public, such as the one at the 1968 Democratic Party presidential convention in Chicago. College campuses became common locations for protests and the scenes of more violent encounters between the police and demonstrators. One of the most widely publicized was the student takeover at Columbia University in New York City, where approximately 2,000 police officers attempted to clear protestors from campus buildings. The military Reserve Officer Training Corps (ROTC) building in the campus of the University of Wisconsin was firebombed in 1970, leading to 500 bombings and arson attacks on college campuses throughout the country. The clashes between the police and student demonstrators during this time period left a lasting negative impression on the national psyche (Dempsey & Forst, 2008).

The 1980s and 1990s led to positive developments in policing, including the greater use of technology, improvements in communications, and a drastic reduction in violent crime. There were many different contributory factors in the decrease in violent crime in the early 1990s, including the use of community-oriented policing, problem-oriented policing, and even the more aggressive zero-tolerance policing, credited to then NYPD commissioner William J. Bratton through the intelligence-led policing initiative of CompStat.[7] But the crime reductions of this era were fouled by several events that gave police throughout the country a public "black eye," including the Rodney King brutality case[8] and the trial of O. J. Simpson[9] (Dempsey & Forst, 2008).

Most modern volunteer police organizations in the United States can trace their history back to the civil defense organizations of the 1940s and 1950s. With increasing crime and violence, civil unrest, and the growth of anti-crime patrols, many jurisdictions turned to volunteers to increase manpower levels, and many governments expanded the use of volunteers, often adopting these civil defense units under the auspices of the police. A major exception, however, was in the northeast of America, where these initiatives to utilize volunteer police were thwarted by strong police unions and associations. In some states the legal actions and challenges raised by these associations have led to strong restrictions on the deployment of unpaid police personnel (Wolf, Albrecht, & Dobrin, 2015). While these states may have active volunteer policing organizations, the legal challenges have resulted in greatly reduced authority and responsibility on the part of those who serve in these positions. Most, for example, do not have arrest authority (beyond that of any citizen).

This same concern about increasing crime and civil unrest led to the creation of the National Neighborhood Watch (NNW)[10] in 1972 by the National Sheriffs' Association through funding by the US Bureau of Justice Assistance, Office of Justice Programs, Department of Justice. While the NNW would not be categorized as a volunteer police organization by the definition in this book, the continued inclusion of citizens in serving as the "eyes and ears" of the police is an important part of understanding the development of these organizations throughout the country.[11] Neighborhood watch, in attempting to reduce opportunities for crime, may also lead to a reduction in crime through enhanced community cohesion, and a greater dialogue with government policing agencies. Neighborhood watch has been consistently associated with reductions in crime, but "it remains unclear whether neighborhood watch deters offenders or enhances police investigation" (Holloway, Bennet, & Farrington, 2013).

Volunteerism in the United States since the Terrorist Attacks on September 11, 2001

After the attacks on New York City in 2001, volunteerism in the United States jumped 28.8 percent, and support for the government and government institutions were at their highest in decades (Zherka, 2014). Americans sought out opportunities to serve in numerous government and non-profit community service agencies, including community emergency response teams, the American Red Cross, Habitat for Humanity, and other organizations. Americans felt compelled during this time period to help those who were unable, to serve altruistically, and to connect to other Americans. Immediately after the 9/11 attacks, thousands of people from all over the United States headed to New York City hoping to volunteer to assist in any way possible (Steffen & Fothergill, 2009). This initial increase could not be sustained, however, and many volunteers left their service.

However, the Great Recession of 2007 forced government agencies to look to volunteers as a way to supplement services. The economic downturn forced 21 percent of American policing agencies to lay off civilian employees and police officers, and another 56 percent to shrink purposefully by not filling openings that resulted from employee attrition. This loss in professional policing was blamed for an increase in crime rates, and fewer police arrests (Yoder, 2012). Volunteers were recruited to assist policing agencies in a wide range of tasks associated with community and the quality of life. Most of these volunteers do not have any law enforcement authority or training, however. Many volunteers are used for non-enforcement functions, including crime scene processing, fingerprinting, working in reception areas, case filing and management, police-managed tourist information centers, and more (Greenberg, 2015).

The use of unpaid volunteers in both sworn and non-sworn, or "civilian," roles has since grown throughout the United States, although certainly not every police agency, nor every state, utilizes them, or utilizes them in the same way. Many agencies use police reserves and auxiliaries who do not have any or extremely limited law enforcement authority. The volunteers play an important role as a force multiplier and act to report crime and suspicious activity to full-time officers. As outlined earlier, this has created a largely geographic difference in how volunteer police are utilized, and it is primarily in the west and south United States that volunteers serve in law enforcement positions with full or partial police powers, and in a variety of policing functions and roles.

Civilianization of the Policing Role

In addition to adding volunteers to support the police role, police organizations have reduced their budgets by replacing positions that were occupied by police officers with non-sworn (or "civilian") employees. Police organizations have successfully changed sworn police positions to civilian positions for posts including reception personnel, communications personnel, driving under the influence (DUI) or evidence technicians, human resources personnel, research and planning staff, and other positions that may be more efficiently handled by less expensive employees (Cordner & Scarborough, 2010). A position in the crime scene unit, for example, may have previously been limited to only those with experience working as police officers and with police authority; however, many policing agencies have replaced these positions with less expensive (because of salary, but also largely due to reduced benefits) trained civilian personnel. "By utilizing civilians to perform duties typically undertaken by sworn staff, police departments are able to save money primarily through lower pay, reduced training requirements, and smaller overheard requirements" (Greenberg, 2015, p. 37).

An advantage of both volunteers and civilians filling roles in police agencies is that it "brings different kinds of people into the police organization" (Cordner & Scarborough, 2010, p. 272). Non-sworn volunteer positions or civilian employee positions may appeal to those who may not be interested in, qualified for, or physically able to hold sworn law enforcement positions. These jobs may be especially exciting to the elderly, individuals with physical disabilities, or those unable to spend the time to get the necessary police training (Cordner & Scarborough, 2010). Some police departments have also utilized paid and volunteer community service officers, uniformed civilians, for routine police duties. These positions, which are very similar to the United Kingdom's police community support officer (PCSO) role, take reports on minor offenses, support frontline policing by dealing with non-enforcement police calls for service, provide minor first aid, and provide crime prevention information and advice to citizens. These uniformed roles have also been used as a recruiting avenue for full-time policing positions (Travis & Langworthy, 2008).

Notes

1 For the early history of tithings, see Mawby (1999).
2 The Bow Street Runners were also employed full-time, and were an exception to the volunteer system, which at the time relied heavily on unpaid constables. Officially called the "principal officers" of Bow Street, the Bow Street Runners, founded in 1749, have been called London's first professional police force. When a crime was reported, Bow Street Runners were sent out by the magistrate

to detect and apprehend the suspect (Old Bailey Proceedings Online, n.d.). By the 1820s, however, lawlessness in London had grown exponentially, and the number of paid constables was totally inadequate (Seth, 2006).

3 The General Strike of 1926 in the United Kingdom lasted from May 4 to 12, and was called by workers' unions in an attempt to force the British government to prevent wage reduction and worsening conditions for coal miners. In an effort to help the police and restore public order, the government swore in large numbers of special constables. The strike involved over 3 million workers, but despite the large number of strikers it passed with "remarkably little violence and no deaths; the most famous incident was the football match played at Plymouth between police and strikers" (Pugh, 2006).

4 A burgh was an autonomous municipal corporation in Scotland, similar to a borough or town, and a police burgh was one that had adopted a "police system" for its government. These local entities had councils, elected magistrates, and commissioners of police. Police burghs were in existence in Scotland from 1833 until 1975.

5 The New York City (NYC) Sheriff's Office, for example, is a division of the New York City Department of Finance. The sheriff is appointed by the mayor of New York City (although other sheriffs in the state of New York are elected), and deputy sheriffs primarily carry out civil law enforcement evictions, warrants, and summons, and ensure the collection of judgments. The NYC sheriff used to oversee the city's jails, but no longer; that is a duty now carried out by the City Department of Corrections. In contrast, the sheriff of Orange County (Florida) has primary responsibility for all law enforcement functions within the county limits of Orange County that are not within municipal jurisdictions. The sheriff of Orange County is elected, but is not responsible for the county jails, that function being handled by the Orange County Department of Corrections; this is an anomaly in Florida, as most sheriffs in the state also have primary responsibility for the county jails.

6 Theodore Roosevelt would later become governor of the state of New York (in 1898) and then the 26th president of the United States (1901–1909). He was not quite 43 years old when the 25th president, William McKinley, was assassinated and Roosevelt rose from the position of vice president to assume the presidency. Arguably his most famous quote was "Speak softly and carry a big stick."

7 CompStat stands for either "Computer Statistics" or "Compare Statistics" and is a process used to reduce crime by emphasizing information sharing, the accountability of managers, and improved effectiveness. CompStat has four core components: 1) timely and accurate intelligence; 2) rapid deployment of personnel and resources; 3) effective use of police tactics; and 4) "relentless" follow up (Bureau of Justice Assistance, 2013).

8 The Rodney King incident refers to the 1991 videotaped beating of an African American by members of the Los Angeles Police Department. The videotape was recorded by a bystander, who recorded the culmination of a 115 mile per hour chase of King through the city. Four police officers were arrested and charges with the assault of King, and were originally found not guilty by the jury in the criminal trial, but later convicted in federal court for violating King's civil rights.

9 O. J. Simpson was a professional American football player and movie star who was tried on two counts of murder concerning the death of his ex-wife and acquaintance. The trial lasted seven months, and may be the most publicized criminal trial ever in history. Simpson's defense team painted the Los Angeles Police Department as bumbling the investigation and as systemic racists.

10 The National Neighborhood Watch empowers citizens to be active in community efforts to fight crime by participating in neighborhood groups that receive training, technical assistance, resources, and other assistance from their local police agency and the NSA. Additionally, the NNW program provides signs to registered programs to mark their community as participating in the national organization.

11 NNW members and local organizations do not have any police powers, but are encumbered with the education necessary to report activity that may be suspicious, criminal, or dangerous. This program also spread to the United Kingdom in the 1980s, and in 2000 there were an estimated 6 million households, or more than 155,000 active programs, participating in the Neighborhood Watch "scheme" in England and Wales.

References

Advisory Committee on Police in Northern Ireland (1969). *Report of the Advisory Committee on Police in Northern Ireland*. Belfast: HMSO.

BBC (2016, September 15). Rural crime: Cost in England and Wales "reaches more than £800m." Retrieved April 15, 2017, from www.bbc.co.uk/news/uk-34250455.

Belfast Telegraph (2015, April 22). Concerns over part-time officers. Retrieved January 10, 2018, from www.belfasttelegraph.co.uk/news/northern-ireland/concerns-over-parttime-officers-31161970.html.

Boehm, B. (2011, December 13). National Guard marks its 375th birthday. US Army. Retrieved January 4, 2017, from www.army.mil/article/70758.

Bureau of Justice Assistance (2013). *Compstat: Its origins, evolution, and future in law enforcement agencies*. Washington, DC: Police Executive Research Forum.

Cain, M. E. (1973). *Society and the policeman's role*. London: Routledge & Kegan Paul.

City of London Special Constabulary (2011). *City of London Special Constabulary, 1911–2011*. London: City of London Special Constabulary.

Cordner, G. W., & Scarborough, K. E. (2010). *Police administration*, 7th Edition. New Providence, NJ: Lexis Nexis.

Dempsey, J. S., & Forst, L. S. (2008). *An introduction to policing*, 4th Edition. Belmont, CA: Wadsworth.

Donnelly, D., & Scott, K. B. (2002). Police accountability in Scotland: (1) The "new" tripartite system. *The Police Journal*, 75(1), 1–12.

Donnelly, D., & Scott, K. B. (2010). *Policing Scotland*, 2nd Edition. Cullompton, UK: Willan Publishing.

Farrell, M. (1983). *Arming the Protestants: The formation of the Ulster Special Constabulary and the Royal Ulster Constabulary 1920–27*. London: Pluto Press.

Gamble, R. (2009). *My service life (1939–1979): William "Bill" Balmer*. Coleraine, UK: Causeway Museum Service.

Giblin, J. (2007). The office of constable: An historical perspective of the "old" and "new" police. Leatherhead, UK: Police Federation. Retrieved January 10, 2018, from www.scribd.com/document/54427522/183-The-Office-of-Constable-An-Historical-Perspective-of-the-Old-and-New-Police.

Greenberg, M. A. (2015). *American volunteer police: Mobilizing for security*. Boca Raton, FL: CRC Press.

Hertfordshire Constabulary (n.d.). Rural special constabulary. Retrieved October 14, 2016, from www.herts.police.uk/hertfordshire_constabulary/special_constabulary/rural_specials.aspx.

Hezlet, A. (1972). *The "B" Specials: A history of the Ulster Special Constabulary*. London: Stacey.

Holloway, K., Bennett, T., & Farrington, D. P. (2013). *Does neighborhood watch reduce crime?*, Crime Prevention Research Review 3. Washington, DC: US Department of Justice, Office of Community Oriented Policing Services.

Kettilby Rickards, G. (1831). *The Statutes of the United Kingdom of Great Britain and Ireland, 1 & 2 William IV*. London: His Majesty's Statute and Law Printers.

Kopel, D. B. (2015). The *posse comitatus* and the office of the sheriff: Armed citizens summoned to the aid of law enforcement. *Journal of Criminal Law and Criminology, 104*(4), 761–850.

Legislation.gov.uk (n.d.). Metropolitan Police Act 1829. Retrieved January 12, 2018, from www.legislation.gov.uk/ukpga/Geo4/10/44/contents.

Mawby, R. I. (1999). *Policing across the world: Issues for the twenty-first century*. London: UCL Press.

Mawby, R. I., & Yarwood, R. (2016). *Rural policing and policing the rural: A constable countryside?* Farnham, UK: Ashgate.

Old Bailey Proceedings Online (n.d.). Policing in London. Retrieved January 10, 2018, from www.oldbaileyonline.org/static/Policing.jsp.

Pugh, M. (2006). The General Strike. *History Today, 56*(5), 40–47.

Seth, R. (2006). *The specials*. Trowbridge, UK: Cromwell Press.

Southgate, P., Bucke, T., & Byron, C. (1995). *The parish special constables scheme*, Home Office Research Study 143. London: Home Office Research and Planning Unit.

Steffen, S. L., & Fothergill, A. (2009). 9/11 volunteerism: A pathway to personal healing and community engagement. *The Social Science Journal, 46*(1), 29–46.

Travis, L. F., & Langworthy, R. H. (2008). *Policing in America: A balance of forces*. Upper Saddle River, NJ: Pearson Publishing.

Wolf, R., Albrecht, J., & Dobrin, A. (2015). Reserve policing in the United States: Citizens volunteering for public service. *The Police Chief, 82*(10), 38–47.

Yoder, S. (2012, August 7). As police budgets are cut, citizens step in. The Fiscal Times. Retrieved January 2, 2017, from www.thefiscaltimes.com/Articles/2012/08/07/Police-Budget-Cut#page1.

Zherka, I. (2014, November 11). Volunteering and service are more than a temporary response to tragedy. The Huffington Post. Retrieved January 2, 2017, from www.huffingtonpost.com/ilir-zherka/volunteering-and-service-_b_5805286.html.

Chapter 5

The Contemporary Role and Functions of Volunteer Police

Beginning a paid, full-time, regular law enforcement career in modern policing requires a community service mindset in both the United States and the United Kingdom. Candidates must be willing to work long hours in varying shifts, work in frequently dangerous or at least questionable conditions, be exposed to both physical and psychological dangers, and usually for less than middle-income wages. Law enforcement officers risk being sued (whether they were in the right or wrong) and investigation by citizen oversight groups (Walker, 2001), and may be the subject of racist or derogatory comments or attack by those in the community who choose to dislike the police (Greenberg, 2005). In England and Wales there is also the regular scrutiny by Her Majesty's Inspector of Constabulary; in the United States there is the possibility of civil lawsuit and investigation by professional standards or internal investigations units.

However, becoming a volunteer law enforcement officer takes these requirements to a new level. Volunteer officers in the United States must "consider such occupational hazards as possible death, physical injury, stress, cynicism, alcoholism, divorce, and other maladies" (Berg & Doerner, 1988, p. 82), but also must enjoy working with people, and learning and using new skills in order to accept such a challenge without economic reward, or even at personal economic expense. In many jurisdictions in the United States they must also be willing to maintain police certification or maintain certain training levels, which may require countless hours of preparation with no pay, and necessitate work within the paramilitary structure of police agencies. Mandatory court appearances or hearings may keep volunteer police from their regular employment, or from their families (Arwood, Hilal, Karsky, & Norman, 2005). The commitment is similar in England and Wales, where the College of Policing oversees all aspects of policing, including the certifications of special constables. At the UK Special Constabulary conference 2016, the focus on volunteering in policing highlighted the difficulties still experienced by SCs from regular officers, whose perceptions of volunteer police often continue to be discursive and disparaging, in spite of the energies and time given freely by the volunteers. This is not limited to special constables in the United Kingdom, however; American volunteer police commonly face full-time regular police officers who see them as "weekend warriors" or "wanna-be cops." In some places in the United States, volunteer police are disdained by full-time officers and supervisors, who complain that they are a liability for the "real" police, who work in policing every day.

While finding a volunteer who is willing to give so much without any monetary reward may be difficult, there has also been an increased demand for volunteers at the local government level. Reductions in government spending, rising populations, and increasing public expectations for better-quality services have led municipal and local police agencies to look to volunteers to fill important functions (Sharpe, 1986; Fredericksen & Levin, 2004). In England and Wales there have been accusations of "policing on the cheap" through the use of SCs and, more recently, PCSOs (see, for example, Whitehead, 2012). Policing agencies may also respond to increasing crime by "expanding the variety of roles in which volunteers may serve" (Sharpe, 1986, p. 86). Volunteer officers may "help bridge the distance between the department and full-time officers, on one hand, and the community, on the other (Fredericksen & Levin, 2004, p. 121). In addition to their community policing role, more commonly in the United States, volunteers in policing can be an important aspect of homeland security, delinquency prevention programs, narcotics enforcement (Greenberg, 2005), and criminal investigations, and may be utilized to respond to natural or man-made disasters. In the United Kingdom specialism roles are less common, but this is on the rise and is a slowly changing issue, as discussed later in this chapter.

It is widely recognized that policing, and the criminal justice system in general, depend on public involvement in the detection and investigation of criminal activity (Gill & Mawby, 1990; Roberg, Novak, & Cordner, 2009). Public crime campaigns such as "See Something, Say Something" count on citizens to be involved in detecting criminal activity and reporting it to the police, while programs such as *Crimewatch* in the United Kingdom represent a synergy between the police and the public. Without the collaboration and goodwill of the public, crimes would not be reported, nor would investigations routinely solve criminal activity; hence the relationship between police and citizens is routinely examined and explored in the literature (see Weitzer & Tuch, 2005; Myhill & Beak, 2008; Sindall, Sturgis, & Jennings, 2012; Perkins, 2016; Sprott & Doob, 2014). It might be argued that British special constables and their counterparts in American volunteer policing can be considered to be closest, along with police support volunteers and police cadets, to the Peelian principles of "citizens in policing" (College of Policing, n.d.). These volunteers often go beyond being merely another set of eyes on the street; volunteer officers in particular are tasked with the authority and responsibility of taking an active role in "the police." While deployment of these volunteers may develop positive outcomes, such as a better relationship between the police and the community, better accountability, and cost savings over an equal number of full-time officers, there is no research to suggest that the addition of volunteer officers acts as a deterrent to criminal activity, and certainly no more than an increase of a similarly small number of regular officers would (Gill & Mawby, 1990).

Volunteer police come from a variety of backgrounds. They may have full-time jobs as doctors, nurses, plumbers, mechanics, educators, corporate business leaders, lawyers, or professional athletes (Williams, 2005; Volunteer Special Constabulary, 1998; *Special Impact*, 2015a). They may also be diverse with regard to age, ethnic group, gender, religion, and culture (Gravelle & Rogers, 2009). The issue of diversity is very important, because the diversity within contemporary policing is regarded as vital in ensuring an improving relationship between minority ethnic groups and support for female victims of crime (Police.uk, 2015). The use of volunteer officers also varies greatly by agency. Volunteer officers may provide basic police services, such as foot patrol, or walking the beat. However, there are other methods of utilizing sworn police volunteers, and American policing agencies in particular make use of volunteers in positions in marine patrol, aviation, transport, special weapons or special response teams, mounted patrol, and canine patrol. In England and Wales, however, the scope for specialist functions is somewhat more limited.

> One of the advantages of Special Constables is the expertise and knowledge many of them bring from their paid employment, which can be utilized for the benefit of the Police Service. A specialized example of this was a scheme introduced by the MSC in February 2003 to recruit qualified accountants to work as plain clothes Special Constables within the Metropolitan Police Specialist Crime Unit. The accountants do not complete the same training as current Specials, but are trained by the Specialist Crime Unit to assist investigators to seize proceeds of crime.
>
> (Seth, 2006, p. 257)

Historically, skills transfer from volunteers into the police has been shunned in the United Kingdom, but there have been movement toward utilizing prior experience and education. In 1995 a force in the southeast of England put in place a patrol of Chichester Harbour using a boat manned exclusively by special constables. This replaced a similar service that had been scrapped 12 years previously due to high costs when regular officers had been used (Howe & Graham, 1995).

As another example of the utilization of specialized skills from professions outside policing, Hampshire Constabulary in Portsmouth in the United Kingdom has begun recruiting highly trained IT workers for positions as special constables and support volunteers. The volunteers are being used to investigate cybercrime, including internet fraud, ransomware attacks, and child exploitation. With their previous specialized training, the volunteers work a minimum of 16 hours every month assisting with relevant investigations and providing digital forensic support. The team of volunteer detectives are called "cyber specials," with the same investigative authority and powers as regular police (Fishwick, 2016). The pilot program was developed to be an extension of other partnerships with the police to reinforce and support the role of full-time police. The project, evaluated by the University of Portsmouth, which holds a newly established Forensic Innovations Centre, is in the force area where Hampshire specials chief officer Tom Haye is the CEO of a broadcasting company and therefore at the cutting edge of digital technology. The cyber specials also are being recruited in Gloucestershire, the location of the Government Communications Headquarters (GCHQ).

The United Kingdom's National Crime Agency (NCA) also recruits volunteer police specials for their expertise in cybersecurity, financial services and markets, accounting, and language skills. The NCA is most similar to the Federal Bureau of Investigation (FBI) in the United States, and was established in 2013 to replace the Serious Organised Crime Agency to investigate human, weapon, and drug trafficking, cybercrime, and economic crime. This is contrary to the United States, where volunteer police are not used at the national level with federal police agencies, although full-time local or state police officers may be dual-sworn with federal agencies for criminal investigations.

The City of London Police, a separate force from the London Metropolitan Police, has developed a very successful Economic Crime Directorate, which is the national policing lead for these types of crimes. The economic crimes unit is internationally recognized for its reputation and is the largest fraud investigation unit in Europe, investigating crimes at the local, national, and international levels (Field, 2007). The force utilizes volunteer special constables in a wide range of areas, including economic crimes.

> Using specialist knowledge from cross-sectional backgrounds as increased our technical cyber capabilities, business expertise and increased our capacity in the fight against economic and cybercrime.
> (City of London Police, 2016)

In another very specific role, however, the City of London Police was the first police force in the United Kingdom to train and utilize special constables in professional standards investigations. Special constables are trained to handle complaints against police officers, including cases of alleged discrimination, use of force, vehicle misuse, and other suspected policy or crime violations by City of London Police officers. Special Constabulary commander Ian Miller is very proud of the expert work that his volunteer officers undertake, allowing them to "use their skills in more and more areas of value and service to the community" (Robinson & Miller, 2016). The City of London has approximately 75 special constables, or slightly more than 10 percent of the regular police force's strength of approximately 700.

With the appropriate level of training, volunteer police can be called upon to do everything that full-time police can do, but there are additional benefits from their use. In the event of natural or man-made disaster, the size of a police force can be (almost) immediately multiplied. In an event that requires significant immediate response by on-duty personnel, volunteer police can be called upon to "back-fill" the normal patrol function of the agency.[1] Some jurisdictions may use volunteer police to form or complete special response teams, which can respond quickly to civil disturbances or large-scale disasters. Other jurisdictions may have planned large-scale events at which volunteer police are needed to handle a substantial influx of people added to the normal size of the population. This might include sporting events, spring break and holidays, or other times when there is a substantial need to increase the police presence and visibility.[2]

As an example of the type of deployment that is possible for volunteer police given the right training and opportunities, in 2015 Bedfordshire special constable Inspector John Power became the first UK special constable to become a police canine handler. John and his dog (Charlie) attended the national training course after John had sold the idea to his command team. The two attended an eight-week residential course at the Surrey Police Dog School, focusing on training for explosive detection. Once they had become certified by the Association of Chief Police Officers (ACPO) as an accredited explosive search dog detection team, they began to donate their time by ensuring that Luton Airport in Bedfordshire was a safe traveling environment, but they also provided support for a joint counter-terrorism unit, providing explosive searches for visiting royalty, dignitaries, and foreign heads of state (*Special Impact*, 2015b). Bedfordshire has approximately 250 special constables, who reported over 500 arrests in 2015 and over 82,000 hours of volunteer service (Bedfordshire Police, n.d.).

In addition to special constables within the 43 police forces in England and Wales, volunteer police can also be found at work with specialized policing services, including the British Transport Police (BTP), which is attached to the rail system. The British Transport Police is overseen by the British Transport Police Authority, which is independent and answerable to the railway companies and the public. They also appoint the chief constable and other senior posts and respond to complaints against the BTP. British Transport Police officers have patrolled railway properties and trains since 1830, with special constables being authorized under the Special Constables Act of 1831. Their implementation was of particular importance at the time new railways were being built, as vast numbers of "navvies"[3] flocked to new employment opportunities, resulting in the building of large shanty towns. Crime became a major problem in such environments, and, as a result, special constables were used to police the problems. However, the costs of all these special constables initially fell on the local ratepayers (taxpayers) until, in 1838, an Act was introduced which put the cost on the railway companies (British Transport Police, n.d.). As with the countrywide forces, BTP special constables also have full warranted powers, though their areas of policing are very different. Not only are the BTP utilized at railway stations in England and Wales, but they also travel on trains, particularly during major sporting and music events, when large numbers of fans use the rail system to travel to and from the matches, meetings, and concerts (see Photo 6).

The Orange County Sheriff's Office in Orlando, Florida, utilizes reserves wherever possible, based on their training. Once reserves complete their initial academy training and their subsequent Field Training Evaluation Program (FTEP), they are required to work their monthly volunteer hours in a patrol capacity. However, just like full-time deputies with the agency, they are allowed to request specialized training to serve in specialty units. Reserves with the proper certification and training can

Photo 6 British Transport Police special constables providing assistance at Paddington train station in London

participate in the horseback unit, marine patrol unit, bicycle patrol, or other specialized patrol units. Additionally, reserves are authorized to assist with investigations and may participate in fugitive apprehension, criminal investigations, or the training section, based on their training, experiences, and interests.

Similarly, the Los Angeles County Sheriff's Department (LASD) Reserve Forces Bureau has over 700 reserve officers of various training and authority (*Monrovia Weekly*, 2015). Reserve deputies with the LASD are provided a US$1 per year stipend to serve their communities, and most often are assigned to patrol stations to perform general law enforcement duties, including responding to calls for service, traffic control, and criminal investigation. Over 150 reserve deputies, however, also participate in search and rescue teams, including swift water rescue teams. During 2015 the LASD search and rescue teams participated in over 450 search and rescue missions, making it one of the most active teams in the nation. "Air Rescue 5," a Los Angeles County Sheriff's Department helicopter, is operated by reserve deputies (Alfonso, 2015), and is on call 24 hours a day, seven days a week. All LASD Special Enforcement Bureau deputies, including those in the search and rescue and "Air Rescue 5" teams, are certified paramedics and rescue divers (*Monrovia Weekly*, 2015). Additionally, LASD volunteer officers are also authorized to participate in the mounted enforcement detail, mounted search and rescue, and reserve mounted posse based on their equestrian training. In 2014 volunteers with the Los Angeles County Sheriff's Department recorded over 450,000 hours of volunteer time, estimated to be worth over US$11 million in savings to the LASD (Wright, 2015).

Special constables in England and Wales have, over the years, proved their worth in time, expertise, effort, and reliability, but the policing of rural areas has, until recently, been regarded as secondary to urban areas, largely due to what has been perceived as low levels of crime in low-density locations. However, more recently the incidence and types of crimes in such locations has come under increasing scrutiny, and, in some areas, the local police service has used innovative methods of policing. For example, in several forces across England, SCs who own their own horses are dispatched to rural areas for their duty; this allows them access across open land and other areas where cars are less maneuverable.

While the fire and rescue service has made use of retained fire officers for many years, it was only in 1996 that the Home Office recommended a study of the potential of special constable recruitment with the collaboration of employers. Employers are encouraged to provide their employees with paid time to serve their community by gaining the training required and then serving in an active role as a special constable or police support volunteer. After a somewhat faltering start to the scheme, employers that now are actively supporting police volunteering range from banks to telecommunications, supermarkets, and councils. Such partnerships can have benefits for the employer, the police service, and the individual. In 2015 a "Give and Gain" day took place in Greater Manchester at which special constables and PSVs who were part of Employer Supported Policing (ESP) gave an entire day to a number of targeted initiatives. They were observed throughout the day by some of the participating employers as they worked with and without their regular counterparts. Among the successes of the day there was the seizing of an air weapon, the confiscation of cannabis, and the recovery of a stolen vehicle, as well as a significant number of lesser offences (Greater Manchester Police, 2015).

Leadership, Management, and Recognition of Volunteers

Volunteer police have very diverse full-time occupations or experiences, and may be successful leaders, entrepreneurs, or public sector employees before even deciding to volunteer for a policing role. They strive to serve their communities and take an active role in society. The typical top-down leadership of the quasi-military structure used in policing may meet with resistance from typical volunteers. In portions of the United States where retired law enforcement officers serve in volunteer policing capacities, for example, the prior experience, knowledge, and leadership need to be nurtured and recognized. Former full-time regular police who become volunteers may bring with them a wealth of leadership experience in that role, but also may have no formal leadership position as a volunteer. Because volunteer police give their time with limited or no formal reward, the agency must consider ways to satisfy personal needs, drives, and skills; this may include an internal management organization, including a rank structure.

Although some agencies in the United States have developed successful volunteer programs that are managed by only one or two paid employees (usually regular law enforcement officers), other agencies have created structures that are similar or mirror the structure of the full-time members of the agency. In the United Kingdom this system is used extensively, with a senior chief special constable who is in command of the special constables of the force, but in the United States there is great variation, as in many other aspects of policing.

Although it is not entirely consistent, most UK police forces utilize a rank structure for volunteer police. The National Policing Improvement Agency has recommended a rank structure for special constables that included the ranks of special police constable, special sergeant, special inspector, special chief inspector, special superintendent, special chief superintendent (when needed), and chief officer of the Special Constabulary. Other forces have added additional senior management ranks, including those of assistant chief officer of the Special Constabulary and deputy chief officer of the Special Constabulary. Most forces in the United Kingdom utilize special constable rank insignia, a move that was not recommended by the National Policing Improvement Agency (which was replaced in 2012 by the College of Policing), and that is not consistent with the regular police forces. The senior ranks are also volunteers, but their degrees of authority vary from force to force.

In recent research a survey was sent to all senior special officers of all 43 police forces across England and Wales, and it drew responses from 39; three failed to provide gender information among senior officers and so are also excluded from the following. In every remaining force, the percentage of male special inspectors outweighed females by between 100 and 65 per cent. In data for special chief inspectors, 13 indicated that their force did not have such a rank while the remaining forces showed that male special chief inspectors outweighed females in every force area but one. According to the findings, in one force with ten special chief inspectors, there were no females of that rank. The data shows that the more senior the rank, the less likely it is to be a female in the special constable role. With regard to the gender at each rank, while female special constables account for almost one-third of all special constables (31.3 percent), female chief officers account for only 8.1 percent of the total (Britton, Knight, & Maloney, 2016)

A recent debate is that of rank and seniority between regular and volunteer police officers. For example, in the case of a regular constable and a special sergeant together at a scene, who has seniority? A leadership review for the College of Policing found that "there continues to be an element of 'us and them'" between regular and voluntary officers (College of Policing, n.d.). While there is a level of hierarchy within the Special Constabulary, it remains detached from the regular service, so that, even when an SC may have strong and proven leadership skills and knowledge, within the policing "family" a regular officer will routinely take authority over that special.

As an example of an American police agency that utilizes a rank structure, the Orange County Sheriff's Office in Florida matches reserve deputy ranks with those of the full-time members of the agency. The unit has the ranks of reserve deputy, reserve corporal, reserve sergeant, reserve lieutenant, reserve captain, reserve major, and reserve chief deputy. The rank insignia of the reserve deputies are identical to the insignia of the full-time counterparts for these ranks; however, reserve deputy ranks are silver in color rather than gold.[4] In addition, while full-time corporals and sergeants have sewn on gold-colored rank insignia on their upper sleeves, reserve corporals and sergeants wear silver-colored collar brass with the identical insignia. Full-time members of the OCSO also have additional ranks, including the ranks of deputy first class and master deputy.[5] These ranks are not supervisory in nature, however, and are used as promotional opportunities for regular members of the agency. The volunteer unit has therefore not incorporated them into the command structure. Reserve deputies of any rank with the OCSO do not outrank full-time members of the agency, however. While reserves who hold supervisory rank are granted the same respect as full-time deputy sheriffs with the same rank, they do not have any authority over any full-time or regular deputy in the course of their duties. When working in an enforcement function with full-time deputies, reserve deputies who hold rank do not wear their insignia, so as not to confuse the public (or full-time deputies) regarding the management authority. However, when working details which are staffed only by reserves or for ceremonial occasions, reserves are authorized to wear their rank insignia.

Another example from Florida is the Saint Lucie County Sheriff's Office reserve unit. This unit is small in size, with only about 15 reserve deputies, with both the equivalent of full-law enforcement certifications and auxiliary certifications. However, this agency has elected to have only two ranks; that of reserve deputy and reserve sergeant. There are no additional ranks and no supervisory authority of the reserve sergeants over the reserve deputies. Hamilton Police Service (Canada) auxiliaries follow this same leadership model, with auxiliary staff sergeants, auxiliary sergeants, and auxiliary constables reporting to a regular full-time inspector with the agency. Auxiliary sergeants are responsible for directed patrol areas, crime prevention teams, and training units. Auxiliary sergeants have authority and responsibility over auxiliary constables who report to their area.

Famous and Celebrity Police Reserves, Auxiliaries, and Special Constables

Elvis Presley (1935–1977)

The "King of Rock and Roll" was not only a star of radio and the big screen; he was also a law enforcement reserve. During his career it was well known that he was a fan of law enforcement, and was often in contact with police and security because of his status and need for security. He collected police badges and memorabilia, and it is often said that, if he had not been a famous rock and roll star, he would have worked in policing. He was friends with many members of the Memphis Police Department before he became famous, and was sworn in as a captain with that agency, and was deputized as a member of the Shelby County Sheriff's Department, and made an honorary captain with the Denver Police Department (Troedson, 2016). On December 21, 1970, Elvis met with President Richard Nixon, when he showed off his police badge collection and asked if it would be possible to get a badge from the Bureau of Narcotics and Dangerous Drugs. President Nixon complied, and the photograph of the two men in the Oval Office became extremely popular after Elvis' death in 1988 of a drug overdose (Carlson, 2010).

Babe Ruth (1895–1948)

George Herman Ruth, Jr., started his career as a baseball pitcher for the Baltimore Orioles in 1914. He died in 1948 after a battle with cancer, but is still known as one of the greatest American baseball players, and he gave hope and a mental escape to millions of baseball fans during the Great Depression. Ruth was sworn in as a member of the New York City Police Reserve, and was provided a uniform and the rank of lieutenant (Garvey, 2004), though it is likely that he never participated in any training or enforcement duties. His role with the NYPD was ceremonial, and in an effort to provide positive public relations (Wagenheim, 2014).

Erik Estrada (1949–present)

Best known for his starring role as Frank Poncherello, or "Ponch," in the television show *CHiPs* in the late 1970s and early 1980s, Estrada is a reserve police officer in many cities throughout the country. In 2006 Estrada and other celebrities trained to become reserve officers for the Muncie Police Department (MPD) in Indiana on the reality television show *Armed and Famous*, which aired on CBS in early 2007. Estrada was sworn in as a reserve police officer with MPD on December 5, 2006, and a full-time deputy sheriff with the Bedford Sheriff's Office in Virginia in 2009, but has since also been sworn in with the St. Anthony Police Department in Idaho. Estrada claims that he wanted to be a police officer even before he became an actor (Real, 2016).

Shaquille O'Neal (1972–present)

This 7 foot, 1 inch tall American former professional basketball player has also stared in numerous movies and has made a name for himself as an actor, rap star, and TV reality star. However, he also attended the Los Angeles County Sheriff's Reserve Academy and became a reserve police officer with the Los Angeles Port Police. He has held numerous volunteer policing positions, including as a Tempe (Arizona) police reserve, Bedford County (Virginia) reserve deputy, a Miami Beach (Florida) reserve police officer, a Doral Police Department reserve officer in Florida, and a reserve police officer with the Golden Beach Police Department in south Florida (Wyllie, 2009). He has also been named an honorary US deputy marshal, and received public accolades for assisting Gainesville police officers in playing basketball with several neighborhood kids after someone called in a noise complaint on the group. The video of his pick-up game with the police and local youth went viral (Karimi, 2016). "Shaq" has reported numerous times that he aspires to someday run for elected law enforcement position, as a sheriff, most likely in Florida.

Steven Seagal (1952–present)

Martial arts expert and movie star Steven Seagal volunteered for over 20 years as a reserve deputy for the Jefferson Parish Sheriff's Office in Louisiana. Seagal had a second home in Louisiana while he worked elsewhere on the movies that made him famous, and began serving as a reserve for the sheriff's office. His reality TV show focusing on his work with Jefferson Parish, *Steven Seagal: Lawman*, premiered on December 2, 2009, and production was halted in April 2010 when the sheriff's office announced that the second season would not be filmed due to a lawsuit filed against the actor for sexual harassment (Lemons, 2011). After leaving his position with Jefferson Parish, reportedly due to the lawsuit, Seagal served as a member of Sheriff Joe Arpaio's "posse" unit in Maricopa County, Arizona. Posse members are not certified by Arizona police standards, and are used primarily in police support positions, not as law enforcement officers (Lemons, 2011). Seagal has been very active in politics, and publicly called for the impeachment of President Barack Obama. In 2016 Segal was awarded Russian citizenship by President Vladimir Putin (Walker, 2016).

Lou Ferrigno (1951–present)

Best known for his portrayal of "The Incredible Hulk," broadcast by CBS in the late 1970s and early 1980s, Lou Ferrigno is also recognized for his two consecutive body-building titles as Mr. Universe. After receiving training in California, he was sworn in as a reserve deputy with the Los Angeles County Sheriff's Department in 2006. Ferrigno was diagnosed with severe hearing loss when he was three years old, and, because of this, he was assigned to duties with the LASD that would not result in arrests, including recruiting new deputies and work with the Special Victims Bureau. He was also sworn in with the Maricopa County (Arizona) volunteer sheriff's posse in 2010, and then with the San Luis Obispo County Sheriff's Office, in California, in 2012 (Linn, 2012). In September of 2013 he was sworn in as a special deputy with the Delaware County Sheriff's Department in Ohio. As a special deputy in Ohio, Ferrigno does not have arrest powers, but he took the position to promote positive ties between the community and police. "He said too many people think officers and deputies are not the good guys. It's a stigma he wants to fight" (Arenschield, 2013). Ferrigno asserts that his interest in policing started because of his father, who was a lieutenant with the New York Police Department.

Carl Edwards (1979–present)

An American stock car racing driver, Edwards competed in the NASCAR Sprint Cup Series, and raced for the final time in 2016. A native of Columbia, Missouri, he won the NASCAR Busch Series championship in 2007 at the age of 28. Edwards served as a reserve deputy sheriff in Boone County, Missouri, and has provided his star support for the "Below 100" campaign, a national effort to reduce the number of law enforcement fatalities in the United States in a single year to below 100. The NASCAR driver spent part of his Christmas holidays in 2004 serving his community in uniform (Walljasper, 2005).

Charles Dickens (1812–1870)

The author famous for such classics as *David Copperfield*, *Oliver Twist*, and *A Christmas Carol* spent a short time in Liverpool and showed interest in the policing of the city, where he was sworn in as a special constable, possibly only for one night. It is thought that he used characterizations and locations where he was "on the beat" in several of his publications. It is said that his service as a special constable aided his research in writing *The Uncommercial Traveller* (O'Keefe & Hull, 2012).

Isambard Kingdom Brunel (1806–1859)

Brunel was one of Britain's most illustrious engineers; in his lifetime he designed and built a number of bridges and tunnels which are still in use almost 200 years after their construction. It was during the building of one such bridge, the Clifton Suspension Bridge, which spans the River Avon in Bristol in the southwest of England, that political unrest and rioting broke out in the city. Brunel signed up as a special constable during these Bristol riots in 1831 because construction work was severely affected, thus delaying the completion of the work (Brunel200, n.d.).

Nigel Mansell (1953–present)

Nigel Mansell was a Formula 1 racing world champion who served as a special constable during and following his career as a racing driver. He lived on the small Isle of Man off the west coast of the United Kingdom, which is a self-governing Crown dependency. As such, the criminal justice system, including policing, is separate from the mainland's laws and delivery; the Isle of Man does have special constables, though, and

Nigel Mansell served as such for several years while a resident on the island. He also served as a special constable in Devon and Cornwall in the southwest of England, during which time he was caught breaking the speed limit on an English road, but was not forced to step down from his volunteering role (BBC, 1998).

Emperor Napoleon III (1808–1873)

Prince Louis Napoleon Bonaparte, the future Emperor Napoleon III of France, was sworn in as a special constable in London in 1848. Due to working-class unrest throughout England, and revolutions throughout Europe, it was greatly feared that there would be a huge revolutionary uprising. In preparation, thousands of troops were positioned on London's bridges and the Bank of England's walls were reinforced. Some 85,000 special constables were recruited and enrolled, including Bonaparte (Working Class Movement Library, 2016).

Notes

1 As an example, in 2005 University of Central Florida Police Department (UCFPD) officer Mario Jenkins was working in plainclothes when he was shot and killed by an Orlando Police Department officer in a case of mistaken identity. The university police department at the time had fewer than 50 sworn police personnel, and the loss of their first officer ever to die in the line of duty was understandably significant. The Orange County Sheriff's Office reserve unit took over all policing for the UCFPD for two days as officers from UCF attended the funeral and other memorial events.
2 The Daytona Beach Police Department (DBPD) in Volusia County, Florida, uses reserves to assist during times of high need for that agency, including Bike Week, spring break, and other major events. DBPD pays its reserve officers to assist with these duties, however. Another example of a beach area that utilizes reserve officers is the Boynton Beach Police Department, also in Florida. BBPD has unpaid volunteer fully certified and volunteer auxiliary officers who work as a force multiplier when there is a need (Keegan, 2015).
3 "Navvy" is an early nineteenth-century abbreviation of the word "navigator," and refers to the laborers who worked on railway, canal and road construction.
4 The Orange County Sheriff's Office uses gold rank insignia and uniform insignia for all full-time deputy sheriffs above the rank of corporal.
5 These ranks fall between the ranks of deputy and corporal.

References

Alfonso, M. (2015, October 30). LASD Air Rescue 5 completes humanitarian mission, saves people. South Pasadena Patch. Retrieved September 23, 2016, from http://patch.com/california/southpasadena/lasd-air-rescue-5-completes-humanitarian-mission-saves-people.

Arenschield, L. (2013, September 21). "Hulk" actor Lou Ferrigno to be strong arm of law here. *The Columbus Dispatch*. Retrieved November 15, 2016, from www.dispatch.com/content/stories/local/2013/09/21/hulk-actor-lou-ferrigno-to-be-strong-arm-of-law-here.html.

Arwood, D. E., Hilal, S. M., Karsky, J., & Norman, M. (2005). Police reserve officers: Structural embeddedness of self-role merger and volunteering. *Great Plains Sociologist, 17*(2), 36–60.

BBC (1998, January 23). Former racing champion banned from the road. Retrieved September 3, 2017, from http://news.bbc.co.uk/1/hi/uk/49787.stm.

Bedfordshire Police (n.d.). Bedfordshire Police: Protecting people and fighting crime. Retrieved September 23, 2016, from www.bedfordshire.police.uk/recruitment/special_constables.aspx.

Berg, B. L., & Doerner, W. G. (1988). Volunteer police officers: An unexamined personnel dimension in law enforcement. *American Journal of Police, 7*(1), 81–89.

British Transport Police (n.d.). Our history: The first railway police. Retrieved February 13, 2017, from www.btp.police.uk/about_us/our_history/detailed_history.aspx.

Britton, I., Knight, L., & Maloney, D. (2016). *Citizens in policing: National benchmarking exercise – phase one*. Northampton, UK: University of Northampton, Institute for Public Safety, Crime and Justice.

Brunel200.com (n.d.). Brunel biography. Retrieved September 3, 2017, from www.brunel200.com/1820s.htm.

Carlson, P. (2010). When Elvis met Nixon. *Smithsonian* (December). Retrieved November 23, 2016, from www.smithsonianmag.com/history/when-elvis-met-nixon-69892425.

City of London Police (2016). *National policing lead for economic crime: Annual review 2015–2016*. London: City of London Police.

College of Policing (n.d.). Special constables and volunteers in policing. Retrieved January 8, 2017, from www.college.police.uk/What-we-do/Development/Promotion/the-leadership-review/Pages/Current-topics.aspx.

Field, M. (2007, December 18). The future of the City of London Police. Mark Field MP. Retrieved September 22, 2016, from http://markfieldmp.com/speeches/freedom-a-security-speeches/the-future-of-the-city-of-london-police.

Fishwick, B. (2016, January 20). Hampshire Police want "geeks" to volunteer for cyber crime fight. *The News*. Retrieved September 22, 2016, from www.portsmouth.co.uk/news/crime/hampshire-police-want-geeks-to-volunteer-for-cyber-crime-fight-1-7170191.

Fredericksen, P. J, & Levin, D. (2004). Accountability and the use of volunteer officers in public safety organizations. *Public Performance and Management Review, 27*(4), 118–143.

Garvey, J. (2004). *Images of America: San Francisco Police Department*. San Francisco: Arcadia Publishing.

Gill, M. L., & Mawby, R. I. (1990). *A special constable: A study of the police reserve*. Aldershot, UK: Avebury Publishing.

Gravelle, J., & Rogers, C. (2009). Your country needs you! The economic viability of volunteers in the police. *Safer Communities, 8*(3), 34–38.

Greater Manchester Police (2015). Give and Gain Day, 2015: Debrief document. Manchester: Greater Manchester Police.

Greenberg, M. A. (2005). *Citizens defending America: From colonial times to the age of terrorism*. Pittsburgh: University of Pittsburgh Press.

Howe, S., & Graham, V. (1995, September 29). Special duties. *Police Review*.

Karimi, F. (2016, January 24). Shaq, Florida officer surprise kids with a basketball game. CNN. Retrieved November 2, 2016, from www.cnn.com/2016/01/24/us/florida-shaq-police-officers-game.

Keegan, C. (2015, December 21). Boynton Beach Police Department expanding reserve officer program: Unpaid volunteers serve as police officers. WPTV.com. Retrieved August 20, 2017, from www.wptv.com/news/region-s-palm-beach-county/boynton-beach/boynton-beach-police-department-expanding-reserve-officer-program.

Lemons, S. (2011, March 18). Steven Seagal resigned rather than face IA investigation, according to Sheriff Newell Normand. *Phoenix New Times*. Retrieved November 2, 2016, from www.phoenixnewtimes.com/blogs/steven-seagal-resigned-rather-than-face-ia-investigation-according-to-sheriff-newell-normand-6499604.

Linn, S. (2012, June 15). Lou Ferrigno, aka The Hulk, sworn in as reserve deputy for Sheriff's Office. *The Tribune*. Retrieved November 15, 2016, from www.sanluisobispo.com/news/local/article39205230.html.

Monrovia Weekly (2015, October 7). L.A. Sheriff Search and Rescue prepares for swift water rescues during rainy El Niño. Retrieved September 23, 2016, from www.monroviaweekly.com/current-news/l-a-sheriff-search-and-rescue-prepares-for-swift-water-rescues-during-rainy-el-nino.

Myhill, A., & Beak, K. (2008). *Public confidence in the police*. London: National Police Improvement Agency.

O'Keefe, J., & Hull, R. (2012). Charles Dickens's Liverpool. *The Merseysider* (2). Retrieved September 3, 2017, from www.merseysidermagazine.com/site/local-history/charles-dickenss-liverpool.

Perkins, M. (2016). Modelling public confidence of the police: How perceptions of the police differ between neighborhoods in a city. *Police Practice and Research: An International Journal*, 17(2), 113–125.

Police.uk (2015, October 22). How diverse are the police? Retrieved January 2, 2017, from www.police.uk/news/how-diverse-are-police.

Real, E. (2016, July 6). "CHiPs" alum Erik Estrada is a real-life police officer now! *US Weekly*. Retrieved November 23, 2016, from www.usmagazine.com/celebrity-news/news/chips-alum-erik-estrada-is-a-real-life-police-officer-now-w212275.

Roberg, R., Novak, K., & Cordner, G. W. (2009). *Police and society*, 4th Edition. New York: Oxford University Press.

Robinson, D., & Miller, I. (2016, September 21). Specials making their mark in the professional standards department. Police Oracle. Retrieved September 22, 2016, from www.policeoracle.com/news/investigation/2016/Sep/20/specials-making-their-mark-in-professional-standards-department_92962.html.html.

Seth, R. (2006). *The specials*. Trowbridge, UK: Cromwell Press.

Sharpe, M. E. (1986). Volunteering in municipal police departments: Some hypotheses on performance impacts. *Public Productivity Review*, 10(2), 77–92.

Sindall, K., Sturgis, P., & Jennings, W. (2012). Public confidence in the police: A time-series analysis. *British Journal of Criminology*, 52(4), 744–764.

Special Impact (2015a). Newcastle Falcons rugby player joins Special Constabulary. *Special Impact* (21), 5. Retrieved September 22, 2016, from www.dutysheet.com/Special_Impact/Special_Impact_Issue_21.pdf.

Special Impact (2015b). UK's first special constable dog handler. *Special Impact* (21), 16–17. Retrieved September 22, 2016, from www.dutysheet.com/Special_Impact/Special_Impact_Issue_21.pdf.

Sprott, J. B., & Doob, A. N. (2014). Confidence in the police: Variation across groups classified as visible minorities. *Canadian Journal of Criminology and Criminal Justice*, 56(3), 367–379.

Troedson, D. (2016, July 24). Elvis Presley and the police. Elvis Australia. Retrieved November 23, 2016, from www.elvis.com.au/presley/police-elvis-presley.shtml.

Volunteer Special Constabulary (1998). *Service to the nation: 50 years of the Volunteer Special Constabulary*. Singapore: Volunteer Special Constabulary.

Wagenheim, K. (2014). *Babe Ruth: His life and legend*. New York: Open Road Media.

Walker, S. (2001). *Police accountability: The role of citizen oversight*. Belmont, CA: Wadsworth.

Walker, S. (2016, November 3). Steven Seagal granted Russian citizenship by Vladimir Putin. *The Guardian*. Retrieved November 15, 2016, from www.theguardian.com/culture/2016/nov/03/steven-seagal-granted-russian-citizenship-vladimir-putin.

Walljasper, J. (2005, February 16). The ride of his life: Columbia driver can't stop smiling on his way to the top. *Columbia Daily Tribune*. Retrieved November 15, 2016, from http://archive.columbiatribune.com/2005/feb/20050216spor007.asp.

Weitzer, R., & Tuch, S. A. (2005). Racially biased policing: Determinants of citizen perceptions. *Social Forces*, 83(3), 1009–1030.

Whitehead, T. (2012, October 9). Police cuts mean more specials and volunteers, chief signals. *The Daily Telegraph*. Retrieved July 15, 2017, from www.telegraph.co.uk/news/uknews/law-and-order/9643289/Police-cuts-mean-more-specials-and-volunteers-chief-signals.html.

Williams, G. (2005). Special report: Reserve officers on bikes. *Law and Order*, 53(4), 82–87.

Working Class Movement Library (2016, December). A special constable is sworn in to help thwart a revolution… Retrieved September 3, 2017, from www.wcml.org.uk/our-collections/object-of-the-month/objects-of-the-month-2016/a-special-constable-is-sworn-in-to-help-thwart-a-revolution.

Wright, T. (2015, March 12). LASD volunteers log 450,000 hours. *The Malibu Times*. Retrieved September 23, 2016, from www.malibutimes.com/news/article_ea5ddfca-c84a-11e4-8136-7ff750f42c9a.html.

Wyllie, D. (2009, October 29). Shaquille O'Neal may be Ohio's next deputy sheriff. PoliceOne. Retrieved November 2, 2016, from www.policeone.com/police-recruiting/articles/1960007-Shaquille-ONeal-may-be-Ohios-next-deputy-sheriff.

Chapter 6

Training Volunteer Police

Individuals in both the United States and the United Kingdom become volunteer police for a variety of reasons, and the amount of training they receive also varies. Although the United Kingdom has a nationalized police force, and training for police throughout the country has been greatly standardized, training for special constables has, until very recently, been more at the discretion of the local constabulary. Police in regular service in forces across England and Wales have, since January of 2010, been subject to national occupational standards of preparation and the Initial Police Learning and Development Programme (IPLDP), which is two years of training leading to the Diploma in Policing (College of Policing, n.d. – a).

In the United States, where every state has different regulations concerning both full-time and volunteer policing, there is no consistency at all for the recruiting, application, screening, or training of police reserves and auxiliaries or for regular police officers. To be a regular police officer, most states require recruits to complete a police academy training program, with minimum standards for law enforcement officers (Discover Policing, n.d.). In 2006 there were 648 state and local law enforcement academies throughout the United States, comprising 213 county, regional or state academies, 292 technical school, college, or university academies, and 143 city or municipal academies (Bureau of Justice Statistics, 2009). Although academy training in many states is acceptable as completed training for application in many other states, there is a lack of uniformity in this as well. While a fully certified police officer in one state may be able to transition to a police officer position in another state by certification through examination, proof of minimal amounts of experience, or meeting a combination of education and experience, the same is not true for volunteer police with less than full certification.

In order to better understand the differences and similarities with regular police training, the following provides a brief description of training as required for full-time policing duties as compared to those of volunteer police. As indicated, this is especially difficult to demarcate for training in the United States, as variations between states and even local jurisdictions within states make it difficult to understand the training needs and the role of volunteer police. In England and Wales, however, training for both regular officers and SCs follows a more homogeneous structure, as defined by the College of Policing.

Regular Police Training

United Kingdom

The College of Policing has been designated as the clearinghouse for information and standards applied to police training in England and Wales. Police forces are provided with modules with learning outcomes, and can choose to use the national materials, or develop localized elements to replace or supplement them. Force trainers, operational tutors, force line managers, and supervisors all participate in the training of recruits.

In England and Wales vacancies are posted online and applicants may apply to only one police force at a time. Beyond the basic requisites of age (18 or over, with no prescribed upper limit) and legal eligibility to reside in the United Kingdom, there are no formal qualification requirements beyond evidence of reasonable written and numeracy skills. Many police forces currently or have previously worked with universities and colleges of further education to provide elements of or all training through the employment of police trainers within the university setting. Other higher education institutions have, in the past, encouraged police force trainers to adopt modules as part of their training program. However, many of these partnerships were short-lived because of the unsuitability of the modules or a lack of understanding of the working practices on both sides. One example of a successful partnership between a police force and university, however, was one that led to a two-year foundation degree which mirrors the theoretical elements of the two-year probation period of a regular officer. Students (self-funded) were required to serve as special constables during the time and, upon successful completion of the program, the student graduated with a nationally recognized qualification (the Certificate of Knowledge in Policing) and was also determined to be competent for independent patrol.[1] Other collaborations have had varying degrees of success. While there is currently no national qualification, police training in the United Kingdom is moving toward a graduate profession with a higher-level apprenticeship in policing, due to be ready in April 2018, and a professional pre-entry degree, to commence in September 2018. While there is currently no national qualification, police training in the United Kingdom is moving toward a graduate profession, with a higher-level apprenticeship in policing, due to be ready in April 2018, and a professional pre-entry degree, to commence in September 2018.

In the first quarter of 2016 the College of Policing produced a consultation paper, "Policing Education Qualifications Framework" (PEQF), which called for responses to the standardization and public recognition of police training. Historically police officers have been trained in the basics of the job along with a range of specialisms. However, on retirement from the service those skills and specialisms, while requisite and necessary for the role of policing, did not carry nationally recognized qualifications (the training did not equate to an educational degree). As a result, ex-officers could not easily demonstrate their abilities and strengths to the wider world regardless of their proficiency. This is true even as the demand on policing, and the knowledge base necessary to serve successfully in that role, continues to widen with increasing and developing technologies, public demands, and economic challenges.

The National Policing Curriculum (NPC) lays down the standards required in every force: "The curriculum provides both a framework and a benchmark for the development of knowledge, understanding, skills, attitudes and behaviours within policing, by means of education and training using a variety of approaches and delivery methods" (College of Policing, n.d. – b).

Historically every police force has been responsible for the education and training of its recruits. The regular police training schedule is significantly longer than the training undertaken by special constables and does not include any specialist training that may be needed in accordance with the demands of the respective force at the time. The training is designed to ensure that the successful candidate is fit for independent patrol in any force within England and Wales. This is because, unlike the United States, police training standards are nationalized and established by the NPC. In Scotland training continues to take place at Police Scotland training and recruitment centres, the Scottish Police College at Tulliallan, and within the individual's division (Police Scotland, n.d.). Training in England and Wales is provided by a range of providers who must each satisfy the requirements of the NPC and the PEQF.

This is a complex and changing time in police professionalism and training in the United Kingdom; in a speech given by the Right Honourable Brandon Lewis of the Home Office in March 2017, he announced that the College of Policing, which was established in 2012, is charged with high standards for policing. The speech, addressed to the Police Education Qualifications Framework conference, stressed the importance of the police code of ethics, a culture of continual professional development, and standards of education. Lewis stressed the importance of the College to ensure that the police force is flexible, professional, and agile enough to adapt. In addition, he recommended that the PEQF work with the College to develop licensure and universal registration for officers who work in certain critical areas, including working with vulnerable populations. Finally, he recognized that the College and PEQF should seek to accredit skills, to give officers access to the knowledge and skills they need to be successful. He stressed that there should continue to be a variety of ways to enter the police service, including the importance of a degree apprenticeship route, which allows diverse populations to raise standards in workplace training (Lewis, 2017).

In 2016 a publication entitled *Developing and Delivering an Education Framework for Policing* concluded that "there should be a national framework of accredited qualifications" (College of Policing, 2016). In short, the report concluded that all future policing staff will attain qualifications commensurate with educational levels so that police community support officers reach level 4.[2] Police constables should achieve either level 5[3] or 6,[4] which is equivalent to an undergraduate degree. In order to successfully achieve the required level within the National Policing Curriculum, training will be through either an apprenticeship or a pre-join professional policing degree from an accredited institution.

The recruitment process for regular officers differs from that for special constables, but there is a fast-track assessment program which is open to SCs, police staff, and university graduates who may bring diversity and new perspectives to the role. Successful candidates on the fast-track program are anticipated to attain the rank of inspector after three years, and therefore training is very much focused on management and leadership. Potentially there may be candidates who apply to join the Special Constabulary and who already have leadership and managerial expertise; these candidates may consider transferring to the regular police service, and might find themselves in a position in which that proficiency could accelerate their advancement, but may have little or no bearing on their role during their time as a special constable.

The program consists of about 35 weeks of classroom instruction blended with a wide range of practical and mentored training. Regardless of who is delivering the training, all courses are quality-assessed through the Qualifications and Credit Framework (QCF). Successful completion of the initial training is followed by two years as a probationary officer, which means that, while new recruits are fit for independent patrol, they must continue to undertake training and complete a professional development portfolio (PDP) to demonstrate their competencies while on duty.

United States

The training provided in US police academies for regular officers has a median length of about 19 weeks (or 761 hours), of which 60 hours is spent on firearms instruction and 44 hours on self-defense instruction (Bureau of Justice Statistics, 2009). Other academy subjects, in descending order of the median amount of time spent on the training for that topic, include: investigations (45 hours), health and fitness (40 hours), patrol procedures and techniques (40 hours), criminal law (40 hours) emergency vehicle operations (36 hours), basic first aid and CPR (24 hours), basic foreign-language skills (16 hours), domestic violence (12 hours), use of non-lethal weapons (12 hours), constitutional law (11 hours), human relations (11 hours), domestic preparedness/terrorism (8 hours), hate crimes/bias crimes (8 hours), community policing (8 hours), juvenile law and procedures (8 hours), ethics and integrity (8 hours), cultural diversity (8 hours), computers and information systems (8 hours), officer civil/criminal liability (6 hours), stress prevention and management (6 hours), and problem solving (6 hours) (Discover Policing, n.d.).

Only about 16 percent of recruits entering the basic academy training are women. Overall, nationwide, about 86 percent of the recruits who start a basic police training class complete it. After completion of the police academy recruits complete field training, or on-the-job training, under the instruction of a training officer. While variations exist across the United States on how this training is conducted, the median time that recruits spend in this on-the-job training is approximately eight weeks, or 320 hours (Discover Policing, n.d.).

As mentioned earlier, academy training undertaken in one state may or may not be accepted toward certification as a law enforcement officer in another state. For example, Florida will accept training received in another state in most cases, providing the applicant for certification has worked for at least one year as a certified officer in another state in good standing. Applicants from other states for certification in Florida, however, must also complete a two-week training course to show proficiency in certain areas (such as defensive tactics, firearms, first aid and vehicle operations). Other states offer similar certification transferability, but not all states participate; some jurisdictions may require a certified individual from another state to attend and pass an entire police academy. Additionally, certification requirements in one state may be different from another, such that applicants may not meet minimum/maximum age requirements, or fail to meet certain background requirements for certification.

Even transferring within a state to another jurisdiction may be problematic. Usually, if an applicant does transfer within a state from one law enforcement agency to another, the academy and state certification are not issues; however, applicants may find themselves having to give up their rank and seniority, and, oftentimes, their retirement benefits. Additionally, some agencies require that all sworn employees must have completed their training academy, and will not accept any other. No matter how much experience or training an applicant has had somewhere else, for example, you cannot work for the New York Police Department, the Los Angeles Police Department, or the Florida Highway Patrol unless you have successfully completed their own academy.

In most of the United States it is not uncommon for full-time police to transfer to positions as volunteer police either within their own agency or to an external one (although, as stated earlier, this does not happen very often in the northeast United States, where volunteer police do not usually have police powers). If the new agency is in another state with full police powers and authority, the same mandatory training required for a full-time officer to transfer will usually apply. If he or she is transferring within the same state, there is usually no problem with transferring the certification, but the officer will likely have to complete some sort of reduced-time field training with the new agency. However, even if transferring within the same agency from full-time to reserve status, the officer may have to give up any earned rank; this is not always the case, though, and police chiefs and sheriffs can make their own decisions regarding these types of transfers.

Many states have "in-house" training programs and academies whereby applicants are selected and the trainee begins as an employee and receives a paycheck from the first day of training at the academy. However, it is now more common in the United States for local and regional academies to charge tuition and "certify" police officers before they begin their first day of employment. Fifty-two percent of training academies from around the United States collected tuition to help meet operating costs (Discover Policing, n.d.), meaning that students must pay out of their own pockets to attend the academy in the hopes of securing a policing position in the future. Police academies can be expensive: the cost for a prospective police officer to attend an academy in Utah can be more than US$6,000 (Utah Valley University, n.d.). However, other states report lower costs, including Georgia and Florida, which both collect tuition and fees of around US$3,800 (Georgia Public Safety Training Center, n.d.; Valencia College, n.d.).

Variation between states occurs at the beginning of academy training for new recruits. In some states (such as Florida, New Jersey, and Michigan) students apply to either a local police agency or directly to the academy for admission. Recruits may be hired by a police agency as "trainees" before the academy begins (this is called "sponsorship"[5]), and are therefore provided with tuition, books, uniforms, and often an hourly pay while attending the academy. Recruits who are not successful in getting hired before attending the academy must pay for their own tuition, books, and uniforms during the academy (these are called "non-sponsored" trainees). These students often rely on financial aid to complete the certification, or must accept outside employment to meet their financial obligations and living costs.

Not all academy graduates in these types of programs will be able to find jobs as police officers, as most academies that accept students to their police academy training programs do only cursory background checks, and more detailed police agency background checks may make an academy graduate ineligible or undesirable for work as a police officer. Candidates with what they may perceive to be minor blemishes in their background may be unable to find work as a police officer; often these blemishes include credit reports or traffic citations.

Florida has 39 police academies throughout the state, and basic law enforcement (BLE) certification in the state of Florida is based on successful completion of an academy, the successful completion of a state exam, and hiring by a police agency within four years of successful completion of the exam. Students in these Florida academies may be either self-sponsored or sponsored by a police agency. Utah separates sponsored recruits from self-sponsored recruits by providing peace officer training at academic satellite facilities for self-sponsored students who have not been hired by a Utah law enforcement agency, and the Utah Peace Officers Standards and Training Academy for police-agency-hired applicants. Colorado utilizes agency academies for sponsored recruits, but also provides community college academies to allow non-sponsored students to attend at their own expense (Utah Department of Public Safety, n.d.; Colorado Peace Officer Standards and Training, n.d.).

Rhode Island requires that applicants first complete the application process for a police agency, and they cannot directly enter an academy without sponsorship. Recruits can attend a police academy only if a police department hires the candidate as a probationary officer. The police agency conducts all background investigations and exams prior to the applicant's enrollment in the academy (State of Rhode Island Municipal Police Training Academy, n.d.). Louisiana is similar, requiring all candidates to be hired at a department and then attend a state-certified police basic training academy for approximately 360 hours, earning them certification with the Louisiana Peace Officer Standards and Training Council (Louisiana Commission on Law Enforcement and Administration of Criminal Justice, n.d.).

Volunteer Police Training

United Kingdom

Today most police forces in the United Kingdom have adopted the Specials National Recruit Assessment Process, a standardized application process for those who wish to serve as special constables. Candidates are required to complete a competency based questionnaire (CBQ), a situational judgement test (SJT), a written skills test, and participate in a competency-based interview. Some forces elect to utilize additional screening for recruits. Candidates must also successfully complete a standardized physical fitness test and a medical screening. While police forces throughout England and Wales provide training and education based on the core requirements of the IPLDP, the training of special constables is based on the Initial Learning for the Special Constabulary (IL4SC) national program (Pepper, 2014; College of Policing, n.d. – a).

Core elements of the initial training include ethics, diversity, health and safety, and first aid, thus providing a foundation for the operational and legislative demands of the role. Unlike in US police agencies, once an applicant for the volunteer role of special constable has been accepted for training the new recruit is sworn in and receives his or her warrant card, providing the holder with the powers of arrest in exactly the same way as those of a regular officer. This occurs even before training begins. They may not go out on patrol, however, until they have completed initial training, and even then they are required to be accompanied while on patrol until they are deemed proficient for independent patrol. Subsequent training in both content and duration varies from force to force, with new special constables being trained to fit local policing needs.

The IL4SC requires approximately 3.5 weeks of direct learning, though delivery can vary from force to force. On successful completion of this part of the training, student special constables are considered fit for accompanied patrol. Training varies from force to force for both regular officers and SCs, which has led to recommendations within a government Home Affairs report in which national standards are presented (Home Affairs Committee, 2016).

United States

Because of the varied ways that states and individual policing agencies have provided authority and responsibilities to volunteer police throughout the nation, there is no single standard or straightforward view that can be gathered about the training with which they are provided. The following describes examples of the many and various ways that policing agencies in the United States train their volunteer police, but there are policing agencies that do not require any specific training for their volunteer police and there are policing agencies that require the same high level of training provided to regular police; other agencies require every level in between. This variation in training is largely based on the eventual utilization of the volunteer officer. States that allow volunteer police very little authority most often provide the least amount of training. States that allow volunteer police full police authority most often provide vastly expanded training, often equal to or similar to full-time academy training.

Some states do not require a specific number of training hours, nor do they require any type of state-level certification for volunteer police. Usually this is because the volunteer police have greatly reduced powers (when compared to full-time officers), or no police powers at all. In states where reserves and/or auxiliary officers cannot carry a firearm or make arrests, it is common to see each police agency responsible for determining the training it requires of volunteers to serve in these positions. As discussed earlier in the book, the New York City Police Department, for example, does not provide any authority to its auxiliary officers. The NYPD auxiliary police are asked to provide uniformed foot, vehicle, and bicycle patrols, but do not have any authority to act on observed criminal activity. These volunteer officers act as additional "eyes and ears" of the police and are trained to observe and report incidents to the regular, full-time police, and assist in non-law enforcement functions (New York City Police Department, n.d.). NYPD auxiliary police officers are not considered police officers, do not carry firearms, and have no power of arrest. They are provided with 54 hours of instruction to carry out their duties as auxiliary police officers (Kelly, Grasso, Esposito, Giannelli, and Maroulis, 2008; New York City Auxiliary Police, 2012), which qualifies them as "peace officers without firearms training. " Peace officers in the state of New York have some law enforcement authority, but are not the same as police officers.

The state of Montana allows reserve officers to be sworn in and immediately begin to serve as volunteers, but requires that they must complete 88 hours of basic training within the first two years in order to continue as a reserve. Police reserves in Montana are considered "peace officers" and not police officers, in that they have the power of arrest only for warrants within the state of Montana and felony warrants issued in other states. Reserve officers are authorized to carry firearms in Montana (if they have qualified on a firearms course conducted by the Montana Law Enforcement Academy, and if authorized by the chief law enforcement officer of their agency), and are considered sworn officers. Reserve officers may assist in patrol duties, security checks, or similar functions. Another classification of volunteer officers in Montana is auxiliary officers, however, who are unsworn, part-time volunteers who may perform "search and rescue, office duties, crowd and traffic control, and crime prevention activities" (Montana Code Annotated 7-32-201, 2015), and they have no arrest authority other than what would be authorized to any citizen in the state of Montana.

Minnesota is another example of a state where reserve officers have no police authority or power. Minnesota state statutes define a reserve officer as "an individual whose services are utilized by a law enforcement agency to provide supplementary assistance at special events, traffic or crowd control, and administrative or clerical assistance, and shall include reserve deputies, special deputies, mounted or unmounted patrols, and all other employees or volunteers performing reserve officer functions. A reserve officer's duties do not include enforcement of the general criminal laws of the state, and the officer does not have full powers of arrest or authorization to carry a firearm on duty" (Minnesota Statute 626.84). Minnesota reserve law enforcement officers are not allowed to carry firearms, and reserve officers are not required to hold any licensure or education requirements with the state of Minnesota, but individual agencies are allowed to establish their own training requirements.

The state of Texas (like many other states) uses the term "peace officer" differently from Montana and New York, in that all police officers in Texas must be certified as peace officers and successfully complete a state licensure exam; this includes all volunteer police officers. In 1989 Texas requirements to serve as a volunteer police officer changed, and all reserve officers now must complete the exact same training as their full-time counterparts. The Texas Commission on Law Enforcement since then has required that reserve police officers receive the same amount of training as full-time regular police officers, over 640 hours, though individual police agencies may require their reserves to do more training (Hallman & Martin, 2015). The City of Dallas Police Department equates that training to over 1,000 hours in a single year including on-the-job training (Dallas Police Department Reserves, n.d.).

The state of Florida has two different categories of volunteer law enforcement officers. The first hold certifications as "auxiliary" law enforcement officers. These officers have received high-liability training (including firearms, defensive tactics, patrol techniques, criminal investigation, first aid, and emergency vehicle operations), but have not completed the entire Florida curriculum for full state law enforcement certification (390 hours of instruction). The second are classified as "part-time" officers by state statute, and they hold full law enforcement powers. These officers are provided with the same training (790 hours) and have the same authority as their regular, full-time, police counterparts, but they usually act as volunteers. Both auxiliary-certified and Basic Law Enforcement (BLE)-certified volunteers in Florida complete "high-liability" areas of training. This training encompasses areas that might be scrutinized in court, and includes first aid, law enforcement vehicle operations, firearms, defensive tactics, and dart-firing stun gun. Auxiliary officers in Florida, because they must always be under the supervision of a BLE-certified officer, receive additional limited training in patrol tactics, traffic control, and investigations. Florida BLE-certified police volunteers receive the same training as their full-time counterparts (and often attend the same academy training as those seeing full-time positions), which also includes instruction in legal issues, communications, crime scene investigations, traffic stops, drunk-driving investigations, traffic crash investigations, and human issues.

California's training is very similar to Florida's in the way that training standards are established. Applicants for reserve positions in California must pay their own academy tuition, as Californian law mandates that aid for training expenses is provided only for full-time regularly paid employees. Level 1 reserves in California are fully certified police officers with the same authority and responsibility as their full-time counterparts. They must take 727 hours of training to hold this California Peace Officer Standards and Training (POST) designation, which costs about US$2,000 (College of the Desert, n.d.). Level 2 reserves, however, have limited authority, and can act only under the immediate supervision of a California police officer. This level of training requires 333 hours of training. Level 3 reserves are provided with 144 hours of training, but may perform only specific support duties. Certification as either a level 2 or level 3 reserve costs about US$1,000 (College of the Desert, n.d). Other states have similar two-tier or three-tier systems for classifying volunteer police by the amount of training they have received and the amount of authority they are given.

Oregon holds reserve academy training for candidates to become reserve officers. This academy training is shorter than the full-time police academy. Some police agencies in the state of Oregon provide the reserve academy training for free, others ask participants to pay tuition to offset the cost of running the academy program. For example, the Marion County (Oregon) reserve deputy academy program tuition was US$400 in 2017 (Marion County, Oregon, n.d.). These reserve academies are part-time, and are usually held several nights a week and on weekends. The reserve academy course is approximately 375 hours in length (compared to approximately 640 hours for the full-time academy) and includes courses on defensive tactics, the use of force, firearms, first aid and CPR, and emergency vehicle operations. Reserve officers are permitted to work with a regular full-time officer after completing the academy training, but cannot work as solo officers until they have completed additional training. The City of Dallas, Oregon, for example, requires that reserve officers provide an additional 960 hours of patrol activity with a field training officer before they are eligible to work in a solo capacity. The City of Dallas allows reserve officers who are authorized to work solo to perform mostly traffic enforcement duties, but may also take minor calls and assist with other patrol needs (City of Dallas, Oregon, n.d.).

South Carolina's volunteer police training is similar to that found in Oregon. In South Carolina, a reserve officer is a volunteer who is appointed by and serves at the pleasure of the agency head, but must also successfully complete the South Carolina Reserve Officer Training Program, which includes an end-of-course written exam. The training academy, which is 162 hours in length and which is provided by policing agencies at no cost, includes classes in South Carolina law, ethics, constitutional law, town ordinances, patrol procedures, defensive tactics, human relations, firearms, and other topics. The successful completion of both the reserve police academy and the state exam certifies the individual as a reserve police officer in the state of South Carolina. Reserves in South Carolina must always be in contact, by radio or another device, with the full-time officer to whom they are assigned, but they may work in a solo capacity once they have completed a minimum of an additional 240 field training hours and have received the approval of the agency head. South Carolina law does allow for a reserve who has been on active status for at least two years to receive additional training in order to become a full-time law enforcement officer (South Carolina Code of Laws §23-28-10; South Carolina Criminal Justice Academy, 2012).

Specialized Training

Police agencies may also allow volunteer police to participate in specialized units, or to carry specialized equipment, which may also necessitate additional training. A good example of this type of training would be for bicycle patrol duties. Many American jurisdictions utilize bicycles for both full-time police and volunteer police to perform patrol duties, but may require that the operators who perform these duties attend additional training. Training courses for police bicycle classes may teach riding in groups, jumping curbs, riding down stairs, riding very slowly, and bicycle dismounts. For volunteer police with law enforcement authority, these classes may also include rapid mounting and pursuit, cover and contact with bicycles, and safe approaches to suspicious subjects and incidents (Mroz, 2001). Another example can be found in emergency vehicle operations. Although most volunteer police in the United States who have full law enforcement authority will have received vehicle operations training in the academy, most UK volunteers must attend extra training to be authorized to drive certain vehicles for their force.

As with the basic volunteer police training mentioned earlier in this chapter, however, the ability to participate in specialized training and utilize the training once received will vary greatly in both the United States and, to some degree, in the United Kingdom. In the United States, although policing agencies that utilize full-sworn volunteer police, may for example, train with specialized patrol rifles or less lethal shotguns, both of these training courses and types of equipment would not be authorized for volunteer police in other states that do not use volunteer police in the same way as, for example, in New York. The Orange County Sheriff's Office in Florida allows reserves to participate in any specialized unit, as long as they have been vetted by the unit's chain of command, and they have received the required training. Reserves in the OCSO participate in the motors unit (motorcycle patrol), mounted unit (horseback patrol), honor guard, aviation (helicopter and fixed-wing aircraft pilots and flight observers), and as investigators. Just like their full-time counterparts, however, reserves in the OCSO need to complete the necessary requisite training, but also must complete on-the-job training under the supervision of the specialized unit (Wolf, 2017; see also Wolf & Beary, 2010).

Notes

1 The University of Chester and Cheshire Constabulary began a partnership in 2009 that provided a foundation degree combined with the initial training for every new officer who joined the police force. The program was designed to train students to be police officers, and allow students to receive formal, transferable, higher education credits. The program was designed to train cohorts of about 15 students six times a year, and students who successfully finished the program could also complete a third year of study to receive an honours degree (University of Chester, 2009).
2 Level 4 qualifications in the United Kingdom are roughly equivalent to associate degrees in the United States. UK degrees usually focus on the main subject area for the entirety of the program, which is different from the American educational system, which usually requires students to have a more liberal arts, broader focus for the first two years of study.
3 Level 5 qualifications may also roughly equate to a two-year university qualification in the United States. The distinctions used in the UK educational system for "levels" and "diplomas" do not directly equate to American educational degrees.
4 Level 6 qualifications in the United Kingdom are awarded upon completion of a bachelor's degree with or without honors.
5 Florida, as one example, uses state colleges and technical schools to provide training to most police officers trained within the state. Sponsorship is provided by police agencies, which will then pay the tuition and employ the academy student during the entire police academy. The hourly rate of pay is less than is paid to a certified police officer, but allows the student to be less concerned about finances while attending a tuition academy.

References

Bureau of Justice Statistics (2009). State and local law enforcement training academies, 2006, NCJ 222987. Washington, DC: US Department of Justice, Office of Justice Programs, Bureau of Justice Statistics. Retrieved December 24, 2014, from www.bjs.gov/content/pub/pdf/slleta06.pdf.

City of Dallas, Oregon (n.d.). Reserve officer program. Retrieved June 5, 2017, from www.ci.dallas.or.us/139/Reserve-Officer-Program.

College of Policing (n.d. – a). Initial police learning. Retrieved December 24, 2014, from www.college.police.uk/What-we-do/Learning/Curriculum/Initial-learning/pages/initial-learning.aspx.

College of Policing (n.d. – b). National Policing Curriculum. Retrieved July 13, 2016, from www.college.police.uk/What-we-do/Learning/Curriculum/Pages/default.aspx.

College of Policing (2016). *Developing and delivering an education framework for policing: The College of Policing response to the consultation.* Coventry, UK: College of Policing. Retrieved March 19, 2017, from www.college.police.uk/What-we-do/Learning/Policing-Education-Qualifications-Framework/Pages/Responding-to-Recommendations.aspx.

College of the Desert (n.d.). Reserve police officer training. Retrieved June 5, 2017, from www.collegeofthedesert.edu/students/ap/psa/Pages/bpot.aspx.

Colorado Peace Officers Standards and Training (n.d.). Colorado POST-approved basic academies. Retrieved September 3, 2017, from www.coloradopost.gov/academy/basic-academy.

Dallas Police Department Reserves (n.d.). Becoming a Dallas Police Reserve officer. Retrieved July 2, 2017, from www.dpdreserves.org/A55CD1/recruiting.nsf/Content/BORS-62NE5G?OpenDocument.

Discover Policing (n.d.). Training/academy life. Retrieved December 24, 2014, from http://discoverpolicing.org/what_does_take/?fa=training_academy_life.

Georgia Public Safety Training Center (n.d.). Basic law enforcement training program. Retrieved September 3, 2017, from www.gpstc.org/training-divisions/basic-training-division/basic-police-officer-training.

Hallman, T., & Martin, N. (2015, April 20). Reserve officers have higher training standards in Texas than Oklahoma. *The Dallas Morning News.* Retrieved September 3, 2017, from www.dallasnews.com/news/news/2015/04/20/reserve-officers-have-higher-training-standards-in-texas-than-oklahoma.

Home Affairs Committee (2016). *College of Policing: Three years on: Fourth report of session 2016–17.* London: House of Commons, Home Affairs Committee. Retrieved January 11, 2017, from www.publications.parliament.uk/pa/cm201617/cmselect/cmhaff/23/23.pdf.

Kelly, R. W., Grasso, G. A., Esposito, J. J., Giannelli, R. J., & Maroulis, A. J. (2008). *Auxiliary police program overview 2008.* New York: New York City Police Department Auxiliary.

Lewis, B. (2017, March 29). Speech to the Police Education Qualification Framework conference. Retrieved April 23, 2017, from www.gov.uk/government/speeches/speech-to-the-police-education-qualification-framework-conference.

Louisiana Commission on Law Enforcement and Administration of Criminal Justice (n.d.). Peace Officer Standards and Training Council (POST). Retrieved September 3, 2017, from www.cole.state.la.us/programs/post.asp.

Marion County, Oregon (n.d.). Enforcement reserve deputy programme. Retrieved June 5, 2017, from www.co.marion.or.us/SO/jointheteam/Pages/reservedeputies.aspx.

Mroz, R. (2001). Cops on bikes. *Police: The Law Enforcement Magazine, 25*(12), 41–45. Retrieved June 5, 2017, from www.policemag.com/channel/vehicles/articles/2001/12/cops-on-bikes.aspx.

New York City Auxiliary Police (2012). Auxiliary operations order. New York: New York City Auxiliary Police. Retrieved June 5, 2017, from www.nycapba.com/files/2012/01/aps_operations_order1.pdf.

New York City Police Department (n.d.). NYPD New York's finest: Who are the volunteer auxiliary police? Retrieved December 22, 2014, from www.nyc.gov/html/nypd/html/careers/auxiliary_police.shtml.

Pepper, I. K. (2014). Do part-time volunteer police officers aspire to be regular police officers? *The Police Journal: Theory, Practice and Principles*, 87(2), 105–113.

Police Scotland (n.d.). Police officers: Training. Retrieved April 26, 2017, from www.scotland.police.uk/recruitment/police-officers/training.

South Carolina Criminal Justice Academy (2012). South Carolina reserve officer training program: Administrative guide. Columbia, SC: South Carolina Criminal Justice Academy. Retrieved June 5, 2017, from www.sccja.sc.gov/Other%20Files/SC%20Reserve%20Officer%20Training%20Program%20Administrative%20Guide%202015.pdf.

State of Rhode Island Municipal Police Training Academy (n.d.). Interested in becoming a police officer in Rhode Island? Retrieved September 3, 2017, from http://rimpa.ri.gov/basicrecruitment/requirements.php.

University of Chester (2009, March 24). Foundation degree trains Cheshire's new police officers. Retrieved September 2, 2017, from http://chester.ac.uk/news/2009/03/19.

Utah Department of Public Safety (n.d.). Peace officer standards and training: POST information. Retrieved September 3, 2017, from https://post.utah.gov/prospective-officers/post-info.

Utah Valley University (n.d.). Cost of the academy. Retrieved September 3, 2017, from www.uvu.edu/criminaljustice/policeacademy/cost.html.

Valencia College (n.d.). Criminal justice: Basic law enforcement academy. Retrieved September 3, 2017, from https://valenciacollege.edu/public-safety/criminal-justice-institute/basic_law.cfm.

Wolf, R. (2017). Civic volunteerism in Orange County (Florida): Sworn police reserves in a metropolitan sheriff's office. In J. Albrecht (Ed.), *Police reserves and volunteers: Enhancing organizational effectiveness and public trust*, pp. 88–92. Boca Raton, FL: CRC Press.

Wolf, R., & Beary, K. (2010). The Orange County Sheriff's Office Reserve Unit: A strong, cohesive unit able to handle multiple functions. *Deputy and Court Officer*, 2(2), 26–30.

Chapter 7

A Comparison of US and UK Volunteer Policing

It is apparent that volunteer law enforcement in the United States has largely been ignored in the literature; only in the past few years have a handful of American researchers begun to focus on this area. The fact that there are so many varied ways of operating and managing volunteers in American police agencies has further hindered investigation and research. However, the National Sheriffs' Association Outreach Committee and Reserve Law Enforcement Task Force have made this a priority and have worked with academic researchers to gather information about the utilization of reserve, auxiliary, and special deputy sheriffs throughout sheriff's departments in the United States (see Wolf, Holmes, & Jones, 2016; Dobrin & Wolf, 2016; Pepper & Wolf, 2015). The International Association of Chiefs of Police has also begun to underscore the importance of volunteer police through the IACP Police Administration Committee (see Wolf, Albrecht, & Dobrin, 2015).

Although there has been more scholarship on volunteer policing in the United Kingdom than in the United States, special constables have also been vastly under-studied. There has, however, been a small number of researchers who have begun to focus on this important, albeit largely academically neglected, area (see Gill & Mawby, 1990; Pepper, 2014; Britton, 2016; Jones & Wolf, 2017; Reay, 2012)

In order to compare volunteer policing in the United States and the United Kingdom, the authors worked with the National Sheriffs' Association in 2013 to write, revise, and distribute a national survey in the United States, and a comparable national survey was developed for the United Kingdom. The NSA does not represent police departments in the United States, and therefore survey responses were collected only from reserve and auxiliary officers in the United States who are linked to sheriff's offices. Sheriff's offices have varying duties throughout the country, in some places having the responsibility only to manage jails or corrections. In much of the United States, however, sheriff's offices are full-service police agencies with an elected sheriff as the chief executive. The UK survey was undertaken in 2016 in England and Wales and commissioned by the National Police Chiefs' Council's business lead for Citizens in Policing and the national Citizens in Policing "Community of Practice." These two national surveys were the largest ever undertaken about volunteer policing in both the United States and the United Kingdom (Wolf et al., 2016).

Sample and Data

The NSA survey was sent out to 3,080 sheriffs, representing all 50 states, who were members of the National Sheriffs' Association on March 18, 2013. Each recipient sheriff was asked to forward the survey to all reserve, auxiliary, volunteer, or special deputies in their agency. Reminder notices went out to all NSA member sheriffs again on April 18, 2013, one month after the original request. By May 18, 2013, there were 1,719 completed responses that had been received. One of the limitations of this study was due to the exploratory nature of the research. Each sheriff was instructed to send the survey to the volunteer law enforcement officers within the agency, thus making it impossible to calculate a response rate. For every initial sheriff contacted by the e-mail request, there was a possibility that there could be multiple responses (Wolf et al., 2016).

Although sheriffs in all 50 states had been part of the initial study population, there were many states that were not represented in the final responses. This may be explained by the varying roles of sheriffs in the United States. The role, responsibility, and authority of the sheriff in the northeast is distinctly different from the role of the sheriff in the south, or in the west. The northeast states was conspicuously absent from the final sample. This may be indicative of the lack of use of law enforcement volunteers within those states, or the minimum responsibilities they do have if they are utilized. Respondents from California, Florida, Ohio, and Washington represented 39 percent of the total sample (n = 668); these states are amongst the states that both have active sheriff's offices and are likely to have active volunteer programs (Wolf et al., 2016).

The UK survey initially was developed for special constables, but was eventually sent to both special constables and police support volunteers. For this current comparison, only the responses from special constables are used. Unlike policing in the United States, all 43 forces in England and Wales follow the same directives, so that, while there may be differences in training, uniforms, and roles, their powers are the same across both countries, thus avoiding some of the complications identified above.

Similar to the distribution methodology in the United States, the survey was sent to senior officers in each of the 43 forces in England and Wales for distribution to all special constables (and PSVs). The survey was sent by e-mail and asked each of the senior officers to distribute to their appropriate volunteers, and then responses were collected electronically.

While there were responses from all the forces, volumes varied, with ten of the larger forces returning approximately 50 percent of the responses. 1,908 total responses were returned, accounting for a little fewer than 12 percent of all special constables in the United Kingdom, though not all respondents had completed the entire survey. While this may not appear to be a large percentage, it is the largest-scale survey ever undertaken among special constables (and PSVs), and its findings provide a tangible foundation for further research (Britton, 2016).

Survey Instrument

The original intention of conducting the surveys in both countries was to mirror, as far as possible, the two versions. However, the UK version was delayed in being distributed (it was originally intended to be circulated in 2013 along with the NSA survey) because of a prolonged review process and the fact that questions were changed/added/omitted. A complete comparison therefore cannot be made for all areas of the survey. There are, however, a large number of areas in which direct analogies can be made, and these are discussed in the following portion of this chapter.

The US survey was designed and data collected through on online survey tool by the authors and in consultation with the NSA, and utilized Qualtrics®, an online survey tool, to collect responses. The survey contained a total of 43 questions collecting basic demographic information and perceptions of volunteer utilization within the agency. The UK survey consisted of 29 questions and was circulated by the National Police Chiefs' Council in January 2016 by email and results were collected electronically. As with the US version of the survey, the UK version collected details on demographics, how volunteers are used, and perceptions on interactions with their police force colleagues.

Results

Sample Demographics

United States

As can be expected in such a male-dominated field as policing, the survey respondents from the United States were mostly male (92 percent, n = 1,311; see Table 1). The respondents reported being mostly between the ages of 45 and 64 years of age (50.3 percent, n = 712). Approximately 78 percent of the respondents reported that they were currently married (n = 1,099), and 19 percent reported being single and never married or divorced (n = 263). With regard to race/ethnicity, 89 percent of the respondents self-reported as white (n = 1,255), with the next single largest ethnic group of respondents being Hispanic (5 percent,

Table 1 US sample demographics

Variable	Value labels	N	Percentage
Gender			
	Male	1,311	92.0
	Female	107	8.0
		1,418	100.0
Age			
	18 to 24 years	52	3.7
	25 to 34 years	153	10.8
	35 to 44 years	291	20.6
	45 to 54 years	361	25.5
	55 to 64 years	351	24.8
	65 years and older	205	14.5
		1,413	100.0
Marital status			
	Single, never married	130	9.2
	Married	1,099	77.7
	Divorced	133	9.4
	Separated	13	0.9
	Widowed	18	1.3
	Living with partner	22	1.6
		1,415	100.0
Race/ethnicity			
	White/Caucasian	1,255	88.6
	African American	21	1.5
	Hispanic	70	4.9
	Asian	20	1.4
	Native American	20	1.4
	Pacific Islander	6	0.4
	Other	24	1.7
		1,416	100.0
Current position outside law enforcement			
	Management/business and financial	325	27.0
	Business operations/financial	63	5
	Farmers and farm managers	14	1.2
	Computer or mathematical	45	3.7
	Legal	36	3.0
	Education	55	4.6
	Health	23	1.9
	Firefighting/public safety	149	12.3
	Other category	497	41.2
		1,207	100.0
Outside employment status			
	Full-time	952	67.0
	Part-time	89	6.3
	Unemployed	22	1.5
	Retired	264	18.6
	Student	47	3.2
	Other	47	3.3
		1,421	100.0

Note: Percentages have been rounded and may not total 100.

n = 70). Respondents reported that they were most often employed full-time outside their law enforcement volunteer work (67 percent, n = 952), and selected every possible career choice available in the survey (which utilized the US Department of Labor's 36 separate job categories). The most common job categories were reported as management or professional positions (27 percent, n = 325), and firefighting or public safety positions (12 percent, n = 149). This was followed by education (4.6 percent, n = 55), and computer or mathematical professions (3.7 percent, n = 45).

The average length of time that the US respondents reported having served as a volunteer law enforcement officer was 11.05 years (n = 1,423). As explained earlier in this book, many American volunteer police come from full-time positions and are moving into retirement or to new careers or positions outside policing. 28 percent of the respondents from the American sample indicated that they had served as full-time law enforcement officers. Those who had served in a full-time capacity had considerable experience; the average for those who reported full-time service was almost 13 years in those positions.

England and Wales

Respondents to the survey in the United Kingdom were also predominately male (79.8 percent, n = 1,509; see Table 2), somewhat higher than the overall proportion of full-time officers, but less than the percentage found in the American survey. More than half the respondents were age 34 or less (61 percent, n = 1,116), and fewer than 1 percent were 65 years of age or older (n = 18). Among the respondents from the United Kingdom, just over 89 percent (n = 1,709) described themselves as white British or white Irish (the same percentage who had reported their race/ethnicity as white among the American respondents), with the next single largest ethnic group of respondents being "from other white backgrounds" (3.6 percent, n = 69).

Law Enforcement Duties and Motivations to Serve

United States

As there is significant variation throughout the United States on what part-time or volunteer law enforcement officers can do, the American survey asked respondents about their authority to make an arrest. While nearly half the respondents (46 percent, n = 701; see Table 3) indicated that they have full power of arrest whether on or off duty, 33 percent of the respondents indicated that they have power of arrest only while on duty (n = 503). This means that 79 percent (n = 1,204) of the respondents have the power of arrest while on duty. Twelve percent of the respondents

Table 2 UK sample demographics

Variable	Value labels	N	Percentage
Gender			
	Male	1,509	79.8
	Female	381	20.1
		1,890	100.0
Age			
	18 to 24 years	525	28.7
	25 to 34 years	591	32.4
	35 to 44 years	373	20.4
	45 to 64 years	318	17.4
	65 years and older	18	1.0
		1,825	100.0
Race/ethnicity			
	White British	1694	88.8
	White Irish	15	0.8
	Other white background	69	3.6
	Mixed white and black Caribbean	11	0.6
	Mixed white and black African	3	0.2
	Mixed white and Asian	8	0.4
	Other mixed background	6	0.3
	Asian Indian	23	1.2
	Asian Pakistani	13	0.7
	Asian Bangladeshi	4	0.2
	Any other Asian background	6	0.3
	Black Caribbean	7	0.4
	Black African	9	0.5
	Other black background	2	0.1
	Chinese	9	0.5
	Other ethnic group	2	0.1
	Not recorded	26	0.9
		1,908	100.0

Note: Percentages have been rounded and may not total 100.

to the American survey indicated that they have no law enforcement powers of arrest at all as volunteer police (n = 183). In obvious contrast to the UK survey, a large majority of the US respondents (90 percent, n = 1,403) indicated that they have law enforcement authority to be armed with a firearm; 69 percent (n = 1,074) of the respondents indicated that they have this authority while both on or off duty, and 21 percent (n = 329) are authorized to be armed by their law enforcement agency, but only while on duty.

The survey also asked American respondents in sheriff's agencies to indicate what motivated them to serve as volunteer law enforcement officers. Seventy-three percent, the largest response, indicated that serving is a way to "contribute to my community" (n = 982). Sixty-nine percent

Table 3 United States: what motivated you to become a volunteer police officer?

Answer	Response	Percentage
I want to contribute to my community	982	73
I see it as a way to develop as a person	938	69
I have an interest in law enforcement and policing in general	878	65
I have skills/knowledge from my daily life that can enhance the agency	834	62
I wanted some volunteer work/part-time work to perform in my spare time	815	60
I want to join the regular police force and this provides an insight into that role	756	56
My employer encouraged/supported me	538	40
I used to be a regular officer and want to make use of my knowledge and/or expertise	485	36
I used to be a regular officer and want to stay in touch with my colleagues	412	30

Notes: N = 1,353 for this question. Respondents could select multiple options.

indicated that they see this volunteering role as "a way to develop as a person" (n = 938), 65 percent indicated that they serve because they "have an interest in law and policing in general" (n = 878), and 62 percent indicated that they feel that they "have skills/knowledge from my daily life that can enhance the policing agency" (n = 834). Thirty-six percent indicated that they used to be a regular officer and wanted to make use of the knowledge from that position as a volunteer (n = 485), and 30 percent used to be a regular officer and wanted to stay in touch with their colleagues (n = 412).

American survey respondents indicated that, on average, they spend 9.8 hours per week (SD = 8.39, n = 1,409) volunteering in their law enforcement position. When working in their volunteer law enforcement function, approximately 30 percent reported that they work alone (n = 474) or with someone else who was not always the same person (41 percent, n = 641). This is consistent with full-time positions in American law enforcement. They were also asked to indicate what types of duties they undertook as law enforcement officers, and those responses are reflected in Table 4. In addition to the responses listed, open responses included working in investigations, warrants, election security, fingerprinting children, dignitary protection, and more.

England and Wales

All special constables in England and Wales have the same warranted powers but the level and amount of training, uniforms and equipment do vary as do some activities. Table 5 indicates the most common

Table 4 US volunteer functions and law enforcement duties

Area of policing activity	Response	Percentage
Routine patrol (on foot)	378	27
Routine patrol (in a vehicle)	1,028	74
Emergency response (e.g., dive team, special response team, etc.)	431	31
Event policing (e.g., crowd control, traffic control)	1,131	82
Site or facility security	559	40
Law enforcement operations (e.g., DUI checkpoints, prostitution stings, etc.)	546	39

Notes: N = 1,353 for this question. Respondents could select multiple options.

Table 5 UK volunteer functions and law enforcement duties

Area of policing activity	Currently do (%)	Would like to do in the future (%)
Neighbourhood policing	49.7	7.5
Emergency response policing	47.1	11.4
Policing events	48.7	12.3
Working in schools with young people	5.3	36.4
Criminal investigation	12.3	46.6
Administration	4.5	6.8
Helping to manage calls from the public	3.6	17.5
Roads policing	14.5	47.2
Specialist operational units	7.5	64.4
Intelligence	6.2	48.7
Public order policing	18.7	44.2
Criminal justice, supporting cases through court and supporting victims	3.4	32.4
Cybercrime	1.2	36.6
Fraud and other economic crime	0.7	32.9
Safeguarding children	6.2	33.3
Mental health issues	12.4	23.8
Managing dangerous offenders	4.1	27.9

Notes: N = 1,908 for this question. Respondents could select multiple options.

undertakings among special constables who completed and returned the UK national survey. There were differences in the England and Wales survey from the US version, and one area that the commissioning bodies focused on was in relation to the utilization of special constables in an environment that has tended to use such officers for public order, community, and events policing. Results suggest that a significant proportion of special constables would like to be active in other areas. While it should be made clear that "wanting to participate" is not the same as "being competent," it is also clear that, in some activities, a substantial number of currently serving special constables would like to be appropriately trained.

Respondents could select multiple responses for this question, but the results indicate that special constables in the United Kingdom are primarily involved in the duties of neighborhood policing (49.7 percent, n = 948), emergency response policing (47.1 percent, n = 898), and policing special events (48.7 percent, n = 929). However, in order of involvement, special constables are also involved in public order policing (18.7 percent, n = 356), roads policing (14.5 percent, n = 276), mental health issues (12.4 percent, n = 236), and criminal investigations (12.3 percent, n = 234).

With regard to the types of duties they would like to be involved in, the largest number of respondents indicated specialist operational units (64.4 percent, n = 1,228), which would include police canine units, marine patrol, mounted patrol, and similar. Other functions that UK special constables would like to be more involved in include intelligence (48.7 percent, n = 929), criminal investigations (46.6 percent, n = 889), public order policing (44.2 percent, n = 843), cybercrime investigations (36.6 percent, n = 698), working in schools with young children (36.4 percent, n = 694), safeguarding children (33.3 percent, n = 635), and fraud and other economic crime (32.9 percent, n = 627).

UK respondents were also asked to indicate what motivated them to become volunteer police officers and work within their local policing service. The question relating to motivation in the England and Wales survey differed from the US version; respondents were asked to indicate what they hoped to achieve in becoming a special constable. Optional responses were provided (see Table 6), and a degree of altruism is readily apparent in the responses provided. The response "I was interested in policing, and wanted to learn more about it, and/or to gain skills and experience to strengthen a future application for a paid policing role" had the highest percentage of respondents (41 percent, n = 782). The response with the second highest percentage was "I wanted to give something back to my local community, and to play an important part in making my local community safer" (19.8 percent, n = 368). The options that came third and fourth were "I wanted to do something exciting with my spare time" (12.6 percent, n = 241) and "I wanted to do something worthwhile with my spare time" (7.7 percent, n = 147).

Compensation

As discussed earlier in this text, volunteers who are not paid for their services are still not cost-free. There is a monetary cost for a host organization; this could be in training, supplies, uniforms, supervision, transportation, or similar. However, some agencies do decide to pay their

Table 6 United Kingdom: thinking back to when you decided to become a volunteer, what did you most hope to achieve from that experience?

Answer	Response	Percentage
I wanted to meet new people	55	2.9
I wanted to do something exciting with my spare time	241	12.8
I was interested in a career in policing, and wanted to learn more about it and/or to gain skills and experience to strengthen a future application for a paid policing role	782	41.0
I thought it would look good to future (non-policing) employers	22	1.2
I wanted to give something back to my local community, and to play an important part in making my local community safer	368	19.3
I was interested in policing and wanted to learn more about it and become directly involved	171	9.0
I wanted to improve the way my local area is policed	27	1.4
I wanted to make the police more visible in my local community	20	1.0
I wanted to do something worthwhile with my spare time	147	7.7
I wanted to be a voice for my local community, and/or to engage my local community so that we are better heard by the police and they work better to address our priorities	8	0.4

Notes: N = 1,908 for this question. Respondents could select multiple options.

volunteers, and this can range from nothing at all to minimal pay or a small stipend for service (Brudney, 1999). In the American survey, 80 percent (n = 1,213) of the respondents indicated that they receive no stipend, reimbursement, or pay for services, 10 percent (n = 151) specified that they receive some sort of meal or travel reimbursement, and 2 percent (n = 35) indicated they receive reimbursement for liability insurance or for specialized training. However, 8 percent (n = 125) indicated that they receive pay at a rate less than a full-time, sworn deputy, but more than the national minimum wage. Although these last responses may not be seen as those of volunteers, this is an indication of the complexity of the utilization of reserve, auxiliary, and special deputies throughout the United States.

Another interesting characteristic of many jurisdictions in the United States is the legal authority for policing agencies to provide, at a financial cost to the requester, additional specific police protection for events, businesses, or specific functions. Most often this type of work is referred to as "off-duty" work, as the full-time police who generally work these types of services are not working in an on-duty capacity. Government agencies authorize the "outsourcing" of government services to retain the services of public workers, in this case the police. The rise of police unions and collective bargaining may have also been influential in providing police officers with additional compensation without direct public expenditure (Brunet, 2008). "Off-duty police officers can provide a wide range of services that are highly valued in both the public and private spheres such as directing traffic, providing security, maintaining order, and deterring crime" (Brunet, 2008, p. 162). Of particular interest to volunteer policing, however, is that many police agencies throughout the United States also allow their volunteer police to perform paid off-duty police roles. This further blurs the lines between volunteer and paid full-time police personnel, but has significant benefits for areas that have more off-duty work than can be performed by the available full-time police. It also creates a ready reserve of paid workers (though not at the expense of the government) for areas that have a need for policing services at different levels at different times of the year. The issue of off-duty work will be discussed more in the final chapter of this book while examining the future of volunteer policing.

The England and Wales survey did not ask about remuneration; special constables do not receive any pay for their service, though recompense may be given to cover travel expenses, meals, and uniform allowances. Special constables may be reimbursed for lodging expenses incurred if working beyond a normal duty period or if engaged on duty away from their normal place of duty. Actual traveling expenses to and from the place of duty can be reimbursed whether using public transportation or private conveyance at a mileage allowance. Unlike anywhere in the United States, special constables may also be eligible to receive an allowance equal to their actual loss of earnings from their primary occupation if they are required to attend duty during normal work hours (Home Office, 2014).

The issue of pay for special constables has been debated by government for some years. In 1967 a working party considered the introduction of a bounty, or allowance, for special constables, but support was low and it was therefore ignored (Robertson, 1993). Then in 1987, at the conference on special constables, the idea of a bounty was discussed, but support was still minimal (Robertson, 1993). The issue was revisited in 1990, when the then home secretary announced a trial bounty scheme be introduced in the Metropolitan Police Force and two regional forces. In the end, however, only Dorset Constabulary piloted the scheme. It was felt that the payment of the bounty would enhance recruitment, encourage special constables to give more of their time, and reduce government waste. Findings indicated that payment did not enhance recruitment (Robertson, 1993). In spite of doubts over such a scheme (Wright, 1989), the Special Constables (Amendment) Regulation was passed and allowed for the payment of a bounty to special constables. A subsequent report undertaken in 1993 concluded that a pilot bounty scheme in one police force area provided scant evidence of its appeal, and, indeed, other forces that were also part of the pilot bounty scheme had withdrawn from it even before it ended (Robertson, 1993).

Considerations and Limitations

This chapter outlines research that sought to obtain perceptions of individuals who self-identified as reserve, auxiliary, special deputy, or similar and who were affiliated with a sheriff's office or department in the United States or as a special constable in the United Kingdom. This survey research is a foundation on which to build future studies related to the utilization of volunteer law enforcement officers in both the United States and the United Kingdom. While there are several associations of reserve and auxiliary officers in the United States, none are able to claim that they are able to communicate with or maintain contact with even a large minority of the many individuals who fill that role. The result was that researchers relied on the vast network of the National Sheriffs' Association in the United States, which has the capacity to reach out to a subset of volunteer law enforcement officers affiliated with sheriff's agencies, and the National Police Chiefs' Council in the United Kingdom. The resultant analysis has allowed an understanding the type of individuals who volunteer to hold these positions in the two countries.

Initially, the authors intended to deploy a nearly identical survey as the one used in the United States in the United Kingdom. However, in the case of the UK survey, once the survey had been proposed the researchers had no level of engagement in either the revised content or the initial analysis of the survey. Two years prior to its distribution a pilot study of the original version was undertaken in which certain questions mirroring the US survey were included. By the time the final version was approved, however, the survey had been amended and delivered without input from the researchers. That said, there is sufficient data to provide useful and informative information.

Because both surveys rely on self-reported data, limitations include attribution (attributing positive measures to one's own agency) and exaggeration (representing outcomes as more significant than they might actually be). As exploratory research, this study is limited in its generalizability. As respondents were self-identified and/or asked to respond by their agency head, the response rate cannot be reported in either the United States or the United Kingdom.

There has been some very limited recent research to compare US and UK volunteer policing in the literature, and that should be mentioned here. Wolf, Pepper, and Dobrin (2017) used exploratory research to compare the confidence of volunteer police in the United States and the United Kingdom, and in the training each received for their roles. That study, while relying on responses from a very small number of respondents (41 from one policing agency in the United States and 32 from a single policing service in the United Kingdom), showed that the survey respondents perceived their training to be very similar; there were some differences, however. The American policing volunteers were slightly more confident in their training than the UK volunteers in each of three vignettes used to describe a policing scenario. UK respondents rated their confidence in their training with regard to interviewing a victim, interviewing a suspect, and completing required paperwork to be significantly less than their American counterparts (Wolf et al., 2017). A related study by Pepper and Wolf (2015) also had a small response rate, but is worth noting. Similar to the current research from this chapter, they found that 95 percent of their American volunteer respondents were male and 33 percent were between the ages of 55 and 64 years. In contrast, the UK sample was 84 percent male and 52 percent were between the ages of 25 and 34. They also found that the average time the volunteers reported having served monthly as volunteer police officers was approximately 28 hours in both the United Kingdom and the United States. Comparable to the current research, they reported that the motivations of the respondents were different depending upon their country of volunteerism. In the United States, respondents were more likely to respond that they had been regular full-time police officers in the past, and volunteered as a way to give back to their agency or community, or to keep in touch with their former colleagues (Pepper & Wolf, 2015).

It is anticipated that the initial research reported here, and the continued analysis of future research in both the United States and in England and Wales, will provide a basis upon which further exploration and comparisons can and will be developed. In the United Kingdom in particular, the role of the police and crime commissioners has, predictably, brought changes to the structure and management of the police service in each of the 43 forces, and may lead to some interesting changes in volunteerism in policing. Additionally, the establishment of the UK College of Policing in 2012 has brought with it ambitious changes and streamlining across the UK policing organization as a whole. While Chapter 8 will discuss some of the varying ways that volunteer police are used throughout the world, Chapter 9 will discuss some of the issues that may affect the way that volunteers police in both the United Kingdom and the United States.

References

Britton, I. (2016). *National survey of special constables and police support volunteers: Initial findings report.* Northampton, UK: University of Northampton, Institute for Public Safety, Crime and Justice.

Brudney, J. L. (1999). The effective use of volunteers: Best practices for the public sector. *Law and Contemporary Problems, 62*(4), 219–256.

Brunet, J. R. (2008). Blurring the line between public and private sectors: The case of police officers' off-duty employment. *Public Personnel Management, 37*(2), 161–174.

Dobrin, A., & Wolf, R. (2016). What we know and what we don't know about volunteer policing in the United States. *International Journal of Police Science and Management, 18*(3), 220–227.

Gill, M. L., & Mawby, R. I. (1990). *A special constable: A study of the police reserve.* Aldershot, UK: Avebury Publishing.

Home Office (2014, April). Home Office guidance on special constable expense and allowance rates. London: Home Office. Retrieved August 27, 2017, from www.gov.uk/government/uploads/system/uploads/attachment_data/file/304488/GuidanceSpecialConstableExpenseAllowanceRates.pdf.

Jones, C., & Wolf, R. (2017). "Special" kind of policing: Volunteer policing in England and Wales. In J. Albrecht (Ed.), *Police reserves and volunteers: Enhancing organizational effectiveness and public trust*, pp. 205–212. Boca Raton, FL: CRC Press.

Pepper, I. K. (2014). Do part-time volunteer police officers aspire to be regular police officers? *The Police Journal: Theory, Practice and Principles, 87*(2), 105–113.

Pepper, I. K., & Wolf, R. (2015). Volunteering to serve: An international comparison of volunteer police officers in a UK north east police force and a US Florida sheriff's office. *The Police Journal: Theory, Practice and Principles, 88*(3), 209–219.

Reay, W. T. (2012). *The specials: How they served London: The story of the Metropolitan Special Constabulary.* London: Ulan Press.

Robertson, N. (1993). Dorset Police Special Constabulary report on the pilot bounty scheme (1st October 1991–30th September 1993). Unpublished report. Dorset Police Special Constabulary, Winfrith Newburgh, UK.

Wolf, R., Albrecht, J., & Dobrin, A. (2015). Reserve policing in the United States: Citizens volunteering for public service. *The Police Chief, 82*(10), 38–47.

Wolf, R., Holmes, S. T., & Jones, C. (2016). Utilization and satisfaction of volunteer law enforcement officers in the office of the American sheriff: An exploratory nationwide study. *Police Practice and Research: An International Journal, 17*(5), 448–462.

Wolf, R., Pepper, I. K., & Dobrin, A. (2017). An exploratory international comparison of professional confidence in volunteer policing. *The Police Journal: Theory, Practice and Principles, 90*(2), 91–106.

Wright, P. (1989). Letter to the Deputy Under-Secretary of State on special constables, 4th September 1989. Sheffield: South Yorkshire Police Headquarters.

Chapter 8

Volunteer Policing around the Globe

Earlier discussions and the focus of this book have been on the similarities and differences between volunteer policing units throughout the United States and in comparison to the United Kingdom. However, governments and policing agencies throughout the world have developed distinct yet similar ways of doing things, especially with regard to volunteer policing. This chapter will review volunteer policing throughout the world, but certainly does not contain an exhaustive list. As described earlier in this text, even the definition of a "volunteer" can be different from one organization to another, and this is certainly true with regard to volunteer policing. If individuals are unpaid, does that make them volunteers? What if they are required to provide several years of service to the government in an unpaid capacity; are they volunteers? If individuals are provided a small level of pay, or a stipend, for their services, are they volunteers? While some may question whether the organizations described in this chapter are volunteer or not, our intent is to provide a snapshot of some of the variations around the globe in this under-studied area of policing.

The chapter starts with examples of volunteer police in the United Kingdom and the United States to create a foundation regarding the similarities and differences, and then provides case studies of other illustrations from around the world.

Special Constables in the United Kingdom

The United Kingdom utilizes volunteers to serve as part-time police officers in each of the 43 police forces in England and Wales. The Scottish police and the British Transport Police also have special constables serving in volunteer capacities (see Photo 7). As described earlier in this text, special constables, or "specials," serve as warranted police officers, the same as their full-time counterparts. Specials are vested with the same powers to enforce the law as full-time police, including the power of arrest. While many specials serve as volunteers, some forces pay an annual stipend to

Photo 7 A British Transport Police special constable patrolling a train station in England

offset costs. Specials can claim travel and expenses, and uniforms are provided by the police force.

The minimum requirements to become a special in the United Kingdom is that the applicant must be a European Economic Area citizen (or have an unrestricted right to remain in the country) and at least 18 years of age. Applicants must pass a health and fitness test during the recruitment process, and must be willing to donate at least 16 hours per month to the police force. Specials may also be assessed on their interpersonal skills, the ability to work in a team, leadership potential, and initiative. Police forces also commonly use the Police Initial Recruitment (PIR) test to screen candidates to judge the ability of the applicant to write clearly and accurately, solve numerical problems, and reason logically.

Currently special constable uniforms generally mirror their full-time counterparts, and specials are provided with the same equipment provided to full-time police officers, including a baton, handcuffs, incapacitating spray, radios, and stab vests. While different police forces carry variations on the same equipment, specials are also authorized to purchase their own additions to the duty gear.

Often specials work in teams with another volunteer special or a regular full-time officer, but, after successful training they can work alone. Specials are involved with all facets of policing, from crime prevention and special events, to working road traffic accidents and dealing with burglaries, fights, and criminal damage. Specials are not usually involved with more specialized functions of policing, however, including traffic police, criminal investigations, search teams, or firearms teams.

The uniform of the special constable is nearly identical to the uniform of the regular full-time officer, but there are some minor differences. In England and Wales some specials wear ranks similar to regular officers, but there are variations, even between forces. Specials in Scotland do not have ranks or grades. Specials often have the letters "SC" on the epaulette to denote their volunteer role and position.

Special constables have been recruited under a variety of initiatives. In 2004 retail shops were asked to sponsor their staff to apply for and train with the local police force as specials, and then carry out some of their special patrol duties during working hours. The idea was to provide more eyes and ears in the merchant's vicinity, and provide some individuals with an added incentive to providing their services. The program, called Employer Supported Policing (ESP), encourages businesses to support an employee to apply for a position with the Special Constabulary. Participating businesses commit to providing the staff member with paid leave to attend initial training and then participate one day every two weeks to provide policing duties. Special constables in this program are therefore being paid to work policing duties, but by their regular paid work position, not the police (Metropolitan Police, n.d.). Another example of specialized recruiting can be found in the 2003 push to recruit certified and qualified accountants to work in an investigatory capacity within the Metropolitan Police Specialist Crime Unit (Seth, 2006). More recently specialist teams have been brought together to deal with offshore and river policing and cybercrime and to provide mounted patrols in rural areas using their own horses.

City of London Special Constabulary

The history of the Special Constabulary in the City of London is colorful, and can be traced to the reign of Queen Elizabeth 1 in the sixteenth century, when the Lord Mayor of London organized bands of freemen to be trained to quell riots. An Act of 1673 authorized temporary police officers when needed, and the Special Constables Acts of 1831 and 1835 authorized naming special constables for the preservation of the peace and protect people and property. In 1911 the City of London formed the Police Reserves, which was renamed in 1935 as the City of London Special Constabulary (City of London Police, 2011). As the uniforms of the volunteer police in London evolved over time, so did their equipment. In 1994 handcuffs were issued to SCs in the City of London for the first time; prior to this they had had to purchase their own. By 1995 SCs were issued expandable batons, handcuffs, defensive spray, and body armor.

Modern-day City of London special constables receive over £1,000 worth of uniforms and equipment, and initial training of over 280

Photo 8 Many volunteer policing units from around the world have developed exchange programs to learn how others perform volunteer patrol functions; pictured here are Sgt. Jay Rosario of the Orange County Sheriff's Office Reserve Unit and Commander Ian Miller from the City of London Special Constabulary in London during an exchange visit

classroom hours and 400 hours of self-study. Special constables provide significant assistance to the regular police for deployments at ceremonial events, demonstrations, and in the case of terrorist acts. However, special constables also perform more routine policing, through volunteer services provided in teams and by officers qualified to work independent patrol to respond to police calls for service, public drunkenness, and traffic control (City of London Police, 2011). City of London specials wear uniforms that are identical to regular police constables (see Photo 8), other than the "SC" designation with their police number, and must perform a minimum of 200 hours of volunteer duty each year. They do not receive a salary, but are reimbursed out-of-pocket expenses for traveling to and from duty, and a meal allowance (City of London Police, 2017).

Orange County (Florida) Sheriff's Office Reserves

Orange County, Florida, is approximately 2,600 square kilometers in size, and has a resident population (not including tourists) of nearly 1.2 million. Orange County is home to the city of Orlando, Walt Disney World, Sea World, and Universal Studios, among other tourist resorts and destinations. Orange County also boasts the second largest convention center in the United States, and one of the largest universities in

Photo 9 Reserve deputies with the Orange County Sheriff's Office provide patrol duties, but also assist with special functions and large crowd events; this is extremely important in this tourist destination of central Florida

the United States. The Orange County Sheriff's Office has approximately 2,000 paid employees, of whom over 1,400 are sworn law enforcement officers, making OCSO the 12th largest sheriff's office in the nation and the third largest in the southeast United States. The agency is responsible for all law enforcement and criminal investigations in the unincorporated areas of Orange County.

In Florida, volunteer law enforcement officers are authorized by statute with arrest powers and to carry firearms. OCSO reserve deputies (see Photo 9) must meet stringent police academy and state of Florida required training, and serve either as "auxiliary" deputies (with over 300 hours of academy training), who perform their law enforcement duties under the control of a fully certified volunteer deputy or full-time deputy, or as fully certified volunteer deputies (who must attend the same certification academy as full-time Florida law enforcement officers, of approximately 800 hours), who have all of the same statutory authority and responsibilities as full-time law enforcement officers. In addition to state-mandated academy training, the Orange County Sheriff's Office requires all volunteer deputies to successfully complete an on-the-job training program. This consists of a six-week orientation, followed by the equivalent of 14 weeks in the Field Training and Evaluation Program under the supervision of a state-certified field training officer.

Applicants for volunteer deputy positions must complete the same physical, psychological, background, medical, and interview requirements as full-time recruits. Applicants for fully certified status must meet the same educational/experience requirements as applicants for full-time positions, though this is not required for auxiliary classification. Reserve unit personnel, in conjunction with the OCSO Human Resources Division, coordinate an agency hire board and provide an orientation for all new recruits to the unit. All new reserve deputies are assigned to an experienced reserve as a mentor to guide them through the training phase. Although many of the unit's new reserves join directly after receiving academy training, the unit also benefits greatly from full-time personnel who retire or resign (in good standing) from their law enforcement positions. Many of these individuals have thousands of hours of training combined with years of experience, and, although they may be pursuing new careers or retirement, they find that they have a lot that they can continue to give back to their community through volunteerism.

The Orange County Sheriff's Office provides the same equipment to volunteer deputies that are provided to full-time deputies, including radios, handguns, Tasers, incapacitating spray, duty gear, ballistic vests, personal safety equipment, electronic control devices, and agency laptops. Reserve deputies may also be authorized to carry additional weapons (such as rifles and shotguns), or be issued additional equipment (such as radar units, specialty unit equipment, etc.) if requested and if the reserve has received the necessary training. The uniforms of all reserves within the unit are the same as the uniforms issued to full-time deputies within the agency. The unit also has ten marked cars that are used solely for reserve unit functions, special enforcement details, patrol, and other approved functions, but look identical to the vehicles used by full-time personnel. These patrol cars are issued to the highest-producing volunteers as take-home vehicles, but are available for any member of the unit to use.

The reserve unit follows an organizational structure that closely mirrors the full-time structure of the agency, in both the amount of authority and responsibility. The reserve unit is led by a chief deputy, and has two majors and four captains, assigned to operations, administration, training, and special details. The unit also has two training platoons (each led by a lieutenant), three operational platoons (each led by a lieutenant), and six operational squads of approximately ten reserves (each led by a sergeant).

There are currently nearly 80 men and women who volunteer to serve as deputy sheriffs within the agency. Policy requires that each member of the unit must provide 16 hours of volunteer time per month, which includes a monthly four-hour training meeting. Primarily, the reserve unit supports the goals of the agency, with a specific focus on uniformed patrol, and reserves are often called upon to fill in on road patrol squads that have manpower shortages or specific functional needs for supplemental manpower. However, members of the unit are also eligible to participate in other non-uniform or specialized assignments, provided that they have had the proper additional training. This includes mounted patrol, marine patrol, SWAT team (medic), bicycle patrol, tourism-oriented policing (TOP), honor guard, background investigations, juvenile arrest and monitor (JAM) unit, problem-oriented policing (POP), fugitive unit, criminal investigations, traffic enforcement, the training section, and others.

As part of a major county sheriff's office, the OCSO Reserve Unit is very much involved with the law enforcement community. The reserve unit has responded for requests for assistance from other law enforcement agencies within the county, but has also played a pivotal part in relief efforts such as that in southwest Florida after the devastation of Hurricane Andrew, and after Hurricanes Charlie, Francis, Jeanne, and Irma in central Florida. The reserve unit also proudly serves as host for national and international conferences for police reserves and volunteers, and welcomes police reserve units from around the world to learn first-hand about volunteer policing in Orange County (Wolf, 2014; Wolf & Beary 2010).

New York City Police Department Auxiliary

New York City is 1,214 square kilometers in size, and has a population of over 8 million. The role of the NYPD Auxiliary is extremely limited, and specifically functions as the uniformed eyes and ears of the police. NYPD Auxiliary do not have law enforcement or police powers, but act more as a voluntary security force, performing uniformed foot, vehicle, and bicycle patrols of neighborhoods and problem areas to report suspicious activity to the regular, full-time police. They also provide some traffic direction and assistance at major events, and provide an additional uniformed police presence for special events, parks, shopping areas, and at subway entrances and exits. The unit primarily performs foot patrol functions, working in pairs throughout the city. If auxiliaries encounter a problem, they are instructed to report the incident by radio or telephone to the local precinct so that regular officers can respond. During weekdays auxiliaries most often patrol during the evenings (Greenberg, 1984). There are over 4,000 members of the NYPD Auxiliary Police, but active membership may actually be half that number (Greenberg, 1984; Albrecht, 2017).

Applicants for the NYPD Auxiliary must be at least 17 years of age, be able to read and write English, pass a background check including a zero-tolerance drug policy, be a US citizen or a lawful permanent resident authorized to work in the United States, live in New York city or one of the six authorized surrounding areas, and possess a valid New York driver's license or identification card. Although the NYPD Auxiliary is the largest auxiliary program in the United States, it has one of the shortest required training programs. Recruits to the NYPD Auxiliary must pass a 54-hour Auxiliary Police Basic Training Course (as a comparison, regular police in NYPD attend a six-month, 960 hour academy), which provides them with peace officer training; however, NYPD auxiliaries do not have on- or off-duty police officer status, nor the power to make arrests (beyond that of any citizen in the state of New York), unless granted during a time of emergency. NYPD auxiliary officers are considered to be civilian, not sworn, at all times, both on and off duty (Kelly, Grasso, Esposito, Giannelli, & Maroulis, 2008). However, they can be granted peace officer status during a declared state of emergency (Albrecht, 2017).

Because of their civilian status, they are not authorized to make arrests for crimes that they did not witness, unless authorized by a regular police officer or a police dispatcher. Auxiliary police officers cannot be assigned to hazardous or dangerous duties, nor to solo patrol assignments or primary response to radio calls (Albrecht, 2017). NYPD auxiliary officers are not authorized to carry a sidearm at any time while on duty, but are allowed to carry straight batons, a radio, and handcuffs, and may detain individuals for certain misdemeanor crimes and felonies. After the fatal shooting of two auxiliary police officers in 2007, the New York City Council authorized funding for ballistic vests for all auxiliary officers, but that funding has not continued, and vests are currently in short supply.

New York City's auxiliary police officers are tasked with increasing the perception of the numbers of police on patrol by the public, and are authorized to patrol in cars, on foot, and by bicycle. NYPD auxiliary police cars are similar to the cars of regular officers, but are identified by the word "Auxiliary." The uniforms of NYPD auxiliary officers are very similar to full-time officers with the NYPD: auxiliary officers and auxiliary sergeants wear dark blue shirts and pants; auxiliary lieutenants and above wear white shirts. The badges of the auxiliary police, however, are distinctly different from regular officers.

The auxiliary force utilizes a rank structure similar to full-time personnel. New York City auxiliary police officers start as auxiliary officers, and can be promoted to auxiliary sergeant, auxiliary lieutenant, auxiliary captain, auxiliary deputy inspector, auxiliary inspector, and auxiliary deputy chief. Auxiliary inspectors command the auxiliary police units in each of the seven New York police boroughs, and the auxiliary captain commands the units in each precinct (Greenberg, 1984). Promotion is based on the recommendations of the full-time auxiliary coordinator, and additional training is required.

California Police Reserves

In contrast to the NYPD use of auxiliaries, California has one of the most progressive reserve programs in the country. Individuals can receive training to serve in one of three different categories as reserve officers. The different amounts of training in each level result in volunteers who have little to no police authority to equivalent levels of police authority as their full-time counterparts.

Reserve police officers in California are required to meet the same selection standards as full-time law enforcement officers, including a reading and writing ability assessment, an oral interview, a background investigation, and medical and physical testing. Applicants must be at least 18 years of age with a minimum of a high school education, and must be either a US citizen or a permanent resident alien who is eligible for and has applied for citizenship.

California breaks its reserve police officer standards into three categories: level I, level II, and level III. Level I reserves, once training has been completed (727 hours of academy training plus 400 hours of field training), are authorized to work alone and perform the same duties and functions as regular, full-time officers. Level II reserves, once training is complete (333 hours), perform law enforcement assignments but must be under the immediate supervision of a level I or full-time police officer. Level III reserves (with 144 hours of training) may perform specific limited support duties, but only those duties that are not likely to result in physical arrest, and must also be under the immediate supervision of a level I reserve officer or a full-time officer. Level III officers may be utilized to transport prisoners without the requirement for immediate supervision. While level III reserves are not required to complete annual professional training, both level I and II reserves are required to complete 24 hours every two years.

While California utilizes level I and level II reserves in uniformed patrol, those who receive the proper training can also work in other areas, including investigations, boat patrol, mounted posse, and search and rescue. The Los Angeles Police Department (LAPD) Reserve Corps is an example of an agency that utilizes California POST-trained reserve officers. LAPD's reserves are one of the largest reserve units in the state, with over 650 active reserve officers. LAPD reserves are issued all of the same equipment and uniforms as full-time officers, and are required to work a minimum of 16 hours every month. Reserves with the LAPD do not get any salary, donating time worth an estimated US$7 million every year (Garrison, 2003; Johnson, Bonner, & Hanser, 2017).

Civil Guard of Israel

Israel's Civil Guard was created in 1974 and includes uniformed and non-uniformed volunteers, who assist the Israel Police with neighborhood watch, patrol on foot and in marked cars, traffic control, police coastguard patrols, crime prevention, manning security barriers and checkpoints, and other duties. The guard claims to be the largest volunteer body in Israel, with as many as 100,000 participants (Israel Police, n.d.). The guard is a component of the Police and Community branch of the Israel Police. Its members are trained to provide initial response to any type of security situation, particularly terrorist attacks, until the regular police units can arrive (Jewish Telegraphic Agency, 1994). Members of the Israeli Civil Guard are under the command of a police station Civil Guard commander. Police station Civil Guard units fall under regional, district, and national Civil Guard commanders.

Civil Guard volunteers are provided with police powers when on duty, though these powers may be limited based on the volunteer's level of training. Volunteers can be armed, based on the training they have received, and can make arrests when on duty (World Police, n.d.). However, Civil Guard volunteers do not have any police powers when they are not on duty. They are forbidden to function as law enforcement officers when off duty, and cannot prevent a crime in progress, nor identify themselves as a guard member to prevent a crime.

Israeli Civil Guard volunteers are provided with a police vest, flashlight, radio, firearm, handcuffs, and other duty gear as may be required for the assignment. The minimum expectation of a volunteer is 12 hours a month, and a shift is usually two to four hours in length (World Police, n.d.). Volunteers can also undergo additional training to serve in additional capacities. "Yatam" volunteers are responsible primarily for traffic control, and "Matmid" volunteers perform all regular police duties, including patrols, investigation of crime, and crime prevention. Both Yatam and Matmid Civil Guard volunteers receive advanced training and wear regular police uniforms (World Police, n.d.).

Full-time police officers in Israel collaborate closely with the Civil Guard. Members of the Civil Guard develop intelligence in the field and share information with regular police to combat crime and in the fight against terrorism.

Volunteer Police Reserves of the Republic of Ireland

The Garda Síochána Reserve is the volunteer, unpaid, reserve section of the police force of Ireland. Reserve Gardaí members wear the same uniforms as the regular police, but their shoulder boards bear the initials "GR" to distinguish them from the full-time force. Reserve Gardaí are not authorized to carry firearms (neither do regular police unless assigned to special duties) and have limited authority of arrest. They are viewed as a force multiplier, and are used to increase police visibility in communities. Members of the reserve are not authorized to work in plain clothes.

Applicants for the Garda Síochána Reserve must be a national or of a European Union member state, or the Swiss Confederation, and must have been a continuous resident of Ireland. The Garda Reserve was established by the Garda Síochána Act of 2005, and became operational in December of 2006. By 2014 there were over 1,100 Garda Reserve members in Ireland (Garda Síochaána, n.d.), but this number had reduced to 870 Garda Reserve members by 2016 (Lynott, 2016).

Members of the Reserve Gardaí Síochána Reserve must complete approximately four weeks of training, and support the regular police, including providing patrol duties, and targeted problem policing (Garda Síochána, n.d.), assisting primarily in traffic checkpoints, monitoring CCTV, foot patrol, station duty, and event policing. Reserves also receive additional training in areas such as domestic violence, internal police policies, child protection, and roadside safety (Raidió Teilifís Éireann, 2015). Members work under the supervision of regular members of the police force (Department of Justice and Equality, 2016). In 2015 the powers of the Garda Reserve were expanded, to allow them to issue penalty points to motorists, serve traffic summons, and seize vehicles.

It is also common for members of the Garda Reserve to seek entry into a full-time position in policing, and volunteer service in the reserves is treated as a way for candidates to gain valuable experience toward application in An Garda Síochána, the regular police force of Ireland (Raidió Teilifís Éireann, 2015).

Civil Guard of Hungary

The Hungarian civil guard, or auxiliary police, was established in 1989 and is reported to have as many as 90,000 volunteers nationwide (Kardos & Szoke, 2017). The civil guard is known by its formal name, the Nationwide Civil Self-Defense Organization, abbreviated in Hungarian as OPSZ. The unit is made up of entirely non-sworn volunteers who participate in various policing-related duties. Members must be Hungarian citizens or be legal residents (Kardos & Szoke, 2017). The goal of the unit is to act as a uniformed police presence to deter crime, keep public order, and increase public safety. Members of the OPSZ participate in neighborhood patrols, foot and vehicle patrols with marked cars, traffic control, and youth crime prevention units. Members of the OPSZ serve as the "eyes and ears" of the police (Selih & Zavrsnik, 2012; Civil Self-Defense Organizations of Budapest, n.d.).

Members of the OPSZ do not have any more authority to make arrests than any other citizen, but can and do hold suspected criminals on the scene for regular police to arrive and investigate. However, they are not authorized to carry dangerous weapons other than pepper spray (Kardos & Szoke, 2017). In addition to patrol duties with regular police, members of the Hungarian auxiliary police also participate in a license plate recognition unit called Matrix Police. OPSZ members work in a patrol vehicle with a webcam that scans vehicle license plate information and compare those to the stolen car database. When a stolen car is located, the OPSZ members report the vehicle to the regular police who investigate (Matrix, 2015).

In the capital city, Budapest, the auxiliary police unit is called the Civil Self-Defense Organizations of Budapest, or BPSZ in Hungarian. Members of the BPSZ are assigned to one of 73 local community units and patrol in marked vehicles which look similar to police vehicles. Members of the BPSZ and the OPSZ are authorized to carry police issued pepper spray, and wear uniforms or vests to identify themselves (Civil Self-Defense Organizations of Budapest, n.d.).

Bermuda Police Reserves

The Bermuda Reserve Constabulary was established by the legislature of Bermuda in 1951. The original reserve officers in Bermuda were issued with gray uniforms to distinguish them from their regular police counterparts. While reserve police initially worked completely as volunteers, in 1991 a small stipend was approved to recognize the members of the unit for their service to their community. Members in good standing with the reserve unit continue to receive this stipend today, for every six months of service (approximately US$1,600/year). In 1995 the unit adopted a new uniform, nearly identical to the regular police officers, and changed its name to the Bermuda Police Reserve (Bermuda Police Service, n.d.). The regular police are not generally armed while on patrol in Bermuda, and Bermuda Police Reserve members do not carry handguns (Bermuda Online, n.d.).

Candidates for the Bermuda Police Reserve must be between 19 and 50 years of age, and be able to pass a battery of written, physical, and medical tests in addition to an intensive background check. The application standards for the police reserve are nearly identical to the regular Bermuda Police Service. The basic training course for police reserves covers all of the same content areas as training provided to regular police officers. There are approximately 80 members of the police reserve unit, and volunteers are required to provide 150 hours a year of volunteer service to the unit (Clifton, n.d.).

Duties performed by police reserves in Bermuda are varied, but mirror full-time police work. This includes duties in traffic control, road patrol and calls for service, responding to traffic accidents, and working with tourists. Bermuda Police Reserve officers are also trained in problem-oriented policing and work with community action teams to prevent crime (Clifton, n.d.). Members of the Bermuda Police Reserve are sworn police officers with the same powers of arrest as full-time, or regular, police officers. Uniforms and equipment are provided to members of the police reserves.

Russian Cossacks

The Cossacks in Russia have a deep and colorful history, which is also controversial. The term "Cossack" is derived from a Turkic word "Kazak," which can be translated into "free man" or "adventurer" (*History Magazine*, 2001). They can trace their ancestry to Turkic-speaking peasants who traveled to west-central Russia and united in the fifteenth century as a loyal warrior arm of the Russian Tsar. Cossacks settled in six different areas in Russia, and had warrior customs and traditions. It is said that Cossack children were taught warrior ways from birth; male newborn children would have their hand placed on a weapon at birth, and would be riding horses by the time they were three years old. Cossacks were used for military purposes, including protecting the borders and expansion of the Russian empire into Siberia (*History Magazine*, 2001). But, depending on who you ask, Cossacks have a very different image. Outside Russia, Cossacks are known as strict Russian Orthodox Christians who maintain order through violence and fear; within Russia, many view Cossacks as individuals who are loyal to their country and who have a rich and proud heritage (Flintoff, 2014).

Since the fall of the Soviet Union, Cossacks have established cadet colleges where Cossack children can learn about their heritage and prepare for military or police careers. In the 2010 census in Russia, Cossacks were listed as their own ethnic group, and about 650,000 Russians declared themselves as Cossacks (Seddon, 2012; Luhn, 2014). Russian President Vladimir Putin has attempted to cultivate the patriotic service of the Cossacks, and has begun authorizing the use of Cossack organizations as volunteer police forces (Flintoff, 2014). Russia began testing out the use of Cossacks as voluntary police as early as 2012, and used them extensively during the 2014 Winter Olympics in Sochi. Cossacks receive free public transportation and uniforms (which are different from their full-time governmental police counterparts) in exchange for serving, and are given limited police authority (Seddon, 2012), including detaining and checking the documents of those who disrupt the peace (Luhn, 2014). However, their work is not always in tandem with governmental agencies, and in 2012 Cossacks volunteer squads were banned from Moscow's southeastern district because of their frequent failure to get official permission for their actions (*Moscow Times*, 2015). Police leaders have also expressed concern about Cossacks acting as auxiliary police, and admit that Cossack patrols often do things that the police are not allowed to do. They have also been labelled as a modern "morality police" who protect Russia's traditionalist values (Luhn, 2014).

Toronto Police Auxiliary

After Hurricane Hazel struck the Toronto area in 1954, government authorities formed the Civil Defence Organization, including the formation of auxiliary police as part of that organization in 1956. The Metropolitan Toronto Police were also formed by merging 13 municipal police forces at this time (Fanfair, 2016). The Police Services Act (PSA) of Ontario formalized the role of auxiliary police in the province in 1990. Auxiliary officers in Toronto wear uniforms that are slightly different from those of regular Toronto police, but look very similar. Regular Toronto police are armed, and wear dark navy blue shirts. Instead of a solid red band on their hats, auxiliaries wear a checked red and black band, their shirts are light blue, and they have "Auxiliary Officer" on their arm patch. Auxiliary police work alongside regular officers, and assist in crime prevention programs, special events, parades, toy drives,[1] and other community events. In addition, they may be called on to provide security at police perimeters, serve on community committees, and operate Toronto Police information boots and community police offices (Toronto Police Service, n.d. – a; Palamarchuk, 2014).

Auxiliary police with the Toronto Police Service have no more authority than that granted to any citizen by law; however, the PSA establishes that an "auxiliary member of the police force has the authority of a police officer if he or she is accompanied or supervised by a police officer, and is authorized to perform police duties by the chief of police," and that "the chief of police may authorize an auxiliary member of the police force to perform police duties only in special circumstances, including an emergency, that the police officers of the police force are not sufficiently numerous to deal with" (Police Services Act (Ontario), 2015). While, generally, auxiliary members are not issued firearms, there is an exception to policy that allows for the Toronto chief of police to authorize firearms for auxiliaries who have competed the approved course of training. Members of the auxiliary must requalify annually in police use of force, which includes training in baton use, handcuffing, and defensive tactics. In addition, auxiliary members must be continuously certified in first aid and CPR.

Applicants for Toronto auxiliary positions must be Canadian citizens or permanent residents of Canada and be at least 18 years of age. In addition to other background requirements, candidates must reside in the Greater Toronto area, and commit to the program for a minimum of one year.

The Toronto Police Service reports that it had over 360 auxiliary officers in 2016, and each is provided with a uniform, equipment and training. Auxiliary officers are not required to complete a police training program or be certified to the same level as police, but they are required to complete a six-week training program which includes procedural and self-defense training. Auxiliary officers are required to complete a minimum of 150 volunteer hours every year (Toronto Police Service, n.d. – b; n.d. – a), but on average provide over 200 hours' service each per year. Toronto police auxiliary officers can also serve in specialized units, such as motorcycle patrol and the marine unit (Palamarchuk, 2013).

Hamilton Police Service Auxiliary

Also located in Ontario, Canada, the Hamilton Police Service Auxiliary has approximately 100 members. Hamilton is located on the western end of Lake Ontario, and the Hamilton Police Service has approximately 800 full-time police personnel. Members of the Hamilton Police Service Auxiliary undergo a seven-week training program, including over 30 hours of use of force instruction. After completing the training program, auxiliary police are required to complete a probationary period, and complete the ongoing training required of all auxiliary personnel every year.

Auxiliary police participate in enforcement functions and to increase the visibility of a police presence. They assist with sporting events, directed patrol and patrol ride-alongs, and the Public Order Unit, and direct traffic, conduct safety presentations in the community, monitor CCTV cameras, attend police recruiting events, and provide support to the Photography Unit and the marching team. Members of the auxiliary unit are required to volunteer a minimum of 12 hours every month, and shifts range from four to 12 hours.

The uniform of the auxiliary police is differentiated from the uniform of regular full-time police personnel, with a light blue shirt (rather than the dark blue shirt for regular officers) and a shoulder patch that states "Auxiliary." As with other police services in Ontario, the auxiliary police for Hamilton have no police power and are not armed. They function to assist the regular police in their duties and serve as volunteers.

The Hong Kong Auxiliary Police Force

The Hong Kong Auxiliary Police Force (HKAPF) was formed at the beginning of World War I, in 1914. Initially it was created as a cadre to replace regular police officers who were on active military service, and was called the Special Police Reserve. By mid-February 1915 the total strength of the Special Police Reserve had grown to 250 men, and was made up of Portuguese, Chinese, British, and Indian men. Training was conducted over several months, and consisted of a musketry course and basic instruction in drill. Initially the members of the Special Police Reserve were not issued uniforms, until a prominent Chinese resident donated money for outfitting them (Volunteer Special Constabulary, 1998; Lam, 1997).

By September 1915, however, the numbers of the regular police force had dwindled, and the trend was continuing. The governor of Hong Kong changed the status of all members of the Special Police Reserve to special constables, requiring these volunteers by law to report for duty, but also authorizing them with arrest powers. "They differed from the regular police force in only one area, namely pay and pensions, to which they were not entitled at all" (Lam, 1997, p. 4). In September 1917 the corps was renamed again, as the Hong Kong Police Reserve, until its disbandment in September 1918.

In 1927, in response to a huge increase in the Hong Kong population, largely from refugees from China, the Police Reserve was revived. All members of the force from 1914 to 1919 were re-enrolled. This force did not provide daily patrol duty or police duty, however. Instead, it provided a stand-by list of names to call upon, such as was needed in November of 1938, when 290 police reservists were called to active duty as a response to Japanese incursions into China which threatened Hong Kong's security.

The commissioner of police called upon 3,000 Chinese men to enroll in the Special Constabulary in 1941. In September of 1941 the Police (Militia Status) Ordinance required all regular police officers, members of the police reserves, and special constables to "'perform combatant duties as militia' if war broke out. They were to remain under the command of the Commissioner but were to 'engage in military operations against the armed forces of any enemy attempting to invade or otherwise carrying our war-like operations'" (Lam, 1997, p. 11). Police reservists worked police and military duties during the invasion of Hong Kong by the Japanese, and were disbanded during the occupation. The Hong Kong Police Reserve sustained significant casualties during this time, to heroic actions, friendly fire, and execution.

In May of 1946 the Police Reserve was re-created, with a Chinese force and commanded by Chinese officers. In 1949 the Special Constabulary was re-created, and, in addition to Chinese volunteers, allowed men of all races to join. In 1951, under the Compulsory Service Ordinance, all male subjects of Hong Kong of 18 years of age or older were required to serve in either the Royal Hong Kong Volunteer Defense Force, the Essential Services Corps, or the Special Constabulary. By 1955 special constables and reserve police performed a full range of policing functions, primarily in relief duties, and were required to work just eight hours a month. The two groups were joined together in 1957 and renamed the Hong Kong Auxiliary Police Force, organized similarly to the regular police force, and required conscription for required service was abandoned. 1965 saw the first women auxiliary police, and in 1969 both the Hong Kong Police Force and the Hong Kong Auxiliary Police Force were given "Royal" titles. The strength of the force rose from 3,761 in January of 1973 to 7,000 in November of the same year. By 1979 the force number had

Photo 10 The Hong Kong Auxiliary Police Force is a paid, part-time police force that serves as a supplement to the full-time police service

reduced to 4,714; but about 20 percent of those turned up daily to assist the full-time officers in their day-to-day duties.

The role of the HKAPF has varied over time, but maintains focus on crowd management duties during major public events and pre-planned operations. In addition, the HKAPF is tasked with the protection of key points, staffing command and control centers, staffing civil defense stations, protecting consular premises, and acting as a ready reserve for times of natural or civil emergencies. As of June 2013 there were approximately 3,850 members of the HKAPF (Information Services Department, 2017). The only difference in the uniform today between regular members of the police force and members of the Hong Kong Auxiliary Police Force is that auxiliary members have a letter "A" on both shoulder badges. Auxiliary recruits must complete a basic training course of 320 hours, then must complete continual annual training of 208 hours each year. In addition to requirements for time in-grade, in order to be eligible for promotion HKAPF members must participate in promotion courses ranging from 76 hours to 226 hours. Hong Kong auxiliary police (see Photo 10) are not volunteers, and are paid for their service, which is limited to eight hours for every 24-hour period (Volunteer Special Constabulary, 1998). The pay for auxiliaries goes from HK$620/day (approximately US$80/ £48) for new recruits to HK$1,436/day (US$185/£110) for senior station sergeants, who are the highest-paid hourly employees. Inspectors, senior inspectors, chief inspectors and above are paid a maximum of HK$1,940 (US$250/£148) per day as salaried employees (Information Services Department, 2017).

The Volunteer Special Constabulary of Singapore

Singapore's Volunteer Special Constabulary (VSC) was originally formed as the Singapore Police Volunteer Reserve (SPVR) in 1938, in response to political and labor disturbances. The unit had approximately 30 volunteer police reservists at that time and was tasked with public order and to assist the police force with cordons during demonstrations, protests, and strikes. Over the next several years the SPVR continued to grow, but it was disbanded in 1942 when Singapore fell to the Japanese. Following the return of the British colonial government the Singapore Volunteer Police Reserve was revived in October of 1946, with between 100 and 150 former members, and was renamed the Special Constabulary. The Special Constabulary was responsible for sentry work, guarding merchant areas, and performing mobile patrols. Members of the Special Constabulary were considered full-time employees, and worked eight hours a day and were paid salaries of S$45 or approximately US$36/£21 per month (Singapore Police Force, n.d.; Volunteer Special Constabulary, 1998; Chia Yeong Jia, n.d.). In 1946 the Special Constabulary was divided into two units with different responsibilities: the Active Unit (also known as the Extra Constabulary), made up of full-time paid officers; and the Reserve Unit (also known as the Volunteer Special Constabulary), which was made up of part-time, volunteer, unpaid officers. Members of the VSC were trained in firearms, and were responsible for one four-hour patrol duty every week (Volunteer Special Constabulary, 1998; Chia Yeong Jia, n.d.).

In December of 1950 the Maria Hertogh racial and religious riots broke out, in which eight individuals were killed and over 130 injured in a week of disturbances. The VSC provided over 11,500 hours of volunteer service during the rioting, and made several noteworthy arrests, including a suspect of a grenade attack on a restaurant. Following the riots the strength of the VSC rose to an unprecedented high of 2,293 officers in 1951. The VSC was tested again with riots in 1955, when the Hock Lee bus riots resulted in the death of VSC Andrew Teo (Volunteer Special Constabulary, 1998; Chia Yeong Jia, n.d.). More riots in 1956 led to further tests of the VSC and an eventual calm through 1967, when the VSC was again reorganized.

In response to what was considered to be a small defense force, in 1967 compulsory national service was instituted, requiring citizens to participate in civil defense. This required all male Singaporean citizens to participate in the Singapore Armed Forces, the Singapore Police Force, or the Singapore Civil Defense Force. The VSC merged with the first recruit class of over 2,000 part-time national service police to form the Special Constabulary (SC). Members of the VSC were called Special Constabulary (Volunteers), or SC(V), while those serving national service were called

Photo 11 The Volunteer Special Constabulary of Singapore is an instrumental part of policing in Singapore

Special Constabulary (National Servicemen), or SC(NS). Members of the SC(V) were called upon to train the SC(NS).

However, the reorganization created a rift between those who served as volunteers and those who were "forced" to serve. "The SC(NS) officers viewed the enthusiastic SC(V) officers with cynicism while the volunteers became disillusioned with their NS colleagues who were generally reluctant to serve. Consequently a number of SC(V) officers resigned. From an average of 300 volunteers on duty per night in 1967, only 110 were left by 1973" (Volunteer Special Constabulary, 1998, p. 17). In 1981 the Special Constabulary was separated from the Volunteer Special Constabulary, and women were also recruited to volunteer. In 1985 VSC members were deployed for duty with the Police Coast Guard (formerly known as the Marine Police).

In October of 1993 official integration of the VSC into the Singapore Police Force began. This included a shift in the roles and responsibilities of the members of the VSC to more closely align them with their counterparts in regular service. In 1997 a unique arrangement was formed with Singapore schools when the Honorary Volunteer Special Constabulary program was begun. The program trains school employees as police officers to fight and prevent crime in the school system (Volunteer Special Constabulary, 1998; Chia Yeong Jia, n.d.).

Throughout the history of the volunteer constabulary, VSC officers wore the letter "V" on their uniforms to distinguish them from the regular officers. There is no difference today in the uniform of the VSC officers from that of regular police officers (Volunteer Special Constabulary,

1998). The VSC currently is staffed with approximately 1,200 volunteer officers, who may remain in active service as long as medically fit, up to the age of 50 for officer ranks, up to the age of 55 for senior officers. VSC officers receive an hourly allowance of S$3.60 (approximately US$2.88/£1.71) to offset expenses, regardless of rank. VSC members work throughout policing in Singapore, including neighborhood policing centers, and patrol the streets in patrol vehicles (see Photo 11) and take part in surveillance and other plainclothes operations (Koo & Tan, 2017).

Phuket Tourist Police Volunteers, Thailand

There are two types of police volunteers in Thailand: the Auxiliary Police Volunteers and the Immigration Police Volunteers. Often used to serve as translators between tourists and the police, Phuket Tourist Police Volunteers assist the regular police in interactions with foreign visitors. Police volunteers must purchase their own uniform, which is distinct from that of regular police officers, and includes a white polo shirt with an embroidered logo of the Auxiliary Police, dark navy pants, and a baseball-style hat. Volunteers must purchase and wear a duty belt, flashlight, and radio, but may also opt to carry pepper spray, handcuffs, and a baton (Phuket Tourist Police Volunteers, n.d.).

The Phuket Tourist Police Volunteers assist tourists in their travels, and promote the travel industry of Thailand. They provide educational information to tourists, and also serve as translators when the police are needed; they are also used to provide tourists with information related to Thai law when it is needed in a criminal case. They are also used as the eyes and ears of the police, but are not authorized to take law enforcement action and do not have the power of arrest. However, Thai auxiliary police have been used to stop bar fights and apprehend thieves if they have approval from a supervising Thai officer (Forgan, 2014).

Applicants for the Phuket Tourist Police Volunteers must hold a non-immigrant "B" or "O" visa, indicating that they are eligible to work or conduct business in Thailand. Additionally, applicants must be a high school graduate or equivalent, and have near fluency in the Thai language and at least one other additional language among other requirements.

Police Volunteer Reserve, Malaysia

As in many Asian countries, the auxiliary police of Malaysia are not volunteer police. Auxiliary police are paid and sworn security police in Malaysia, and are more similar to private security officers in the United States than to voluntary police organizations. Malaysian auxiliary police are authorized to carry firearms, but are largely privatized and authorized by statute to have certain police powers, including the power to make arrests and carry out minor investigations.

However, the Police Volunteer Reserve (PVR; Malay: Sukarelawan Polis) is a supporting unit of the Royal Malaysian Police Force utilizing volunteers. Members of the PVR have the same duties and powers as full-time police officers in Malaysia, including the authority to carry a firearm and to make arrests. There were approximately 1,200 members of the PVR in 2014, providing services in patrol, criminal investigations, and traffic. Malaysian PVR members must be full-time employees in Malaysia between the ages of 18 and 45; males must be at least 5 feet 4 inches tall and women must be at least 4 feet 11 inches tall. While PVR officers serve voluntarily, they are paid a small hourly stipend and an annual honorarium for providing certain levels of annual service (*Borneo Post*, 2014; Malaysian Times, 2013). The stipend is paid hourly, but only for the first 96 hours per month. After that, all time is completely voluntary.

All PVR members must receive standard police training of approximately six months in length, and must participate in regular annual local training throughout their service. When participating in training, however, members of the PVR are authorized to receive salary and allowances equal to the pay received by a full-time police officer of equivalent rank. Members of the PVR work on special details with their full-time counterparts and serve on patrols in residential areas, particularly high-crime areas. They also serve as the "eyes and ears" of the regular police and provide local information to assist in criminal investigations.

South African Reserve Police Service

The history of volunteer policing in its present format is relatively new and aligned to the South African Police Service (SAPS) and the Interim Constitution of the Republic of South Africa (Act 200 of 1993). There are two categories of reservist: category 1 is "Functional Policing," for which successful candidates undertake policing functions at station level and other areas as required. As in the United Kingdom, these reserves work in the area of community safety and function under the supervision of a regular officer or a reservist who has a minimum of three years' service. The second category of reservist, "Specialized Operational Support," has particular skills that can be utilized by SAPS, may or may not be uniformed, and is trained to ensure that the reserve adheres to "relevant legal aspects, policy and instructions applicable to his or her specific functions" (South African Police Service, 2014). As in England and Wales, reservists are required to give at least 16 hours each month to their particular sector, but, while applicants in the United Kingdom are required only to have the legal right to reside within the county, South African applicants must be born in the country. Former full-time members of

SAPS are particularly encouraged to become reservists upon leaving the service.

Like the United Kingdom's special constables, South African reservists are perceived to be fundamental to their communities and policing of same, and so are provided an opportunity for community members to become involved in the policing of their neighborhoods without becoming full-time members of SAPS (Civilian Secretariat for Police Service, n.d.).

Members of the SAPS reserves serve under the command of the national commissioner, in line with regular officers. The ownership of firearms is permitted in South Africa in a number of circumstances, one of which is under Firearms Control Act (FCA) regulations §2–12, which permit members of relevant government institutions to carry guns (Library of Congress, 2015). Unlike in England and Wales but in common with states within the United States, reservists may be permitted to carry guns subject to appropriate permissions and training. Reservists are viewed as being supportive of the regular force, particularly with regard to crime prevention. A significant variation from policing in England and Wales is that, in South Africa, reservists are on duty *only* when required by the service. At all other times they are not regarded as being on duty unless a reservist happens upon an incident either en route to or from his or her scheduled duty. Reservists are therefore only warranted as police officers during their duty hours.

Conclusion

Although this chapter has focused on some interesting para-policing units throughout the world that may or may not be considered volunteer policing units by the definitions provided in this text, there are also many other similar programs throughout the world that should be identified. While several American policing examples were provided, there are thousands of different volunteer policing units in the United States, and these examples are only a small snapshot of the work being done by volunteers in large and small communities. The City of London Special Constabulary was provided in this chapter as an example of the type of volunteer program within police services in the United Kingdom, but there are numerous examples of outstanding work provided by other constabularies as well.

Other examples of para-policing units throughout the world that may be of interest include the South Korean Auxiliary Police, the Royal Cayman Islands Police Service auxiliary and special constables, volunteer police in the Netherlands, the Royal Bahamas Police Force Reserves, Bermuda Reserve Police, and the Western Australia Police Auxiliary Officer program.

The South Korean Auxiliary Police consists of males between the ages of 18 and 35 who have not yet fulfilled obligatory military duty. Service in the Auxiliary Police is an acceptable alternative to the military mandatory service, and lasts 21 months. Auxiliary police in South Korea assist the national police with routine police activities, including traffic control and crowd control. The volunteer police in the Netherlands take their structure from the English model, and volunteers work alongside regular members of the Dutch police. However, regular police and police unions have been critical of volunteer police work, and their historically similar but paid police reserve program. Volunteer police in the Netherlands wear police uniforms and carry handcuffs, a truncheon, and defensive spray, and are not equipped with firearms, though regular police in the Netherlands are (Torn & Verbiest, 2017).

The Royal Bahamas Police Force first established a Police Reserve in June of 1965, and it is still being utilized today, with some 1,000 men and women serving as police reservists in the Bahamas (Maura, 2011). The Royal Cayman Islands Police Service utilizes volunteer special constables who have full police powers and wear a similar uniform to full time police. They also use auxiliary constables who wear the same uniform as specials but work within the court system. Western Australia utilizes police auxiliary officers in protective services, custody support, and property management, who may have select policing power while on duty, and may include the power to stop, search, and detain as well as carry and use a firearm. However, Western Australia police auxiliary officers are not volunteers; they are paid for their services.

Note

1 Toy drives are community events at which donations of toys are collected, usually around significant holidays, for children who may be in foster homes or orphanages, or in families that do not have the financial means to purchase them.

References

Albrecht, J. (2017). Abundance of auxiliary police and volunteer personnel in the NYPD. In J. Albrecht (Ed.), *Police reserves and volunteers: Enhancing organizational effectiveness and public trust*, pp. 51–56. Boca Raton, FL: CRC Press.

Bermuda Online (n.d.). Welcome to Bermuda. Retrieved March 13, 2015, from www.bermuda-online.org/abcbda3.htm.

Bermuda Police Service (n.d.). Making Bermuda safer. Retrieved March 13, 2015, from www.police.bm/content/reserve-history.

Borneo Post (2014, June 25). Interested to join police volunteer reserve? Retrieved September 1, 2016, from www.theborneopost.com/2014/06/25/interested-to-join-police-volunteer-reserve.

Chia Yeong Jia, J. (n.d.). Volunteer Special Constabulary. Singapore Infopedia, National Library of Singapore. Retrieved May 7, 2014, from http://eresources. nlb.gov.sg/infopedia/articles/SIP_1141_2010-05-07.html?s=volunteer%20 special%20constabulary.

City of London Police (2011). *City of London Special Constabulary*. London: City of London Police.

City of London Police (2017, December 11). Specials. Retrieved September 3, 2017, from www.cityoflondon.police.uk/careers/specials/Pages/default.aspx.

Civil Self-Defense Organizations of Budapest (n.d.). Budapest and agglomeration civilian guard. Retrieved March 13, 2015, from www.bpsz.hu/?page_id=32.

Civilian Secretariat for Police Service (n.d.). *South African Reserve Police Service: Policy framework and guidelines: Establishment and functioning*. Pretoria: Civilian Secretariat for Police Service. Retrieved January 20, 2017, from www. policesecretariat.gov.za/downloads/policies/reservists_policy.pdf.

Clifton, K. (n.d.). Hugh Lewis: Commandant Bermuda Reserve Police. ClubRunner. Retrieved March 13, 2015, from http://portal.clubrunner.ca/ 2044/Stories/hugh-lewis-commandant-bermuda-reserve-police.

Department of Justice and Equality (2016, February 20). Garda Síochána Reserve: Minister outlines Garda commissioner's proposal. Retrieved August 25, 2016, from http://justice.ie/en/JELR/Pages/PR07000880.

Fanfair, R. (2016, October 28). Auxiliary celebrates 60 years. Toronto Police Service News. Retrieved January 12, 2018, from http://tpsnews.ca/stories/ 2016/10/auxiliary-celebrates-60-years.

Flintoff, C. (2014, February 22). Russia's Cossacks ride back from history as "patriots." National Public Radio. Retrieved August 24, 2016, from www.npr.org/ 2014/02/22/280964932/back-from-history-russias-cossacks-ride-as-patriots.

Forgan, D. (2014, July 4). A night out with the foreign tourist police in Thailand's seediest city. Vice.com. Retrieved August 31, 2016, from www.vice.com/en_uk/ read/a-night-out-with-the-foreign-tourist-police-in-thailands-seediest-city-704.

Garda Síochána (n.d.). Garda Reserve. Retrieved March 11, 2015, from http:// garda.ie/Controller.aspx?Page=165&Lang=1.

Garrison, J. (2003, October 23). LAPD has protection in reserve. *The Los Angeles Times*. Retrieved February 9, 2015, from http://articles.latimes.com/2003/oct/ 23/local/me-reserves23.

Gill, M. L., & Mawby, R. I. (1990). *A special constable: A study of the police reserve*. Aldershot, UK: Avebury Publishing.

Greenberg, M. A. (1984). *Auxiliary police: The citizen's approach to public safety*. Westport, CT: Greenwood Press.

Greenberg, M. A. (2005). *Citizens defending America: From colonial times to the age of terrorism*. Pittsburgh: University of Pittsburgh Press.

History Magazine (2001). The Cossacks. *History Magazine* (October/November). Retrieved January 12, 2018, from www.history-magazine.com/cossacks.html.

Information Services Department, Hong Kong Special Administrative Region Government (2017, July). The police. Retrieved January 12, 2018, from www. gov.hk/en/about/abouthk/factsheets/docs/police.pdf.

Israel Police (n.d.). Structure. Retrieved March 10, 2015, from www.police.gov.il/ english_contentPage.aspx?pid=4&menuid=5.

Jewish Telegraphic Agency (1994, November 30). Behind the headlines: Olim join Israeli Civil Guard to help bridge culture gaps. Retrieved March 10, 2015, from www.jta.org/1994/11/30/archive/behind-the-headlines-olim-join-israeli-civil-guard-to-help-bridge-culture-gaps.

Johnson, M. S., Bonner, M., & Hanser, R. D. (2017). "Doing more with less": The professional model of the Los Angeles Police Department. In J. Albrecht (Ed.), *Police reserves and volunteers: Enhancing organizational effectiveness and public trust*, pp. 101–112. Boca Raton, FL: CRC Press.

Kardos, P., & Szoke, B. (2017). Auxiliary police in Hungary. In J. Albrecht (Ed.), *Police reserves and volunteers: Enhancing organizational effectiveness and public trust*, pp. 137–142. Boca Raton, FL: CRC Press.

Kelly, R. W., Grasso, G. A., Esposito, J. J., Giannelli, R. J., & Maroulis, A. J. (2008). *Auxiliary Police Program Overview 2008*. New York: New York City Police Department Auxiliary.

Koo, W., & Tan, D. (2017). Effectively using police volunteers in the "little red dot" Singapore. In J. Albrecht (Ed.), *Police reserves and volunteers: Enhancing organizational effectiveness and public trust*, pp. 181–194. Boca Raton, FL: CRC Press.

Lam, C. B. (1997). *Looking back with pride and glory*. Hong Kong: Hong Kong Auxiliary Police Force.

Library of Congress (2015, July 30). Firearms-control legislation and policy: South Africa. Retrieved January 22, 2017, from www.loc.gov/law/help/firearms-control/southafrica.php#t29.

Luhn, A. (2014, February 21). The Sochi soldiers: Morality police or outdated vigilantes? A look at the Cossacks patrolling the games – and whipping Pussy Riot activists. *The Independent*. Retrieved August 24, 2016, from www.independent.co.uk/news/world/europe/the-sochi-soldiers-morality-police-or-outdated-vigilantes-a-look-at-the-cossacks-patrolling-the-9145387.html.

Lynott, L. (2016, July 23). Garda reserve numbers drop 26 per cent in two years, figures show. *Irish Mirror*. Retrieved August 25, 2016, from www.irishmirror.ie/news/irish-news/crime/garda-reserve-numbers-drop-26-8477875.

Malaysian Times (2013, January 10). Volunteers hand-in-hand with police officers. Retrieved September 1, 2016, from www.themalaysiantimes.com.my/volunteers-hand-in-hand-with-police-officers.

Matrix (n.d.). What is the Matrix police ANPR system? Retrieved March 13, 2015, from www.anpr.hu/matrix-police.

Maura, M. (2011, August 10). Ranks of Police Reserves to be increased. BahamasNational.com. Retrieved September 3, 2017, from http://bahamasnational.com/?q=node/977.

Metropolitan Police (n.d.). Employer supported policing (ESP). Retrieved September 3, 2017, from www.met.police.uk/esp.

Moscow Times (2015, December 1). Cossack volunteers to guard Moscow's Arbat Street. Retrieved August 24, 2016, from https://themoscowtimes.com/news/cossack-volunteers-to-guard-moscows-arbat-street-51012.

Palamarchuk, A. (2013, November 14). Veteran auxiliary police officer Hayward has served for 56 years. InsideToronto.com. Retrieved August 25, 2016, from www.insidetoronto.com/news-story/4207800-veteran-auxiliary-police-officer-hayward-has-served-for-56-years.

Palamarchuk, A. (2014, December 1). Kennedy Road BOA members donate cash and toys to Toronto police holiday food drive. InsideToronto.com. Retrieved August 25, 2016, from www.insidetoronto.com/news-story/5164631-kennedy-road-bia-members-donate-cash-and-toys-to-toronto-police-holiday-toy-drive.

Phuket Tourist Police Volunteers (n.d.). Join our team. Retrieved from www.phuket-tourist-police-volunteers.com/join.html.

Police Services Act (Ontario) (2015). Section 52 (1): Auxiliary members of municipal police force. Retrieved September 3, 2017, from www.ontario.ca/laws/statute/90p15#BK75.

Raidió Teilifís Éireann (2015, February 20). Garda Reserves to receive greater powers. Retrieved August 31, 2016, from www.rte.ie/news/2015/0219/681492-garda-reserve.

Seddon, M. (2012, November 27). Russia's Cossacks start patrolling Moscow streets. *The Washington Times*. Retrieved August 24, 2016, from www.washingtontimes.com/news/2012/nov/27/kremlin-tests-cossacks-as-an-auxiliary-police-forc.

Selih, A., & Zavrsnik, A. (2012). *Crime and transition in central and eastern Europe*. New York: Springer.

Seth, R. (2006). *The specials*. Trowbridge, UK: Cromwell Press.

Singapore Police Force (n.d.). A member of the home team. Retrieved May 7, 2014, from www.spf.gov.sg/about/org/vsc.html#vsc.

South African Police Service (2014). How to become a reservist. Retrieved January 20, 2017, from www.saps.gov.za/services/reservist.php.

Torn, P., & Verbiest, R. (2017). Reserve Police Force in the Netherlands: From a "reserve" to a "volunteer" police force. In J. Albrecht (Ed.), *Police reserves and volunteers: Enhancing organizational effectiveness and public trust*, pp. 171–180. Boca Raton, FL: CRC Press.

Toronto Police Service (n.d. – a). Frequently asked questions. Retrieved August 25, 2016, from www.torontopolice.on.ca/careers/aux_faq.php.

Toronto Police Service (n.d. – b). Toronto Police Auxiliary. Retrieved August 25, 2016, from www.torontopolice.on.ca/community/auxiliary.php.

Volunteer Special Constabulary (1998). *Service to the nation: 50 years of the Volunteer Special Constabulary*. Singapore: Volunteer Special Constabulary.

Wolf, R. (2014). The Orange County (Florida) Sheriff's Office Reserve Unit. *Special Impact* (16), 12–13.

Wolf, R., & Beary, K. (2010). The Orange County Sheriff's Office Reserve Unit: A strong, cohesive volunteer unit able to handle multiple functions. *Deputy and Court Officer*, 2(2), 26–30.

World Police (n.d.). Israel Police and auxiliary. Retrieved March 10, 2015, from http://world-police.com/?page_id=142.

Chapter 9

What the Future Holds for Volunteer Policing

Throughout this book we have identified and explored volunteer policing in the United States and the United Kingdom with particular emphasis on England and Wales. During the course of this review we have endeavored to identify similarities and differences both between the three nations as well as variances between American jurisdictions, and provide insight into the many different ways that volunteer police are used around the globe. There is such great diversity in volunteer policing programs in the United States that it is a nearly impossible task, however, to make direct comparisons between the United States and anywhere else, programs within the United States, or even within the same state. As identified earlier in this text, what one state calls an auxiliary police officer another state would call a citizen on patrol; what one state authorizes in terms of volunteer police powers and authority is completely unsuitable for volunteers in other states. This variation in the ways that volunteers are utilized in the United States has become a source both of pride and of concern.

The principles of policing and volunteering alike have been addressed in this book and shown to have progressed in waves, with volunteering increasing during periods of greater need, such as during wars and natural disasters, and most recently the growth of cybercrime and the dangers from extremism and terrorism. In the latter part of the second decade in the twenty-first century global economic concerns[1] have led to a tightening of budgets and a constriction of services, particularly in the public sector. This has, in turn, caused growing pressures on the policing sector in both the United States and the United Kingdom, in varying ways, and the future of volunteer policing may rely on the response to these political and economic threats.

The Future of Volunteer Policing in the United States

Local Control versus National Concerns

Police chiefs and sheriffs who utilize volunteers are often quick to point out that they have shaped their volunteer programs in the way that their communities support. Some localities and police agencies are encouraging of volunteers who have police authority, while others are concerned that providing volunteers with police training and authority creates potential safety, employment, and control concerns. Heavily unionized states often react to volunteer policing with the disdain of a striking worker to someone who crosses a picket line. In these states it is likely that volunteer police have very little authority or training; in fact, some police departments do not utilize reserve or auxiliary officers, as their union contracts specifically prohibit the use of volunteers with police powers (Bartels, 2013).

The circumstances involving Robert Bates in Tulsa, Oklahoma, in April of 2015 (which were discussed earlier in this book) have also created some concern for the future of volunteer policing throughout the United States. Not only was Mr. Bates sentenced to four years in prison after the guilty finding of manslaughter in the case of his mistaken use of a firearm that he thought was his Taser, but the sheriff of Tulsa was criminally indicted, and resigned because of the incident. A grand jury indicted Sheriff Stanley Glanz on misdemeanor charges, including unlawfully withholding e-mails related to requests for the release of internal investigations regarding the Tulsa Reserve Deputy program. Nearly one year later Glanz pled guilty to willful violation of the law, and pled no contest to refusal to perform an official duty[2] for failing to turn over a report on the 2009 investigation of favoritism regarding Bates to the press (Killman, 2016). The sheriff's office in this case, as in other examples throughout the past, has been plagued with criticism that its reserve or volunteer policing units are *pay-to-play*[3] programs that allow political supporters to perform law enforcement functions. In the Tulsa incident, the sheriff had been accused of allowing Bates to continue to participate as a volunteer officer even though he did not complete the required training, because Bates was a friend of Glanz and because Bates had made donations to the agency (Krehbiel-Burton & Pérez-Peña, 2015).

The Tulsa incident has rightfully caused many law enforcement agencies in the United States to review their policies and procedures regarding volunteer policing programs, but has also caused some police leaders to reconsider their level of involvement in volunteer policing, or the possibility of withdrawing from it altogether. The incident has also caused the US Commission on Accreditation for Law Enforcement Agencies (CALEA), a non-regulatory credentialing private organization, to require all accredited agencies to change their practices with regard to sworn police volunteers. Since April 1, 2017, CALEA has no longer accredited police agencies that have "levels" of sworn reserve officers; all reserves must have the same training required of full-time police personnel. CALEA requires this of their accredited agencies, even if state law allows otherwise, as in California and Florida (Commission on Accreditation for

Law Enforcement Agencies, 2017). Agencies in the United States are not required to hold accreditation, and many agencies and researchers have questioned whether the expensive routine of the accreditation process actually helps them avoid litigation or increases their community trust (Hougland & Wolf, 2016). How this will affect volunteer policing in the long term remains to be seen. Some police and sheriffs agencies with current CALEA accreditation have threatened to leave CALEA because of this and other requirements (in addition to the financial burden of accreditation), but others feel that this move will increase professionalism among volunteer police officers and is a move in the right direction. It should be noted, however, that most law enforcement agencies that utilize volunteers in the United States will not be concerned with the accreditation requirements of CALEA,[4] and will likely just ignore the requirements (Hougland & Wolf, 2016).

If they are adopted by accredited agencies, however, the CALEA restrictions may create significant hardship for agencies that count on the volunteer time and community linkages that are provided by less than fully certified law enforcement volunteers. An example of this would be the Florida Highway Patrol Auxiliary (FHPA). The Florida Highway Patrol (FHP) is a CALEA-accredited agency, and the significant restrictions that the new CALEA regulations place on auxiliary-certified volunteers may make it impossible for FHP to continue operating its volunteer program. The FHPA already reports a downward spiral in membership strength, from a high in the 1970s of more than 1,000 members to a current strength of fewer than 300 auxiliaries. Sheffer (2017) reported that part of this decline may be due to the increasing training requirements for volunteer policing in Florida.[5]

The National Sheriffs' Association Reserve Law Enforcement Subcommittee of the Outreach Committee has also reacted to the Tulsa incident. The committee has been working on proposing standardized recommendations for sheriff's departments and offices that utilize reserve deputies. The roadblock that the situation has created has a familiar theme: there are far too many diverse ways of dealing with volunteer sworn officers throughout the United States to be able to develop one single recommended policy that will work in all jurisdictions, in all states, and for all elected sheriffs. The International Association of Chiefs of Police has also struggled to find a way to address volunteer policing. Through various articles in its magazine *The Police Chief*, the IACP has addressed the leadership, organization, training, and functions of police reserves; but the bottom line is the same: there are too many varied ways of implementing these programs currently. At least one article has suggested that there needs to be standardization, at least in what volunteer police are called based on their functions (Wolf, Albrecht, & Dobrin, 2015), recommending that, because of the variation throughout the country and because of the varied roles and levels of training, it would be better to identify common tiered categories for police volunteer resources (see also Albrecht, 2017):

Level 1 – police agency volunteer (unarmed)/no arrest or law enforcement authority: this would include those with very minimal or no police training, who are uniformed or non-uniformed personnel, and who assist the agency with administrative duties, public relations events, minor traffic control duties, or other non-law enforcement functions.

Level 2 – community patrol (unarmed)/no arrest or law enforcement authority: this would include those with some level of documented training, who are uniformed or non-uniformed personnel who perform patrol activities and act as the "eyes and ears" of their policing agency. This level of personnel would not have any type of law enforcement function or authority granted.

Level 3 – police patrol (unarmed)/some law enforcement powers: this would include those with partial to moderate levels of documented training, who are uniformed or non-uniformed personnel, who perform patrol activities and act as the "eyes and ears" of their policing agency, but have some type of law enforcement function or authority. This might include the ability to issue parking citations, write simple police reports, or similar functions.

Level 4 – sworn volunteers (armed)/most law enforcement powers: this would include those with a significant amount of documented training who are uniformed or non-uniformed personnel who provide, or can provide, a law enforcement function. Their law enforcement authority or functions may be limited. For example, this might include individuals who have no authority to work alone or to take police action while off duty.

Level 5 – sworn volunteers (armed)/all law enforcement powers: this would include those who are uniformed or non-uniformed personnel who serve in a capacity equal to that of a full-time, career law enforcement officer. These individuals are not limited in their authority or responsibility and follow the same regulations, and have the same training, as full-time law enforcement personnel.

(Wolf et al., 2015, p. 47)

A national model, such as the one described above, would allow local police and county sheriffs' offices to maintain local control over what they want volunteer police to be able to do, but would also create a nationwide terminology for when discussing the authority and powers of those who serve in the various "levels." If the United States moves toward nationwide standardization, this model would allow for specific training requirements based on the job functions that are authorized by state law.

Selection

The prerequisites for serving as a volunteer police officer in the United States vary at least as much as the level(s) of training required. The same is true for full-time policing. Most states require that full-time police have completed a high school education, though August Vollmer advocated as early as 1916 that, if police have higher education,[6] very few police agencies require it. While there have been studies that have pointed to the positive effect that a college degree can have on critical decision-making skills, positive attitude, less authoritarian behavior, and being more accepting of other ethnicities (Carter & Sapp, 1990; Weiner, 1976; Dalley, 1975), there have also been studies that showed that college-educated officers were less satisfied with working in policing, and can be more cynical about their role (Hudzik, 1978; Regoli, 1976; Lefkowitz, 1974). Lastly, there have been studies which indicate that college-educated officers were no different from those with less education when it came to professionalism and job satisfaction (Miller & Fry, 1976).

Even in light of the fact that requirements for employment as police officers in the United States have barely increased in the last 100 years,[7] there has been significant movement in getting higher-educated officers into the field. Hilal & Densley (2013) found that 48 percent of the 964 officers in their study in Minnesota[8] and Arizona held at least a four-year degree, and 54 percent of their study respondents indicated that they had achieved college credits since beginning their law enforcement career. Paoline et al. (2015) found that, of the seven police agencies utilized for their study,[9] none required a four-year degree, but 45 percent of the 2,109 officers in their study voluntarily held bachelor's degrees or higher, and most of these had been received before they started in their policing career.

For those American agencies that aspire to or that do hold CALEA accreditation, volunteer police with at least partial law enforcement authority are required to have the same educational minimum standards as their full-time counterparts.[10] However, most states (and therefore most agencies) do not have any educational standards required for volunteer police. While full-time officers may voluntary earn college degrees in order to be competitive applicants for their positions or in order to increase their chances at promotion (Hilal & Densley, 2013), volunteers may not have the same concerns. Volunteers who serve in policing come from all public and private careers, including mechanics, lawyers, ministers, teachers, school administrators, business owners, firefighters, accountants and airline pilots, and therefore have all levels of formal education, and many hold graduate degrees. Certainly, the requirement to maintain the same minimal educational standards for the selection of volunteer officers as full-time applicants is a positive step in keeping up the professionalism of reserve and auxiliary units throughout the country.

However, is there a negative impact from higher education requirements on certain demographics? If an agency wants to select individuals for what was earlier described as a level 3 volunteer, could a requirement for a high school education keep an important part of the community from getting involved, particularly in lower socio-economic jurisdictions? The US Equal Employment Opportunity Commission (2016) recommends that policing agencies build partnerships with educational institutions to provide internships and a pipeline of potential minority applicants who will have college degrees. These partnerships may also help to address the historically negative perceptions that minority individuals may have of the police (US Equal Employment Opportunity Commission, 2016).[11] It is impossible to know what increased educational requirements would do if applied to volunteer policing. Very little is known about volunteer police demographics in the United States (see Dobrin & Wolf, 2016). In fact, recent research into volunteer policing in American sheriffs' offices indicates that minorities may be even more under-represented in volunteer policing than they are amongst regular police. In that study, respondents were almost entirely male (92 percent), and almost entirely white (89 percent), while whites represent approximately 80 percent of sheriffs' deputies nationwide (Wolf, Holmes, & Jones, 2016).

Training

Policing in the United States is under intense scrutiny. This scrutiny seems to ebb and flow, but, as we approach 2020, the police (which may include anyone related to government-organized policing, including volunteer reserve and auxiliary programs and even neighborhood watch programs) have seemingly never been under such an intense microscope.[12] Almost half the nation's nearly 18,000 law enforcement agencies have fewer than ten officers, and many states do not have specific requirements on initial training or annual retraining. Of those states that do, there is great variation. There is a great discrepancy not only in the amount of requisite training between police agencies but in pre-employment requirements, background checks, minimum standards, and – for full-time, paid police (maybe most importantly) – in pay.[13] Reforms to training requirements are being discussed at the national level, but not without controversy. While a source of American pride can sometimes be the decentralization of government, it is this same decentralization that is creating conflict for a national standard for training for regular police. One example can be found in the "Guiding Principles on Use of Force," developed in the hopes of creating national standards related to police use of force by the Police Executive Research Forum (PERF), a Washington, DC, nonprofit organization. This document intended to impact the way that the police response to force in the United States is conveyed to police personnel in training, but it has been met with significant resistance from police leadership throughout the country (O'Linn, 2016). If the police leadership cannot agree on an appropriate direction for training that is as important to the profession as is police use of force, it stands to reason that there is very little likelihood that there can be a national agreement on the training required for volunteer police officers.

Training also comes with a price. The immense cost of providing additional mandatory training is a contradictory argument used by many underfunded police agencies regarding standardized police training, but is also a concern for volunteer police units. As mentioned earlier in this book, volunteers may work for free, but that does not mean that they come without cost to the agency. It can be appealing for potential volunteers to learn that they can volunteer to serve as a police officer with only a couple of weeks of training, while another agency might require months and months of academy training followed by a year or more of on-the-job training. But what recruits cannot realize is that the highest level of training possible would actually lead to a more professional organization, increased trust by the community, and – possibly most importantly – a decrease in the chance that the volunteer will be sued, especially for acting improperly in a law enforcement capacity.[14]

Use of Prior Full-Time Personnel as Volunteer Police

A major difference between UK and US volunteer policing is the ready use of former full-time officers by some agencies in the United States. This happens at retirement, or after a career change, and the "corporate knowledge" of the individual officer that otherwise may be lost is utilized by the agency. This role is not limited to uniformed patrol. Many agencies have allowed former full-time officers who continue as reserve officers to continue to serve as field training officers, academy instructors, detectives and investigators, or school resource officers. As discussed in Chapter 7, a nationwide survey of sheriffs' offices indicated that 28 percent of the volunteer police respondents indicated that they had prior experience as a full-time law enforcement officer. Those who reported prior full-time experience as deputies or police officers had served an average of 12.7 years in that role (Wolf et al., 2016). The sample was limited in scope due to self-selection bias, but provides some insight into the utilization of those with prior service by law enforcement agencies. This is geographically limited in the United States. As discussed earlier, it is most common in the south and west United States, but is very unlikely to occur in the east and north (due to the aforementioned issue with police unions).

One example of the possible utilization of former full-time personnel can be seen in reviewing what happened after September 11,

2001, with the New York City Police Department. The NYPD Auxiliary Police program, as described in several places earlier in this text, is a great supply of volunteer personnel to act as the eyes and ears of the police – but they do not have any law enforcement authority. Therefore, on 9/11, unlike agencies in other parts of the country, the NYPD did not have a formal method for retirees and former full-time officers to serve as a "ready reserve" of civilians with policing experience or police authority. After the terrorist attack on New York in 2001, the NYPD was inundated with calls from retired and former officers who wanted to assist in the efforts to bring normalcy back to the city. Unfortunately, much of this goodwill could not be put to use, because there was no strategic way to coordinate this effort and no pre-existing plan in place to do so (Mormino, 2001; Tobin, 2017). In 2005 the City of New York launched the Retiree Mobilization Plan (RMP), which uses a list of "actively retired" police to mobilize resources in the event of an emergency. While not a true reserve police program (the retirees do not have law enforcement authority), this step shows the value that former police officers can have for their agencies (Reuss, 2005), and allows retired members with special skill sets to volunteer their services during critical incidents.[15] Although there have been cities in the United States that have begun short-term programs to rehire retired officers[16] to full-time police positions, very few agencies in the northeast, specifically, have focused on the potential for the continual training and volunteer nature of sworn reserve programs.

There is hope in the federal government for developing legislation that could standardize at least some portions of volunteer policing in the United States. After years of debate throughout the United States on whether a police officer from one state could or should legally carry a firearm in another state, the federal government stepped in to create the Law Enforcement Officers Safety Act (LEOSA). This is a federal law that allows both qualified current law enforcement officers and qualified retired law enforcement officers to carry a concealed firearm anywhere in the United States (with some exceptions), regardless of and superseding all state laws.[17] There is a possibility that federal intervention might also help to standardize the capability of police agencies to utilize former/ retired officers as reserves, reducing the corporate "brain drain" that happens when a full-time officer leaves a position in good standing that might otherwise be able to be put to good use.

Annual Data on Volunteer Programs and Participants

The Bureau of Justice Statistics of the US Department of Justice currently collects data on all police and sheriffs' agencies throughout the United States. This data is collected through mandatory reporting, and is collated every few years through the Law Enforcement Management and Administrative Statistics (LEMAS) survey. LEMAS compiles data from all local law enforcement agencies that employ 100 or more sworn officers and from a nationally representative sample of smaller agencies. Only the number of unpaid reserve and auxiliary police in each participating agency is collected. Demographic data, such as education level, sex, and race, and data on unsworn volunteer police numbers are not collected or reported. The Uniform Crime Reporting system of the FBI also collects data on full-time paid employees of policing agencies, but does not collect any data on either part-time or volunteer officers. Additionally, nearly half the states in the United States that have volunteer police programs report that they do not keep any data or collect any information on them (Dobrin & Wolf, 2016). Current limitations on available data have made it impossible to calculate state-level and nationwide estimates of the economic impact that volunteer programs may have on local communities and government budgets.

It is imperative for the future of volunteer policing in the United States that a method of data collection and reporting be formalized at the national level, including the demographic information of participants and the level of training completed. The usefulness of the data would be increased by also capturing the amount of participation that volunteers provide to their program. The utilization of the previously mentioned "level" system of identifying the scope of responsibilities of the volunteers would also aid in the worth of this data. The collection of data that allows analysis of the utilization of volunteer police is also important. As discussed in this book, volunteer police are used in a variety of roles in addition to traditional patrol duties. Data which collects information on the extent to which volunteers are used in the investigation of crime, the service of warrants, in specialized units (such as marine patrol, mounted patrol, canine units, search and rescue teams, dive teams, etc.), driving under the influence checkpoints, school and youth programs, and other non-patrol activities would allow policing agencies to determine the usefulness of such programs in their jurisdiction.

The Future of Volunteer Policing in the United Kingdom

Compliance by most people with law and order is well decided, and, in early pronouncements such as Sir Robert Peel's 1829 "Principles of Law Enforcement," includes a dependence "upon public approval of police existence, actions, behavior and the ability of the police to secure and maintain public respect" (Peel, 1829). "Policing by consent" has been an important and long-standing principle of policing in England and Wales, so that confidence in the police service by the public is an important factor in the maintenance of law and order. In addition, crimes are frequently solved because of the cooperation and willingness of the public to pass on information to the police.

Jackson, Bradford, Hough, and Murray (2012) provided a detailed debate on police legitimacy and justice which relates to police/public confidence. The importance of confidence in the police continues to be an important element of the criminal justice system in England and Wales, and the public have been consistently surveyed through the Crime Survey for England and Wales (formerly the British Crime Survey) since 1981, in which the subject of confidence in the police is routinely addressed. While the question does not specifically mention SCs but, rather, police in general, there is much evidence to suggest that members of the public often have little or no knowledge of this volunteer category.

The State of Policing in the United Kingdom

The United Kingdom has not recently faced the same types of problems that US local police agencies have encountered with negative public perceptions.[18] However, adverse publicity against the police for shootings are rare in England and Wales, where armed police are not commonplace. The perceptions of crime and policing for most people are derived from the media, wherein newsworthiness and political mores steer the "interpretation" of the story (Reiner, 2002). In July 2017 government statistics indicated that, in spite of reductions in policing numbers, confidence in local policing had risen from 63 percent in 2005/6 to 78 percent in 2016/17 (Flatley, 2017). The press has endeavored to paint a much bleaker picture, however, by focusing on reductions in police numbers and increases in police firearm incidents. For example, news reports show that there are currently just over 123,000 police officers in England and Wales, which is a reduction of 20,500 full-time officers since 2010 (Hargreaves, Husband, & Linehan, 2017). Similarly, the number of special constables fell from 14,544 in 2008 to 13,503 in March 2017 (Hargreaves et al., 2017). The number of specialist armed police officers also fell during the same time period, from 6,796 in 2010 to 5,639 in 2016 (Mason & Walker, 2017; see also Bletchly, 2017). However, in August 2017 it was reported in the news that firearm-trained officers were on the increase in response to increases in firearms incidents (Jones & Rodger, 2017). As reported in March 2017: "There were ten incidents in which police firearms were discharged in the year ending 31 March 2017, up from seven incidents in the previous year" (Home Office, 2017).

This well-publicized picture shows a significant decline in police human capital, and puts the regular full-time police levels at their lowest since 1985. The news outlets have also focused on the effect the reduction in policing numbers has placed on full-time officers. One report indicates that this decrease in full-time officers has been exacerbated by the 47 percent increase in police officers who have taken time off from work for stress, anxiety, and depression since 2012 (Sutherland, 2017), and a reduction in police funding of 20 percent since 2011 while Her Majesty's Inspectorate of Constabulary (HMIC) has reported that there is a "national crisis" regarding the severe shortage of detectives and other investigators (Grierson, 2017).

Watch groups have warned that, if riots to the scale of those in 2011 were to occur in London today, the police would be ill-prepared to handle them. Amber Rudd, the British home secretary, has acknowledged that overextended resources for the police could not continue, especially in light of the terrorist attacks that occurred in London and Manchester in 2017. Vast police financial and personnel resources were required to respond to the mayhem, compelling forces to use budget reserves (Grierson, 2017). Unfortunately, statistics about police force strength and police funding is ultimately a political question – one which, according to media reports, put UK prime minister Theresa May on the defensive in June 2017 when talking about cuts to policing and the number of armed officers (Mason & Walker, 2017).

The future of regular policing is unclear in the United Kingdom. The media has continually fed the conversation with a call for more armed officers, more uniformed patrol officers, more investigators, and better budgets. While fewer than one in 20 police officers in England and Wales is armed (Northern Ireland, a part of the United Kingdom, does have an armed police force), and in spite of recent events, a study among Metropolitan police officers conducted in 2017 found that only 26 percent of the members of the police service felt that they should routinely carry firearms (Rathi, 2017; Walker, 2017). However, almost half (43.6 percent) of police officers in London responded to the same survey that they believe that there should be more firearm specialists (indicating that the number of firearm-trained police officers with the availability to respond to high-risk incidents should be increased), and 12 percent of the respondents to the survey said they never want to carry a firearm on duty (Walker, 2017).

The arming of police officers in England and Wales is a debate that has re-emerged recently, most routinely among members of the Metropolitan Police, who maintain law and order in a large and diverse area of the country including the London metropolitan area (but excluding the City of London).[19] The carrying and use of firearms in England and Wales is very different from the embodiment of the American policing style. As of March 31, 2017, for example, there were 6,278 authorised firearms officers (AFOs) in England and Wales. However, most of these are not routinely deployed readily armed but, rather, will be called upon to attend incidents in an armed response vehicle (Hargreaves et al., 2017). This figure equates to only one-fifth of all full-time police officers. That said, armed response officers are not generally deployed other than in specific, high-risk areas such as airports, seaports, and large crowd events. They are utilized only where they are deemed to be necessary. Only in extreme circumstances are such weapons drawn or, with even less frequency, fired. Police data from March 2017 showed that there were 15,705 police firearms incidents in the prior year, 84 percent of which were by armed response vehicles. Of this total, only ten incidents resulted in the discharge of a weapon (Home Office, 2017).

How the matter of future firearm training and increased numbers of AFOs will play out in the United Kingdom remains to be seen, and is dependent on numerous factors, including public perception, police funding, and the leadership of the UK police forces. How these issues will affect the way that special constables perform policing duties also remains to be seen. If the UK regular police were to move toward arming more police officers in response to national concerns (and this is by no means assured, based on prior surveys), will this affect the current status that no special constables may train as AFOs?

In a very limited fashion, police forces in the United Kingdom have already seen the advantages of utilizing special constables in non-traditional roles,[20] but will this continue to expand? Special constables are routinely assigned to help the regular police forces in times of need (after quelling riots, for example, or for major events such as the Olympics), but most of their duties "revolve around fairly unglamorous grunt work, pounding the beat in highly visible numbers, thus making the public feel safe" (Duerden, 2010), though individual forces do permit their SCs to train in specialist areas, as indicated earlier in this work.

The closest example in the United Kingdom in recent history when "volunteers" have been permitted to bear arms was in the case of badger culling in areas of England where some experts maintained that bovine tuberculosis (bTB) was being carried to cattle by badgers, and that culling (the killing of the animal) was the quickest and most efficient way of reducing the risk. In spite of questionable research (Carrington, 2016) regarding the relationship between bTB and badgers, local farmers in the United Kingdom who already held shotgun licenses were registered with five-year licenses to undertake the shooting of badgers as part of the government program (Department for Environment, Food and Rural Affairs, 2016). It has been reported that more than 14,000 badgers have been killed since the culling began in 2013. While these volunteers receive no police or government training per se, this is the only example found in the United Kingdom wherein someone, other than the police, have such authority to utilize firearms (Department for Environment, Food and Rural Affairs, 2016; see also Carrington, 2016).

Perceptions of and about Special Constables

Training for special constables in the United Kingdom is largely standardized, though their utilization is not. Regular UK police officers (similarly to their counterparts in some agencies in the United States) may view SCs as undertrained, amateur, and less professional. Although the Special Constabulary scheme in the United Kingdom relies on standardization, there are still force differences in how special constables are utilized, trained, or authorized to participate in law enforcement functions. One example is that certain forces do not allow special constables to be trained in or perform police driving functions. Other forces, however, do not have this same restriction, and SCs are authorized not only to drive police vehicles but to drive them in high-risk emergency situations.

A British police officer who writes under the pseudonym of Police Constable Ellie Bloggs wrote a book about her experiences as a regular police officer in 2007 called "Diary of an On-Call Girl." She also spoke to a reporter about special constables and the lack of respect that a special constable may receive from regular police in the United Kingdom. "Most of them [special constables] work just one day a week," PC Bloggs stated. "Not all police like them, no, it's true. Special Constables cannot follow cases through to court, for example, and so they cannot really help with investigations. And many Specials can't even take statements properly because they don't know how to. If you can't take a statement, then you don't fully understand the law" (Duerden, 2010).

In a 2016 qualitative study of special constables in London, many of the participants felt that there was a need for additional training (in this study, the focus was on first aid); they indicated that annual training was not enough, and that training every three or six months would better prepare them for dealing with emergency situations. Special constables in this study felt also that the presence of a second full-time police officer or volunteer special constable was a source of physical and emotional support (Chandan & Meakin, 2016). Other studies have shown that UK special constables are confident in their professional ability to handle issues at a policing scene, but less confident about interviewing and the administrative police paperwork (Wolf, Pepper, & Dobrin, 2017).

Research in 2014 by the Institute for Public Safety, Crime and Justice (IPSCJ) at the University of Northampton of special constables in Northamptonshire found that a key factor that motivates SCs to volunteer is that they desire to become full-time police officers in the future. In the past SCs who wanted to become regular officers found that, routinely, their experience as a volunteer was not taken into account when they applied to their chosen force. This situation has changed radically in recent years, however, and it is often the case that an applicant *must* become a special constable in the training process. The IPSCJ study found that those of a younger age were more likely to intend to move to a full-time post, and that this motivating factor may be a long-term problem for the Special Constabulary in maintaining personnel (Institute for Public Safety, Crime and Justice, 2014). This may also tend to lend itself to the perception that SCs are less professional than their counterparts in regular full-time service. Although specials may have individual skills, knowledge, and abilities that they bring to their role, many feel that these are wasted with a system that assigns tasks based on availability. Effective utilization of these skills, as discussed in the next section on cybercrime, could help police forces use specials more effectively (Institute for Public Safety, Crime and Justice, 2014).

Some special constables have noted concerns about the lack of proper equipment, and a failure of the police service to provide them with body-worn cameras (BWCs). From force to force, SCs are equipped according to the priorities and available funding of that force, so that, while some SCs will be provided with much of the equipment given to full-time officers, in other forces they may carry little with which to defend themselves or complete their assigned duties.

There have also been reports of specials leaving their volunteer positions because they do not feel respected by the police organization and that "the lack of help and support for the special constables is mind-boggling" (BBC, 2017). Certainly, not all special constables agree that there is a lack of respect for their volunteer role, but future research needs to delve into the disparate motivations, loyalty, and morale amongst individuals who serve.

Cybercrime

Previously held within the realm of full-time investigators and detectives, the area of cybercrime has now been opened to special constables. The then British home secretary, Theresa May, announced changes in 2016 that allow volunteers to work in computing or accountancy investigations for police forces. May stated that "we want to encourage those with skills in particular demand, such as those with specialist IT or accountancy skills, to work alongside police officers to investigate cyber or financial crime, and help officers and staff fight crime more widely" (Barrett, 2016). The Hampshire and Gloucestershire Constabularies were the first police forces in the United Kingdom to announce that they were using highly trained IT workers to support a 12-month pilot program of five special constables and five police support volunteers.[21] The Cyber Special Constable and Cyber Volunteers (CSCV) program may become a national model if the pilot scheme is successfully completed, but it has been met with criticism by some leaders in policing. Opponents feel that the government would be better served by providing training and resources for full-time paid personnel to fight the growing cybercrime problem.

Additional Issues Facing Volunteer Policing

The United States has seen an increase in demonstrations against police as well as ambush situations that have left law enforcement officers dead or injured over the past several years. This has been reflected in a concern that it will be more difficult to hire new officers and that current full-time police may decide to pursue other careers. This may also be reflected in the role of volunteer police. It is likely that those who volunteer to serve as police officers may be affected by negative social pressures to at least the same extent as those who get paid to serve in these positions.

The United Kingdom is facing pressures in policing as well, though they come from economic cutbacks rather than from attacks. According to the National Police Officers' Roll of Honour, between 2010 and July 2017 there were 42 deaths in the 43 police forces, but only one when the officer was killed as a result of a terrorist incident, and three in shootings (two of them in the same incident) (National Police Officers' Roll of Honour, n.d.). Only one special constable is listed since 2010, and that was as a result of an off-duty collision.

An increase in high-profile terrorist incidents against police in London and against civilians in Manchester[22] has left police officers either dead or gravely wounded (Tacopino, 2017; Sheth, Mark, & Edwards, 2017; Mills, 2017). The potential influence that this will have on those who serve as special constables remains to be seen. Will these incidents be an encouragement for more civic-minded community members to step forward to receive the training necessary to serve as a member of their Special Constabulary in light of the attacks, or will it function to discourage citizens from serving in a policing role?

While this book has sought to demonstrate the immense intrinsic value that volunteer police can provide to communities and policing agencies, it is nearly impossible to measure the actual fiscal value that a volunteer may save an agency. Many police agencies rely on hourly wage figures to multiply by the number of hours that their volunteers provide to develop a cost-saving figure. However, these estimates are largely inaccurate. An agency does not, for example, receive a true hourly cost saving when a volunteer police officer spends a day in a training class. While there may be additional costs for the agency in training the volunteers, the training class itself is not a cost saving for the budget. The saving is realized only when the volunteer works in a position that would otherwise be filled by a paid employee. The future for volunteer policing will need to include the development of cost-saving accounting measures, so that the true value of having volunteers can be understood by agency leaders (Dobrin & Wolf, 2016).

Off-Duty and Moonlighting Roles

Political (and fiscal) mores, along with increases in scope and opportunities for crime, have, in the last 20 years or so, seen a marked increase in specialisms in policing and a greater demand for policing in public/private spaces such as shopping malls, airports, and entertainment venues. However, it is the primary requirement of the management of these facilities to make profits for the shareholders (Bonnet, De Maillard, & Roché, 2015). In the United States, many full-time regular police officers participate in "off-duty" or "moonlighting" roles as police officers with the support of their police forces. Private companies, homeowner associations, shopping malls, and other venues pay police agencies to provide them with an assigned officer (or numerous assigned officers). The payment made to the police force (or even sometimes directly to the police officer, with a portion going to the agency for overhead costs) acquires a fully uniformed police officer, with all of his or her police authority and powers intact, to serve in an assigned area with a specific purpose (for example, watching out for possible car burglars, prosecuting shoplifters, providing security at a professional sporting event, etc.). Many police forces throughout the United States have these formal programs for providing extra police services when normal government-provided services may not meet the demand or perceived need, but not all police services allow this.

The Los Angeles Police Department, New York City Police Department, Orlando Police Department, Tempe Police (Arizona), and the Orange County Sheriff's Office (Florida) are among the police agencies in the United States that allow these services, and they have developed formal oversight programs for these "off-duty" services. While police officers for one of these departments may be working an assignment that is specific to the need of the organization or private company that is paying a fee for their use, they are still police officers and still have full police authority. Although many agencies in the United States allow and oversee off-duty work, some agencies in the United States do not authorize it. The Orange County Sheriff's Department in California, for example, does not allow its officers to work off duty. The agency feels, as has been reported for most agencies that do not allow the practice, that when a police officer works for another employer the lines between protecting the interests of the public and protecting the interests of a singular entity become gray, and may create ethical challenges (Jenkins, 2016).

Of particular interest to this book is the fact that there are some agencies in the United States that have taken the issue of off-duty police work one step further. Some agencies allow volunteer sworn police officers to receive pay for working in an off-duty capacity. This means that a private entity or organization may pay a fee to a local policing agency for additional police services, and someone who normally serves as a volunteer police officer may perform the required job functions and, most importantly, receive pay for his or her services. This adds an extra dimension to the volunteer police role. One of the many benefits that a full-time police officer may receive is the ability to work for extra money in an off-duty capacity. When retirement approaches, the ability to continue working for extra money jobs in exchange for providing minimal volunteer time to the agency may be very appealing. There are both positive and negative dimensions in this scenario: the police agency keeps hard-working employees as volunteers in exchange for the opportunity to work paying off-duty jobs when they are available; however, regular full-time personnel may see the volunteer police in their agency as "taking away" their opportunity for additional income if there are not enough off-duty positions to go around.

In English and Welsh forces, full-time officers can undertake paid employment during their free time and be paid by the hiring organization. As members of one of the 43 forces, their warranted status means that they have full powers of arrest at any time. Of course, they may "police" only private spaces, so as to alleviate the risk of conflicts of interest. SCs may similarly undertake such roles, and, as with full-time officers, they are paid directly by the hiring agency.

The utilization of part-time, paid, "volunteer" police is not a new concept globally. The Volunteer Special Constabulary of Singapore, the Hong Kong Auxiliary Police, and the Police Volunteer Reserve of Malaysia are all examples of "volunteer" police who receive pay for their specialized duties. The ability of a police force to provide remuneration for the service of part-time, well-trained personnel may be a significant factor in having a ready reserve in the case of planned large-scale public events, or unplanned natural or man-made disasters.

Earlier in this book we identified and discussed the trials and implementation of "payments" or bounties for SCs in individual police forces. In fact, the Special Constables Regulations of 1965 stated that, "except as provided in these Regulations, a special constable shall not be entitled to any remuneration in respect of his service as such" (Legislation.gov. uk, n.d., p. 2). However, in 2013 the United Kingdom considered introducing a £1,000 annual payment to special constables who met certain requirements. The news media represented the plan as not being received warmly, even by members of the Special Constabulary, who were credited with stating that they were worried that, if specials were to start receiving pay for their work, it might attract a different type of individual to the position (Beckfor Thed, 2013). The future of stipends, allowances, or honorariums for special constables in the United Kingdom, and of reserves and auxiliaries in the United States, remains to be seen.

New Technology and the Cost of Equipment

Police work in recent history required only certain limited tools. In the United States that consisted of a firearm, a set of handcuffs, a uniform, and a means to get around. In the United Kingdom it was even less extensive: handcuffs, a truncheon, and a uniform. In the past 50 years, however, there have been numerous and expensive items added to the policing kit in both the United States and the United Kingdom. A police radio (a marvel of modern communication equipment), a bullet-resistant vest in the United States, and a knife-resistant vest in the United Kingdom are expensive, but necessary, protective gear. But there are also laptops, specialty first aid equipment (including NARCAN®[23] and QuickClot Combat Gauze®[24] for many agencies in the United States), specialty weapons, electronic control devices (Tasers), and – the most recent item added to the officer's deployment – the body-worn camera.

While many police agencies are still in the process of acquiring BWCs, the true cost of purchasing and using them is not low. Not only does an agency need to select a platform and train officers on how to use them, there are costs associated with storing the data acquired, redacting information from files that have been requested by public information requests, and uploading for criminal prosecution purposes. While nearly every large police department in the United States has plans on deploying BWC devices in their agency, only 18 percent of the agencies that plan on using them have them "fully operational" (Maciag, 2016), and many have excluded volunteer police from their plans. Police leaders need to consider the function of volunteer police and the necessity of their participation in BWC programs. This is true in the United Kingdom as well, where many police forces deploy BWCs to full-time personnel, but not to special constables (West Yorkshire Disclosure Logs, 2016), while other police forces have been more inclusive, and have also been able to provide them to special constables (Compston, 2016).

Tasers are controversial when it comes to issuance to special constables in the United Kingdom, and also to volunteer police in the United States. In the United States, deployment to volunteer police is largely limited to those jurisdictions where volunteer police have law enforcement authority, and are armed. Arming a volunteer police officer with a Taser gives officers, just like their full-time counterparts, another tool to react properly to a given situation. However, Tasers are expensive, and the technology continues to change; this means that, even when an agency has deployed the device to all of their sworn personnel, there is a high likelihood that the agency may develop a need to upgrade, and absorb the cost all over again (the same can be said for laptops, body-worn cameras, radios, and other types of technology).

The United Kingdom began to issue Tasers to full-time police officers in England and Wales who were authorized firearms officers in 2004. Initially use of the Taser by these officers was extremely limited, but in 2007 firearms officers who carried Tasers were approved to use them in a greater number of operations, including incidents where the use of a firearm would not be sanctioned. At the same time, UK forces deployed the Taser to specially trained officers: non-firearms officers, but who would follow the same limited rules of engagement as their firearms operators; the Taser could be deployed only when "they were facing violence or threats of violence of such severity that they would need to use force to protect the public, themselves, or the subject" (National Police Chiefs' Council, 2015). Today every chief constable is able to deploy specially trained officers with Tasers, and those officers are held accountable for the amount of force they use. Many specials feel that because they face the same risks as their regular colleagues they should be equipped with the same tools for the job, "as long as they are appropriately trained, appropriately selected, and appropriately deployed" (Greenwood, 2014). Special constables might encounter the same subjects as their full-time counterparts, but the National Police Chiefs' Council has specifically limited training on the device to full-time members of the police service (National Police Chiefs' Council, 2015).

Conclusion

The utilization of volunteer police in both the United States and the United Kingdom remains in a state of fluctuation. Although there is considerable certainty that the utilization of citizen police officers will continue in all countries, the specific way that these volunteers will be engaged by their respective policing agencies depends on a variety of factors. One single publicized event could change volunteer policing forever; incidents such as the shooting incident in Tulsa, or the volunteer sheriff's deputies who bravely answered the call to an active shooter in Orlando, can significantly sway public opinion and therefore change policies, rules, and laws. Incidents in London and Manchester during 2017 may increase public support for better equipped volunteer police on patrol in the United Kingdom. Volunteers in policing are a relatively inexpensive way to increase community support of the role that police play in society, but they are not free; if policing agencies are willing to take on the extra burden of providing training, equipment, and the investment of time into well-organized volunteer programs, they may find a significant return on this investment. However, a volunteer program that is not well managed may lead to negative perceptions by the regular police and the communities in which they serve, while an undervaluing of reserve officers may result in reduced numbers and poor recruitment. Whatever the reason, a reduction in numbers also has financial implications for tightly resourced policing agencies.

Notes

1 Of the G7 countries (Canada, France, Germany, Italy, Japan, the United Kingdom, and the United States), the United States and the United Kingdom showed the slowest economic growth in the first quarter of 2017. The United Kingdom has been hit by inflation and slow consumer spending, coupled with uncertainty about Brexit and the national political scene. The United States has also experienced slow consumer spending, and the effect the presidency of Donald Trump will have on the long-term economics of the nation remains a large concern for many Americans, though it was apparently positive in the first year of the new administration (Nelson, 2017).

2 Glanz's plea to "refusal to perform an official duty" was the result of his failing to respond to lawful requests from the media to turn over a report on an earlier (2009) investigation into Robert Bates. The indictment against Glanz was that he had told his employees to "hold on to it" even though the report had been requested (Killman, 2016).

3 It has been argued by critics of volunteer policing programs that poorly managed programs may become a patronage benefit for those who desire to hold policing authority but do not have the requisite training. Big donors to a sheriff's re-election fund, for example, may be given the benefit of serving as volunteer sheriff's deputy and be given the accompanying accoutrements of office – including a gun, badge, ID cards, and often the legal ability to carry a concealed firearm as a police officer.

4 Very few agencies in the United States choose to participate in the CALEA accreditation process. Since the formation of the commission, in 1984, CALEA has awarded accreditation to just 623 US state, local, and national law enforcement agencies, accounting for slightly more than 3 percent of the nation's 18,000 policing agencies. For the last ten years this number has remained static. This means that almost 97 percent of police managers in the United States have chosen to not participate in this voluntary accreditation process, which can be demanding, problematic, expensive, and time-consuming (Hougland & Wolf, 2016).

5 In 2017 the Florida Department of Law Enforcement (FDLE) announced that it would be increasing the total number of hours required to hold auxiliary law enforcement officer certification in the state from the previous academy training requirement of 319 hours to the new 364 hours. At the writing of this book, the FDLE was considering allowing a blended approach to the auxiliary academy of online self-paced interactive learning coupled with traditional academy coursework to deliver this new training requirement.

6 August Vollmer was an outspoken advocate for and the first proponent of college education for all police officers. Vollmer felt that higher education would increase the professionalism in policing, and also the ability of

the police to be smarter in their crime-fighting work (Paoline, Terrill, & Rossler, 2015).

7   Fewer than 1 percent of police agencies in the United States require a four-year degree as a hiring requirement (Hilal & Densley, 2013).

8   Minnesota requires a two-year degree for police officer certification.

9   Albuquerque Police Department, Charlotte-Mecklenburg Police Department, Columbus Police Department, Fort Wayne Police Department, and Knoxville Police Department required a high school education for police employment, while the Colorado Springs Police Department and the Portland Police Bureau had a two-year college degree requirement (Paoline, Terrill, & Rossler, 2015).

10 "The selection criteria for reserves are the same as that for full-time sworn officers. This ensures that sworn reserve officers have the same pre-employment testing as full-time officers" (CALEA, 2017).

11 Regardless of education requirements for competitive policing jobs, the percentage of minority police officers working in more than 12,000 local police departments in the United States nearly doubled between 1987 and 2013, increasing from about 78,000 officers (making up approximately 15 percent of the workforce) in 1987 to about 130,000 officers (making up approximately 27 percent of the workforce) in 2013 (Reaves, 2015).

12 The negative national rhetoric in the United States putting the "Black Lives Matter" movement against the police has been blamed for ambush shootings of police, and an increase in what has been called an anti-police rhetoric. The political atmosphere has been called the "YouTube effect," in that officers may be continuing to do their job, but take fewer extra steps in pro-actively confronting problems that may lead to arrests – for fear that any such encounters might be caught on video and uploaded to the internet to be picked apart by the public (see Davis, 2015).

13 In many areas of the United States, particularly in the small towns and rural areas where the small departments are most likely to be, pay for full-time officers can be less than US$11 per hour, which is less than many fast-food workers make (Johnson, 2015).

14 Lawsuits in American policing are, unfortunately, a normal occurrence. When a police department is sued for a law enforcement officer's action, the individual officer is often sued as well. This causes significant stress for the officer, and volunteer police officers are not immune to these lawsuits nor the accompanying stress. Many cases against officers are dismissed based on the immunity that a police officer has in doing his or her job, but this is not always the case (Schott, 2012). *The Wall Street Journal* reported that the cost of police litigation has grown considerably since 2010, and the costliest claims were allegations of civil rights violations and other types of misconduct, followed by civil claims against the police as the result of car collisions. The ten American cities with the largest police departments paid US$248 million in settlements and judgments in 2014, compared to US$168 million in 2010, an increase of 48 percent. *The Wall Street Journal* reported that the increase in video footage available in civil cases may be having an effect on the increase, as is a rise in cities paying for wrongful imprisonment cases as a result of wrongful convictions (see Elinson & Frosch, 2015).

15 Volunteers with the RMP do not have law enforcement authority, but they are provided certain "uniforms" by the NYPD, including a RMP shirt, traffic vest, whistle and flashlight. The NYPD alerts members of the RMP to respond to staging areas, primarily through e-mail and phone. Although RMP members do not received police training, the NYPD does have "drills" in which RMP members can participate to learn about their functions in the event of an emergency. Members of the RMP who respond to a mobilization can receive coverage for medical, lost wages, and funeral and survivor benefits through the same law that covers members of the NYPD Auxiliary Police (Tobin, 2017).

16 The city of Atlanta, Georgia, is one example. The city faced a shortfall of officers and in 2013 began a program to rehire retired police officers for a maximum of three years – avoiding the costs of pensions, life insurance, and Medicare, which were already covered for the employees because of their retirements. The program is called the "Recapture" program (see Beech, 2015).

17 This federal law has also created great debate among volunteer law enforcement officers as to its applicability to their positions. Originally written to exclude most part-time and volunteer police officers, the current language of the legislation allows for "employees" of governmental agencies who are "authorized by law to engage in or supervise the prevention, detection, investigation, or prosecution of, or the incarceration of any person for, any violation of law, and has statutory powers of arrest" to carry a firearm concealed (please see the most updated Law Enforcement Officers Safety Act language to determine current eligibility). Many police agencies consider volunteers with police authority to be "employees" for the purposes of worker's compensation laws, and therefore interpret this law as applying to those positions as well as to full-time personnel.

18 Although the negative public perception appears worse in the United States, the United Kingdom has not been without conflict between the police and the communities they serve. In 2011 the London Metropolitan Police called upon other UK police forces to assist with widespread rioting following the death of Mark Duggan, a suspect who was killed by police. What initially began as a gathering of peaceful protesters grew into a citywide riot. This riot, the largest in the country since the 1995 Brixton riots, was in response to complaints that the police were not communicating about the shooting, or were lying about the circumstances (Lewis, 2011), and is eerily familiar to the incidents that occurred in the United States after the shooting of Michael Brown in Ferguson, Missouri, in 2014. Officers in both the London and Ferguson incidents were cleared of any wrongdoing.

19 It should be indicated that the "Met" is the largest police force in the country, responsible for a very diverse and transient population, and covers sensitive locations including St James's Palace, Buckingham Palace, the Houses of Parliament, and 10 Downing Street, as well as famous shopping streets and the entertainment district of Soho.

20 As discussed in Chapter 5, in 2015 Special Constable John Power became the first UK special constable to be certified as a police dog handler. This K9 police team is able to locate explosives. This is an example of the utilization

of special constables in non-traditional roles in uniform policing. The United Kingdom is also experimenting with other non-traditional investigative roles for special constables, including the cybercrime unit discussed later in this chapter.

21 Police support volunteers have no law enforcement powers, generally speaking, but the investigatory role given in the cybercrime unit scheme allows police chief constables to give these volunteers the ability to perform certain police functions, such as handing out fixed penalty notices and taking witness statements (Barrett, 2016).

22 Cheshire Constabulary's Detective Constable Elaine McIver was killed in Manchester, but was not on duty at the time and therefore not in uniform. She was, along with the other victims, a random choice by the perpetrator.

23 NARCAN is a nasal spray approved by the US Food and Drug Administration for the emergency treatment of known or suspected opioid overdose. Administered through the nose by a first responder, the spray counteracts the life-threatening effects of overdose, including respiratory depression, but the recipient must still be provided emergency medical care.

24 QuickClot is a hemostatic agent that activates platelets and increases coagulation of the blood in emergency care of severe bleeding wounds, including gunshot wounds.

References

Albrecht, J. (Ed.) (2017). *Police reserves and volunteers: Enhancing organizational effectiveness and public trust*. Boca Raton, FL: CRC Press.

Barrett, D. (2016, January 20). Volunteers to be handed police-style powers in war on cyber crime. *The Daily Telegraph*. Retrieved July 27, 2017, from www.telegraph.co.uk/news/uknews/crime/12108994.

Bartels, E. C. (2013). *Volunteer police in the United States: Programs, challenges, and legal aspects*. New York: Springer.

BBC (2017, April 6). Northamptonshire Police special constable numbers have "halved." Retrieved July 30, 2017, from www.bbc.com/news/uk-england-northamptonshire-39503807.

Beckfor Thed, M. (2013, November 23). "Policing on the cheap" row over plan to pay special constables to make up for cutting full-time officers. *Daily Mail*. Retrieved August 6, 2017, from www.dailymail.co.uk/news/article-2512554.

Beech, B. (2015, August 27). Atlanta renews recapture program, hires retired police officers. Retrieved July 25, 2017, from http://news.wabe.org/post/atlanta-renews-recapture-program-hires-retired-police-officers.

Bletchly, R. (2017, March 28). After London terror attack – should all police be armed? Arguments for and against. *Daily Mirror*. Retrieved July 26, 2017, from www.mirror.co.uk/news/uk-news/after-london-terror-attack-should-10087838.

Bonnet, F., De Maillard, J., & Roché, S. (2015). Plural policing of public places in France: Between private and local policing. *European Journal of Policing Studies*, 2(3), 285–303.

Carrington, D. (2016, December 16). Badger cull kills more than 10,000 animals in three months. *The Guardian*. Retrieved September 5, 2017, from www.theguardian.com/environment/2016/dec/16/badger-cull-kills-more-than-10000-animals-three-months-bovine-tb.

Carter, D. L., & Sapp, A. D. (1990). The evolution of higher education in law enforcement: Preliminary findings from a national study. *Journal of Criminal Justice Education*, 1(1), 59–85.

Chandan, J. S., & Meakin, R. (2016). Do special constables in London feel that they are adequately prepared to meet their first aid responsibilities? A qualitative study. *BMJ Open*, 6(1), doi:10.1136/bmjopen-2015–010082.

Commission on Accreditation for Law Enforcement Agencies (2017). Reserve officer program in the 6th edition. Retrieved July 21, 2017, from www.calea.org/content/reserve-officer-program-6th-edition.

Compston, T. (2016, September 19). Weighing up the evidence for body worn video cameras. UK Security Expo 2018. Retrieved July 30, 2017, from www.uksecurityexpo.com/security-news/weighing-up-the-evidence-for-body-worn-video-cameras.

Dalley, A. F. (1975). University and non-university graduated policemen: A study of police attitudes. *Journal of Police Science and Administration*, 3(4), 458–468.

Davis, A. C. (2015, October 8). "YouTube effect" has left police officers under siege, law enforcement leaders say. *The Washington Post*. Retrieved July 29, 2017, from www.washingtonpost.com/news/post-nation/wp/2015/10/08/youtube-effect-has-left-police-officers-under-siege-law-enforcement-leaders-say/?utm_term=.ada9e0bd85f9.

Department for Environment, Food and Rural Affairs (2016, December). Guidance to Natural England on licensed badger control to prevent the spread of bovine tuberculosis. London: Department for Environment, Food and Rural Affairs. Retrieved September 5, 2017, from www.gov.uk/government/publications.

Dobrin, A., & Wolf, R. (2016). What is known and not known about volunteer policing in the United States. *International Journal of Police Science and Management*, 18(3), 220–227.

Duerden, N. (2010, April 9). Hobby bobbies: On the beat with the special constables. *The Independent*. Retrieved July 30, 2017, from www.independent.co.uk/news/uk/crime/hobby-bobbies-on-the-beat-with-the-special-constables-1938251.html.

Elinson, Z., & Frosch, D. (2015, July 16). Cost of police-misconduct cases soars in big U.S. cities: Data show rising payouts for police-misconduct settlements and court judgments. *The Wall Street Journal*. Retrieved July 29, 2017, from www.wsj.com/articles/cost-of-police-misconduct-cases-soars-in-big-u-s-cities-1437013834.

Flatley, J. (2017, July 20). Crime in England and Wales: Annual supplementary tables. London: Office for National Statistics. Retrieved August 13, 2017, from www.ons.gov.uk/peoplepopulationandcommunity/crimeandjustice/datasets/crimeinenglandandwalesannualsupplementarytables.

Greenwood, C. (2014, July 21). Special constables' chief says officers should be armed with Tasers because they "face the same dangers" as regular police. *Daily Mail*. Retrieved August 6, 2017, from www.dailymail.co.uk/news/article-2700739.

Grierson, J. (2017, March 1). Watchdog says police cuts have left forces in "perilous state." *The Guardian*. Retrieved July 26, 2017, from www.the guardian.com/uk-news/2017/mar/02/inspectorate-police-engaging-dangerous-practices-austerity-cuts-diane-abbott.

Hargreaves, J., Husband, H., & Linehan, C. (2017). *Police workforce, England and Wales, 20 July 2017*, Statistical Bulletin 10/17. London: Office for National Statistics. Retrieved August 10, 2017, from www.gov.uk/government/uploads/system/uploads/attachment_data/file/630471/hosb1017-police-workforce.pdf.

Hilal, S. M., & Densley, J. (2013). Higher education and local law enforcement. *FBI Law Enforcement Bulletin*, 82(5), 1–3. Retrieved July 23, 2017, from https://leb.fbi.gov/2013/may/higher-education-and-local-law-enforcement.

Home Office (2017, July 27). Police use of firearms statistics, England and Wales: April 2016–March 2017. Retrieved August 11, 2017, from www.gov.uk/government/publications/police-use-of-firearms-statistics-england-and-wales-april-2016-to-march-2017/police-use-of-firearms-statistics-england-and-wales-april-2016-to-march-2017.

Hougland, S., & Wolf, R. (2016). Accreditation in police agencies: Does external quality assurance reduce citizen complaints? *The Police Journal: Theory, Practice and Principles*, 90(1), 40–54.

Hudzik, J. K. (1978). College education for police: Problems in measuring component and extraneous variables. *Journal of Criminal Justice*, 6(1), 69–81.

Institute for Public Safety, Crime and Justice (2014, December). The Specials "experience" in Northamptonshire: A critical review. Northampton, UK: University of Northampton, Institute for Public Safety, Crime and Justice. Retrieved July 27, 2017, from www.empac.org.uk/wp-content/uploads/2016/02/Specials-summary-report-final.pdf.

Jackson, J., Bradford, B., Hough, M., & Murray, K. H. (2012). Compliance with the law and policing by consent: Notes on police and legal legitimacy. In A. Crawford & A. Hucklesby (Eds.), *Legitimacy and compliance in criminal justice*, pp. 29–49. Abingdon, UK: Routledge.

Jenkins, J. (2016, December 27). Study finds that police officers moonlight regularly to earn extra income. KUAR Public Radio. Retrieved July 30, 2017, from http://ualrpublicradio.org/post/study-finds-police-officers-moonlight-regularly-earn-extra-income#stream/0.

Johnson, K. (2015). Lack of training, standards means big problems for small police departments. USA Today. Retrieved July 25, 2017, from www.usatoday.com/story/news/nation/2015/06/23/small-police-departments-standards-training/28823849.

Jones, J., & Rodger, J. (2017, August 6). How the number of armed West Midlands Police officers is soaring. *Birmingham Mail*. Retrieved September 4, 2017, from www.birminghammail.co.uk/news/midlands-news/how-number-armed-west-midlands-13437889.

Killman, C. (2016, July 16). Former Sheriff Stanley Glanz pleads guilty to one misdemeanor charge and no contest to another. *The Tulsa World*. Retrieved July 20, 2017, from www.tulsaworld.com/news/courts/former-sheriff-stanley-glanz-pleads-guilty-to-one-misdemeanor-charge/article_f0648017-282e-571a-89bc-392966e06e25.html.

Krehbiel-Burton, L., & Pérez-Peña, R. (2015, September 30). Tulsa sheriff to resign over killing by deputy. *The New York Times*. Retrieved July 23, 2017, from www.nytimes.com/2015/10/01/us/tulsa-sheriff-indicted-on-misconduct-charges-in-killing-by-a-deputy.html.

Lefkowitz, J. (1974). Job attitudes of police: Overall description and demographic correlates. *Journal of Vocational Behavior, 5*(2), 221–230.

Legislation.gov.uk (n.d.). The Special Constables Regulations 1965. Retrieved August 12, 2017, from www.legislation.gov.uk/uksi/1965/536/introduction/made.

Lewis, P. (2011, August 7). Tottenham riots: A peaceful protest, then suddenly all hell broke loose. *The Guardian*. Retrieved July 26, 2017, from www.theguardian.com/uk/2011/aug/07/tottenham-riots-peaceful-protest.

Maciag, M. (2016, January 26). Survey: Almost all police departments plan to use body cameras. *Governing* (online). Retrieved July 30, 2017, from www.governing.com/topics/public-justice-safety/gov-police-body-camera-survey.html.

Mason, R., & Walker, P. J. (2017, June 5). Under-fire Theresa May hits back over police cuts. *The Guardian*. Retrieved July 26, 2017, from www.theguardian.com/uk-news/2017/jun/05/karen-bradley-police-cuts-armed-officers-bbc-today-programme-london-bridge-attack.

Miller, J., & Fry, L. (1976). Reexamining assumptions about education and professionalism in law enforcement. *Journal of Police Science and Administration, 4*(2), 187–198.

Mills, J. (2017, May 25). Female police officer killed in Manchester bombing named as Elaine McIver. *Metro*. Retrieved September 3, 2017, from http://metro.co.uk/2017/05/25/female-police-officer-killed-in-manchester-bombing-named-as-elaine-mciver-6661049.

Mormino, B. (2001). Police Reserve Program proposal. New York City Police Department. Retrieved July 23, 2017, from www.nycop.com/Jan_02/Police_Reserves_Program/body_police_reserves_program.html.

National Police Chiefs' Council (2015). ACPO questions and answers on Taser, January 2015. Retrieved August 6, 2017, from www.npcc.police.uk/ThePoliceChiefsBlog/201410TaserBlog.aspx.

National Police Officers' Roll of Honour (n.d.). Indexes. Retrieved July 31, 2017, from www.policerollofhonour.org.uk/national_roll/roll_intro.htm.

Nelson, E. (2017, June 1). The US and the UK are now the slowest growing economies in the G7. Quartz. Retrieved July 29, 2017, from https://qz.com/996097/the-us-and-uk-are-now-the-slowest-growing-economies-in-the-g7.

O'Linn, M. (2016, February 14). Response to PERF's "30 Guiding Principles" document. Law Officer. Retrieved July 25, 2017, from http://lawofficer.com/exclusive/perfresponse.

Paoline, E. A., III, Terrill, W., & Rossler, M. T. (2015). Higher education, college degree major, and police occupational attitudes. *Journal of Criminal Justice Education, 26*(1), 49–73.

Peel, Robert, Sir (1829). Principles of law enforcement. Durham Police. Retrieved August 12, 2017, from www.durham.police.uk/AboutUs/Documents/Peels_Principles_Of_Law_Enforcement.pdf.

Rathi, A. (2017, June 4). Even with all these terror attacks, it's still very rare to see police with guns in England. Quartz. Retrieved July 26, 2017, from https://qz.com/998266/london-attack-how-the-uk-police-deal-with-a-terrorist-attack-when-most-officers-dont-carry-guns.

Reaves, B. A. (2015). Local police departments, 2013: Personnel, policies, and practices, NCJ 248677. Washington, DC: US Department of Justice, Office of Justice Programs, Bureau of Justice Statistics. Retrieved January 10, 2018, from www.bjs.gov/content/pub/pdf/lpd13ppp.pdf.

Regoli, R. M. (1976). The effects of college education on the maintenance of police cynicism. *Journal of Police Science and Administration*, 4(3), 340–345.

Reiner, R. (2002). Media made criminality: The representation of crime in the mass media. In M. Maguire, R. Morgan, & R. Reiner (Eds.), *The Oxford Handbook of Criminology*, 3rd Edition, pp. 302–340. Oxford: Oxford University Press.

Reuss, E. D. (2005, October 25). NYPD retiree mobilization plan. New York City Police Department. Retrieved July 25, 2017, from www.nycop.com/Fall2005/RMP_PLAN/body_rmp_plan.html.

Schott, R. G. (2012). Qualified immunity: How it protects law enforcement officers. *FBI Law Enforcement Bulletin*, 81(9), 22–32. Retrieved July 25, 2017, from https://leb.fbi.gov/2012/september/qualified-immunity-how-it-protects-law-enforcement-officers.

Sheffer, S. (2017). Florida Highway Patrol Auxiliary. In J. Albrecht (Ed.), *Police reserves and volunteers: Enhancing organizational effectiveness and public trust*, pp. 57–66. Boca Raton, FL: CRC Press.

Sheth, S., Mark, M., & Edwards, J. (2017, July 4). Police arrest 12 people in London attacks that killed 7 and left 3 attackers dead. Businessinsider.com. Retrieved September 3, 2017, from www.businessinsider.com/british-police-investigating-london-bridge-incident-after-reports-of-van-hitting-pedestrians-2017-6.

Sutherland, J. (2017, July 24). Time for a Royal Commission? Why we need to talk about policing. *Policing Insight*. Retrieved July 26, 2017, from https://policinginsight.com/opinion/time-royal-commission-need-talk-policing.

Tacopino, J. (2017, March 22). Police officer killed in London attack identified as 48-year-old father. *The New York Post*. Retrieved September 3, 2017, from http://nypost.com/2017/03/22/police-officer-killed-in-london-attack-identified-as-48-year-old-father.

Tobin, T. C. (2017). NYPD's retiree mobilization plan: Keeping retired officers active. In J. Albrecht (Ed.), *Police reserves and volunteers: Enhancing organizational effectiveness and public trust*, pp. 241–248. Boca Raton, FL: CRC Press.

US Equal Employment Opportunity Commission (2016, October). Advancing diversity in law enforcement. Retrieved July 29, 2017, from www.eeoc.gov/eeoc/interagency/police-diversity-report.cfm.

Walker, P. J. (2017, February 12). Nearly half of Met police officers want more firearms specialists. *The Guardian*. Retrieved July 26, 2017, from www.theguardian.com/uk-news/2017/feb/13/half-met-police-officers-firearms-specialists-union-survey.

Weiner, N. L. (1976). The educated policeman. *Journal of Police Science and Administration*, 4(4), 450–457.

West Yorkshire Disclosure Logs (2016). Reference number 1510/16. Retrieved July 30, 2017, from www.westyorkshire.police.uk/sites/default/files/files/disclosure-logs/foi_1510-16_body_worn_cameras.pdf.

Wolf, R., Albrecht, J., & Dobrin, A. (2015). Reserve policing in the United States: Citizens volunteering for public service. *The Police Chief*, 82(10), 38–47.

Wolf, R., Holmes, S. T., & Jones, C. (2016). Utilization and satisfaction of volunteer law enforcement officers in the office of the American sheriff: An exploratory nationwide study. *Police Practice and Research: An International Journal*, 17(5), 448–462.

Wolf, R., Pepper, I. K., & Dobrin, A. (2017). An exploratory international comparison of professional confidence in volunteer policing. *The Police Journal: Theory, Practice and Principles*, 90(2), 91–106.

Index